Further Studies by the
Brunel Social Services Unit

ORGANIZING
SOCIAL SERVICES
DEPARTMENTS

Brunel Institute of Organization and Social Studies (BIOSS)

Further Studies by the
Brunel Social Services Unit

ORGANIZING SOCIAL SERVICES DEPARTMENTS

David Billis
Geoffrey Bromley
Anthea Hey
Ralph Rowbottom

Heinemann · London

Heinemann Educational Books Ltd
22 Bedford Square, London WC1B 3HH

LONDON EDINBURGH MELBOURNE AUCKLAND
HONG KONG SINGAPORE KUALA LUMPUR NEW DELHI
IBADAN NAIROBI JOHANNESBURG
EXETER (NH) KINGSTON PORT OF SPAIN

ISBN 0 435 82085 0 (Cased)
ISBN 0 435 82086 9 (Paper)

Filmset by Northumberland Press Ltd
Gateshead, Tyne and Wear
Printed in Great Britain by Richard Clay (The Chaucer Press) Ltd
Bungay, Suffolk

Contents

Acknowledgements

We would like to acknowledge with gratitude the financial support from our sponsors, the Department of Health and Social Security, which has provided the climate of security and continuity so necessary for the sort of activity whose fruits are described here.

Help and stimulation of a different, but equally necessary, kind has been constantly forthcoming from our colleagues in the Brunel Institute of Organisation and Social Studies. We have been truly fortunate in the steady support over the years of our Unit administrative staff, Anita Rubins, and Pam Erickson and Zena Pereira (who have shouldered the secretarial work in this particular production).

Last but not least must be our thanks to the many hundreds of people employed in social services throughout the country without whose enthusiastic collaboration none of this work would have been possible.

Preface

In 1974 our *Social Services Departments: Developing Patterns of Work and Organization*,[1] summarized the results of four years' research work in local authority social services. We offered it in effect as a report of work in progress. Thanks to our many willing collaborators in the field, and to our sponsors in the Department of Health and Social Security, work has continued. We are now able to make a report of findings from another five years of research.

This second book, unlike the first, has been developed from a collection of separate papers written by various of us individually or together. Some chapters are reprints of articles already published and some appear in print for the first time (at least in their present form).

As is normally the case in such collections, the viewpoints of the contributors differ to some degree, and each writer, of course, takes final responsibility for his or her own particular work. At the same time, as will be evident, there is much that we four hold in common – we are all members of the same research unit, and have worked closely together for many years; we share a common method of research, and to a large extent we draw upon a common stock of basic ideas, values and assumptions.

The Brunel Social Services Unit

The origins of the material lie in a project started in 1969 with the sponsorship of the Home Office, to explore problems of organization and management in the then existing children's departments. A management training programme for staff of the children's service was launched at the same time. With the advent of Seebohm the brief was extended to welfare and mental health work. The Department of Health and Social Security took over the sponsorship and a proper research unit was formed in 1971, with four to five full-time research staff which was given the name 'Social Services Organization Research Unit'. This was changed in 1978 to the simpler 'Social Services Unit' at a time of further extension of the brief to span a wider range of management and planning issues. (The first book

[1] Subsequently referred to in footnotes as *Social Services Departments*.

carried the former name on its title page: the second carries the latter.)

The Unit is part of a research institute, the Brunel Institute of Organization and Social Studies. This was formed within the School of Social Sciences of Brunel University in 1970, in order to create a common focus for a wide range of applied research work in a variety of fields including health, social services, education, housing, youth work, employment and industry. Over the whole of its existence, the Social Services Unit has had strong links with a sister-unit within the Institute, the Health Services Organization Research Unit, which is also financed by the DHSS. There is much sharing of ideas between the two Units, and work across the boundary by members of either Unit is encouraged.

We can now look back over many years of work together studying social services organization within this setting: two of us, Anthea Hey and Ralph Rowbottom, since the start in 1969, David Billis since 1970, and Geoffrey Bromley over the five years from 1973 to 1978.

Method and scope of work

The second feature which the various contributions in this book have in common is the particular method of research from which they derive. This method, which is called 'social analysis', was described briefly at the start of the first book, *Social Services Departments*, and has been expounded more fully elsewhere.[2]

Two main kinds of activity are undertaken, *field projects* and *conferences*.

All projects start with an invitation from an individual or group who works in the field concerned, in this case local authority Social Services Departments (SSDs), to help them examine some current problem (rather than starting with an approach by the researcher for permission to explore an issue which he believes to be of general interest).

In the preparatory stage the method of work is fully explained, the willingness of all potential participants is tested more thoroughly, and any necessary sanction from other interested parties is obtained.

[2] The method was first developed and named by Elliott Jaques in the course of the Glacier Project which started in 1948 – see Jaques, E., 'Social Analysis and the Glacier Project' in Brown, W. and Jaques, E. (1965), *Glacier Project Papers*. Its aims, assumptions, procedures, limitations and claims to scientific status have been discussed at length in Rowbottom, R. W. (1977) *Social Analysis*, (hereafter referred to in notes only by its title).

Exploration of the particular problems in hand is then started in earnest, in successive discussions with individuals and groups. The aim of the researcher in these discussions is to help to analyse the true nature of the problems and their circumstances, and also to help tease-out various possible 'models' of organization, system, or procedure which might be adopted in order to deal with them. No specific recommendations are made however. It is up to the prime actors themselves to decide, or to recommend to higher authorities, what particular line of action to take, and how far any general model needs to be modified to accord with given personalities, financial constraints, or other local and specific circumstances.

The general approach is thus an 'action research' one. However, it is one in which work proceeds by what may be described as 'collaborative exploration' rather than by the more conventional route of objective study (in which there is precise pre-definition of the problem followed by extensive data-collection, followed by independent analysis and recommendation in some lengthy, formal, report).[3]

To stress the point, the particular aim of the researcher in 'social analysis' is not to offer specific *solutions*, but to try, in collaboration with the prime actors, to discern the general features of the problem concerned, and to try and help construct general models (of organization, systems, procedures, etc.) of an 'if ... then' kind. If the actors are willing and able to try out one of these models (or something close to it) this then provides an opportunity to test its validity as a scientific proposition, by seeing if the predicted links between the 'ifs' and the 'thens' really do hold in practice – and if not, discovering how ideas have to be modified. A straightforward example of the kind of 'models' we are talking about is to be seen in Chapter 6, where a model procedure for admission of clients into residential care is described on the assumption of certain fundamental relationships between fieldworks and residential staff. In fact, examples of models of this 'if ... then' type are to be found in practically every chapter of the subsequent text.

There are of course limitations with this research method, as with any other. One is the difficulty (if not impossibility) of arranging to undertake a systematic study of any given list of topics, or indeed to undertake a series of simultaneous comparative studies of any one topic. All depends on just what range of invitations actually materializes. If nobody wants help from us in looking at issues of com-

[3] See *Social Analysis*, Chapter 4, for elaboration of this contrast between 'collaborative exploration' and 'objective study'.

munity work (say) at any time, then there is a real limit on how far invitations to explore this particular topic can be actively solicited, regardless of how much the researcher might wish to study the area, either in depth in one place, or comparatively. Fortunately, the longer the research programme goes on the more comprehensive it becomes. The range of problems researchers are invited to consider steadily widens, and the opportunities to look again at some given problem in a new setting steadily increase.

The advantages of a determined orientation to expressed problems are considerable, despite the limitations mentioned above. In the first place it helps to overcome the perennial problem of access in social research – that is, of simply being able to get into the area of interest in order to study important and sensitive matters at close quarters. Beyond this, it secures the commitment of those working in the field not only to get the 'facts' straight, but to delve to the bottom of the problem at issue. The staff concerned are not simply sparing some of their precious time to help a research programme 'out there'. They are actively inviting an analyst to come in and help them deal with pressing matters already engaging their attention and energy.

Over the ten years of our work since 1969, we have been invited to undertake substantial field projects in some fourteen local authorities in England and Wales: (five Counties, eight London Boroughs, and two Metropolitan Boroughs). Work in about half of these authorities has in fact continued over many years, moving from one project to another, or returning on occasion to analyse the new problems arising from earlier changes. Contacts for shorter projects or briefer discussion of local problems have also been made with a number of other authorities.[4]

The second main element of the research method is the running of conferences. The aim of these events is to test further the adequacy and generality of the analysis, concepts and models that have emerged from field projects, and at the same time to disseminate knowledge of these developing ideas. A continuing programme of such events has taken place each year since the social services research started. Some (particularly the earlier ones) have run to two weeks in length; in later years we have tended to prefer shorter 'workshop'-type events on specific topics, running for perhaps two or three days. Altogether over the whole period some two thousand senior staff have attended, drawn from a wide variety of posts in virtually every one of the hundred and sixteen SSDs in England and Wales, from various central government agencies, and from some of the large voluntary

[4] During the period, Anthea Hey has undertaken similar project work in Scotland.

organizations. A number of these people have returned one or more times, thus furthering the opportunity for continuous testing and retesting of ideas.

The basic framework of ideas

The third feature which unifies the various contributions that follow is that they all share, to a large degree, a common system of views, theories and assumptions about the nature of organization in general, and social services organization in particular, a system which has been gradually developing over the years.

An extended exposition of many of these basic ideas, as they appeared in the light of the first four years of work, is to be found in our earlier book, *Social Services Departments*. It is impossible to reproduce here the detailed argument and evidence, but the main points may be summarized as follows:

In that book we took what may be described as a *pluralistic* view of the world of local authority social services. Rather than portraying a dualist world of administrators-versus-professionals, agencies-versus-clients, establishment-versus-workers (or whatever), we offered a picture of many systems and many actors, sometimes in collaboration, and sometimes in conflict. At the centre was the employment system in which staff of the service, however senior or junior, all work. Immediately adjacent lay the membership of the local authority itself, with its very different structure of council, committees, and sub-committees. Directly impinging on this second system were the various political parties, the pressure groups, the news media, etc. Beyond lay other community groups, voluntary associations, statutory agencies, professional associations and trade unions. All these systems were seen in constant interaction, sometimes competing, sometimes working together. In addition, any individual worker – say a social worker – was seen as potentially not just with one role, but with many – as an employee, a member of a professional association, a member of a trade union, a member of a political party, a citizen, and so on. Here too was potential conflict, this time for each individual to resolve as best as he or she could, if, as, and when it materialized.[5]

We also reported that the reality of the central employment structure in SSDs of the day was basically that of a *managerial hierarchy*. Senior staff and ultimately one person, the Director, carried accountability in principle for everything that went on, and carried the authority, if required, to zoom into all matters resting with more

[5] See *Social Services Departments*, Chapter 2.

junior staff, however 'professional' such matters might appear to be. This we contrasted sharply with other existing and possible organizational forms, for example the current way in which health service doctors are organized.

Within these central managerial hierarchies, there appeared to be some optimum number of levels to be aimed for in order to avoid overcrowding and excessive 'bureaucracy' (in the pejorative sense of the word) on the one hand, or failure to undertake essential managerial work on the other. Most larger SSDs appeared to require four full-managerial levels, that is five main levels of work in all.[7]

We pointed out, however, that 'managerial' relationships were only one of a rich and varied range to be discovered within the employment structure of SSDs, or in various systems of collaboration with other agencies. We described other important types of *organizational relationship* that research had unearthed: 'co-ordinative', 'monitoring', 'prescriptive', 'supervisory', and so on.[8]

More particularly, many situations were noted where staff inevitably found themselves in what we described as 'dual-influence' situations: for example where administrative officers, home help organizers, or occupational therapists were attached to area social work teams; or where social workers were attached to general medical practices, to schools, to child guidance teams, or to specialist medical teams.[9] We suggested that it was, in general, no answer to deny the reality of either of the two 'lines', and that there was therefore a necessary job to be done in spelling out various possible models in terms of the different split of functions and authority between the two lines, which might suit various and different circumstances.

Elsewhere we discerned regular elements of what is now commonly called *matrix organization*; as for example when working parties or project teams were established to pursue topics which cut across the main lines of managerial accountablity, whether the latter was divided in terms of different functions, places, clientele, or occupations.[10]

We suggested that however much those in SSDs might contribute to local authority plans to enhance the general quality of life of the locality, their own particular brief was the prevention and relief of

[6] See *Social Services Departments*, Chapter 2 and Appendix B.
[7] See *Social Services Departments*, Chapter 4.
[8] See *Social Services Departments*, Appendix A.
[9] See *Social Services Departments*, Chapters 5, 7 and 9.
[10] See *Social Services Departments*, Chapter 2. See also Hey, A. (1977), 'Local Authority Social Services Departments, Examples of Matrix Organization' in Knight, K. (ed.), *Matrix Management*.

social distress: social distress in individuals, in families, and in specifically-identified neighbourhoods.[11]

Within this specific brief three main kinds of operational activity were identified:

(*a*) carrying out *basic social work* with individuals or groups, in which the aim was to help them to achieve a better mode of functioning in their particular social environment.

(*b*) providing *basic services*, i.e. accommodation, food, goods, help in daily living, recreation, etc.;

(*c*) providing *supplementary services* of various kinds, e.g. communication and mobility training, sheltered employment, medical and para-medical work (in certain circumstances), education (in certain circumstances), etc.[12]

As far as identifying natural occupational groupings in this particular field was concerned, and selecting, training and organizing their various members, we suggested that this threefold distinction was more fundamental than the more conventional work descriptions like 'casework', 'group work', 'fieldwork', 'residential work', 'day care', and so on.

Five years later we still believe these ideas to be basically sound and descriptive of the realities of life, though now we have various important elaborations and refinements to add.

At this point, for example, we still find a *pluralistic* image of the social services world to be a more useful conception than any of the simpler *dualist* ones which still have currency. It seems too, from our continued work, that the reality of central employment systems in SSDs is still that of a managerial hierarchy – accompanied as it invariably is with overlays of other organizational relationships so as to form the typical 'matrix' pattern mentioned above. As in the earlier book, however, it needs to be stressed that we do not regard managerial hierarchies as the only or, in any sense, ideal form of employment organization. Indeed, we explicitly consider (see Chapers 3 and 4) how other forms of organization might become necessary, in limited areas at any event, as certain distinct kinds – or levels – of work in social services develop more strongly. In this connection too we are able now to offer a much more extensive analysis of the general effect of developing professionalism on management structure, and on rela-

---

[11] See *Social Services Departments*, Chapter 3.
[12] See *Social Services Departments*, Chapter 3.

tions between different kinds of professionals in multi-disciplinary work (see Chapter 2).

Although managerial hierarchies persist, our discussions and investigations strongly suggest that the problems of getting the right number of levels, neither too many nor too few for the organization in question, is still a crucial one, and in many departments still unresolved. As will be seen (Chapter 1) we are now able to offer a much extended and deeper approach to this whole subject, and one which offers a description of 'level' which applies equally to administrative and to professional work.

It still seems just as important – as will be illustrated – to recognize the rich diversity of roles and relationships required to do justice to the complexities of organizational life, and to avoid at all costs simplistic beliefs that terms like 'line' and 'staff' will provide all the necessary definition. Moreover, further experience has strengthened the belief that what we described above as 'dual-influence' situations are widely and unavoidably prevalent, and that detailed definition of the nature of the 'two lines' is regularly called for. Our model definitions of various basic types of organizational role and relationships continue to evolve (see, for example, Chapter 8).

Finally, we continue to find that within the broad aim of dealing with social distress the operational work of SSDs is more usefully conceived for a variety of purposes in terms of the provision of social work, basic services and supplementary services, than in other more conventional terms. (Further discussions of this particular framework and its detailed implications for careers, training and organization are pursued in Chapters 3 and 4.)

The changing social service scene

In the five years since the publication of our first book, there have of course been considerable changes in the social services world. For a start, since local government reorganization in 1974 nearly all the very small departments have disappeared. This trend to larger size was accentuated by the rapid expansion of resources put into social services during the early 1970s.

New questions have arisen about the kinds and grades of staff needed in SSDs. The issues are no longer primarily to do with the amalgamation of children's officers, welfare workers and mental health workers into one profession (though special problems of a related kind arose with the transfer of all hospital social workers to

SSDs in 1974). They are now to do with such things as the need for specialization within generic social work; the development of career grades; proper training and careers for residential social workers; and generally, whether 'social work' comprehensively describes the full range of necessary activities of social services departments, and (if it does not) what alternative variety of basic professional training and career paths might be called for.

Flowing alongside all this has been the rapid growth of trades unionism, the advent of widescale 'industrial action', and the impact of much pioneering legislation in the field of industrial relations and health and safety at work. In the public services as a whole, it has become abundantly evident that staff are no longer to be regarded as ever-obedient agents, willing to shoulder whatever burden they are given, for whatever wage can be 'afforded'. Employees – professional and other – are increasingly conscious of just where they stand in the national pay league. They have their own views on public policies and programmes. They are prepared to fight and, if necessary, to strike; even if their own clientele suffer in the process.

There has been growing realization that social services departments cannot go it alone. Social distress is unending. It intertwines in-extricably with ill-health, educational failure, delinquency, un-employment and other social discomforts and personal sorrows. Not only are hard priority choices having to be faced day in, day out, in sharing out limited services, but every opportunity is having to be grasped for organizing the distressed to help themselves, for recruit-ing volunteers, and for devising schemes of common action with the staff of other statutory and voluntary agencies. Ever more work goes beyond traditional activities into such things as 'group homes', 'street warden schemes', 'professional fostering', 'intermediate treatment', joint day-centre/clinics, and the attachment of social workers to general medical practices.

Difficult issues of professional borderlines and relationships have come to the fore, particularly in activities where much multi-disciplinary collaboration is necessary, like providing for the elderly, the physically handicapped, and the mentally disordered, or dealing with child abuse. All this has required, of course, hard consideration of more effective ways of planning new developments jointly with other parallel departments and agencies, particularly with health services. And it has required thoughts about better methods of cor-porate planning within local authorities themselves.

There has been the well-heralded trend to greater community care, with a marked increase in the provision of home help, other domiciliary services, and day care of various kinds. At the same time (and sometimes as a result) there have been new problems in residential provision. Trying to keep clients in their own homes whilst dealing with a greater range of their problems has meant that any that have eventually come into residential care have been far more demanding of skilled attention. At the same time residential staff have shown themselves increasingly unwilling to accept unmanageable kinds or numbers of residents into their establishments, or to continue to spend extraordinary lengths of time on duty or on call as they often did in the past.

The Unit's work during the last five years

Our work over the last five years has in fact taken us deeply into many, though not all, of these more recent developments and pre-occupations. Some of this work is described here, and some of it has already been published elsewhere. (Some again has yet to reach the stage of publication.)

As will be seen, we have been very concerned, for example, in discussions about the relation of social workers to other existing and emerging groups and occupations in SSDs like home helps, social services officers and occupational therapists, and to the various patterns of training, organization and career structure which are called for in each of these groups (see Chapters 3 and 4).

In conjunction with colleagues from the Health Services Organization Research Unit we have also undertaken considerable work on interactions between health and social services in the fields of mental illness, mental and physical handicap, services for the elderly, child guidance, hospital social work and joint planning. Some of this work has already been published.[13]

As regards the relation of social services to other public agencies, we have done some work in the educational welfare field, we have done a little work on links with housing and with voluntary organizations, and (as described in Chapter 9) we have looked at the special area of 'intermediate treatment'.

[13] See Rowbottom, R. W. and Bromley, G. L. (1978), 'The Future of Child Guidance – A Study in Multi-Disciplinary Teamwork'; and Rowbottom, R. W. and Hey, A. M. (1978), 'Collaboration Between Health and Social Services' in Jaques, E. (ed.), *Health Services*, (hereafter referred to in footnotes only by its title). Both these papers, given their subjects, might well have been published in this book as well as in *Health Services*, but it was decided not to do so in order to avoid undue overlap, and because there were already two other papers – Chapters 1 and 2 in this book – which it was felt essential to have in both books.

Not all our invitations in the past five years have been specifically restricted to the newly-emerging topics identified above. Many of the requests we have received have in fact been to explore or re-explore issues of much longer standing. Moreover, familiar though some of them may be, it is not our sense that problems of this latter kind are necessarily felt by those who have raised them to be less important or demanding. We have frequently received requests to help review, or review again, the most appropriate form of general departmental structure for example, and how systematic development, policy-making and planning can best be undertaken. We have continued to be asked for help in exploring the management of large residential and day care divisions, or of particular establishments within them. We have continued to be invited to look at the organization of administrative, personnel and other support work. Discussions of some of these perennial concerns therefore take their place alongside discussions of more recent issues in the pages that follow – for example, in looking at the continuing problems of managing large residential divisions (Chapter 5); of developing effective and human procedures for taking people into residential care (Chapter 6); of managing 'community homes with education' (Chapter 7); of employing advisers, development officers and the like (Chapter 8); and of undertaking 'development' in general (Chapter 10).

The structure and scope of the book
The book is divided into four parts. Part I is about fundamental issues. The theory of Work Strata which is introduced in the first chapter is employed in most of the subsequent chapters, and provides therefore one of the main theoretical bases. Part II starts from the idea of the three basic components of social services work (already mentioned above) and uses it to explore developing occupational and professional groups, their organization and career patterns, in two components of fieldwork – social work and basic services work. Part III looks at several different aspects of residential work and organization, and Part IV looks at a variety of problems and choices in the general area of 'development'.

It will be evident from what has already been said that there is no pretence of providing any complete treatment of the problems of social services, old or new. What is presented must be regarded much more in the nature of a second report of 'work in progress', a report which must be set alongside the earlier book and, indeed, alongside other publications,[14] in order to obtain any comprehensive overview.

One of the main threads that run through these various writings is the continuing preoccupation with what may be described either loosely as 'organization' or more exactly, as the whole framework of *enacted social institutions* within which specific services – in this case social services – are planned and provided. In 'social institutions' here we include not only formal organization structures in the narrow sense, but all the continuing working assumptions about roles, relationships, and procedures of interaction, between workers, managers, elected members, etc. We include also various agreements and working assumptions about relative status, conditions of service, and levels of pay.

Now we make no claim that the study of organization (or more broadly, of enacted social institutions) is the most important thing in present day social services. Nor do we suggest for a moment that other things such as, say, priority-setting, or resource-allocation decisions, should not be studied with equal care.[15] What we do suggest, however, is that the study and development of social institutions (or organization) *is* important; that it *does* call for special methods; and (last but not least) that it does have a very considerable bearing on the quality of service eventually delivered.

Many readers of our earlier book were obviously put on their mettle by this last issue. For 'organization' still remains a strange if not threatening concept to many of those in social services, tinged as it appears to be with suggestions of incipient managerialism, industrialism and autocracy. The emphasis in much social work training has tended to rest heavily on the personalized elements in social interaction at the expense of the institutionalized (though elements of the latter kind are in fact present in all social relationships, and are indeed particularly prominent in those social settings we describe as 'organized' or 'organizational'). On the other hand, the main emphasis in social administration has tended to rest on studies and analysis of various types of need and provision, rather than on the detailed organizational framework within which provision is secured.

For all these reasons then, it was not perhaps surprising that several

[14] We have in mind here particularly the recent book on *Health Services* already mentioned, to which we all contributed; the book on our research method, *Social Analysis*; and beyond this a whole range of literature, some old, some new, spreading back for over thirty years, all in the general 'social analytic' tradition. (See *Social Analysis*, Appendix B, 'The Social Analytic Literature'.)

[15] Indeed, at the time of writing, the Unit has recently decided to broaden its scope *beyond* social institutions into some of these other important matters.

critics raised questions about the absence of direct references to con-
sumers or clientele in our work, as well as lack of attention to the
'human factors' (that is, presumably to the psychological and social-
psychological elements of life). A lengthy theoretical analysis of these
issues having been published elsewhere,[16] we would propose at this
point to deal shortly with the matter by suggesting that the questions
might rather be reversed. It seems self-evident to us that good
organization is crucial both to good service provision and to good
human relations. The sheer waste of talent, energy, and enthusiasm
that one stumbles across in almost any SSD that one visits because
of a lack of any systematic or well-informed approach to organization,
forces itself continually to the attention. The question we suggest is
not so much why studies like ours do not look directly at consumer
needs and views, or at psychological attitudes and problems as well
as at organization. It is whether there should not be more systematic
study of the organizational factors in service provision, more trial and
development of new organizational forms, more discussion and dis-
semination of clearly thought-out organizational ideas and models.

We might well perhaps have taken for our epigraph the following
thought from one of the reviews of our earlier book, for it expressed
the matter in a nutshell – 'collective caring needs the organization
man'. The 'organization man' required at the end of the day is not
one of us. He, or she, is the sort of worker in social services who is
just as well armed with skills in organizing collective responses as he
is in assessing the nature of individual problems. We trust that this
book will provide some additional contribution to that necessary
armoury.

Ralph Rowbottom
David Billis
Geoffrey Bromley
Anthea Hey

---

[16] *Social Analysis*, particularly Chapters 3, 8 and 9.

PART I

Basic Ideas

Introduction

by Ralph Rowbottom

The two chapters in Part I examine two fundamental characteristics of large-scale social services organization – differences in *levels of work*, and the various effects of *professionalism*.

On the first topic, there can be little doubt of a widespread appreciation not just of the existence of different *kinds* of work within social services (as between, for example, social case work, teaching of the mentally handicapped, research, or training) but of different *levels* at which any of these activities might be undertaken. There is a widespread sense, for example, that a social worker in an area office is typically performing work at a higher level than that of the typical social security clerk, whilst a typical medical consultant is perhaps working at a higher level than either, although all three can reasonably be described as 'front-line' workers.[1]

There is clear recognition in practice that not all social workers (even the so-called 'fully-qualified') are capable of tackling problems of the same depth or complexity: the less experienced are inevitably 'down here', whilst others (properly described as senior social workers perhaps) are 'up there'. Over and above this, there are of course the indications of a wide span of levels manifested in almost every organization chart of social services departments with directors conventionally shown at the top, area officers in the middle, and social workers at the bottom.

Moreover, these differences in level matter. They affect people's sense of relative status and feelings about appropriate pay. They have obvious implications for selection and training. They have implications for how authority is vested, and where the main burden of responsibility is carried. The more we can understand about such a fundamental feature of organizational life the better.

[1] The slightly different concept of 'front-line organization' (see Smith, G. (1970), *Social Work and the Sociology of Organization*) in which certain workers (for example, social workers) are seen by their situation as invested with more discretion and power than others (for example, production workers) also recognizes, if implicitly, real differences in level amongst those loosely describable as 'in the front-line'.

The question is: how can such intuitively-grasped distinctions be described in objective terms, and preferably in terms which are general not only to all the many occupations and sub-occupations in social services, but also across a wider range of other professions and agencies? Grading structures are no help. They are (or ought to be) the *end* product of a process which starts with a clarification of different work levels, not the beginning. Alternatively, the attempt to use terms like 'professional', 'administrative', 'clerical', 'middle management', 'top management', etc., in order to distinguish levels is at best wildly imprecise, and at worst grossly misleading. Nor is there much guidance to be gained from the existing literature (in either social administration, or organization or management theory). Apart from the work now to be described, the general absence of rigorous investigation or analysis of this basic aspect of organization is most striking.[2]

In *Social Services Departments* we made conscious attempts to get to grips with the problem, drawing heavily upon Elliott Jaques' earlier work on time-span measurement and growth of individual capacity, which posited the universal existence of at least seven distinct possible levels in all organized work.[3] Following him, we carefully distinguished the idea of organizational level from that of grade. However, we could do no better at that time than to pin the exact definition of the former on the highly specific notion of 'managerial level'. This had the weakness first that it limited the clear identification of levels to managerial roles only (thus leaving doubt about how to place various practitioner or support roles); second, that in counting the levels it assumed that not too many (nor too few) levels had already been built into any given hierarchy.

The first chapter in Part I, in our view, represents a major theoretical advance. It describes how a general method of identifying distinct levels in work came to be developed, a method which cuts not only across professional practice and administration in the full range of social services but also (it would appear) across an extremely wide range of other services and occupations as well.

[2] There is, of course, the general literature on 'social stratification' which is referenced briefly in Chapter 1. As regards actual schema for practical use in describing levels in organized work however, the only exception to this general dearth known to the author is the scheme developed by Professor Patterson, which indeed bears some interesting similarities to the Work Strata theory about to be described. Significantly, it arises from the field of 'job evaluation' (see Patterson, T. T. (1972), *Job Evaluation*).

[3] A full and generalized statement of this particular material is conveniently provided in Jaques, E. (1976) *A General Theory of Bureaucracy* (hereafter referred to by its title only).

This new theory of 'Work Strata' (as we call it) has proved extremely powerful both in developing further theoretical ideas and in application to immediate problems. As will be seen, it is employed at some point or other in most of the subsequent chapters. We have used it in innumerable discussions in projects and conferences as a tool of analysis in dealing with such pressing current issues as how 'social workers' (*sic*) should be graded; whether senior practitioners should ever equate in pay and status to team leaders; what distinguishes the work of social work assistants from social workers; whether residential workers are underpaid in comparison with field workers; and many other similar issues. None of them can be dealt with adequately without taking proper account of levels and relative levels, and therefore of using or developing a vocabulary to do this job. It is interesting to note that the Work Strata theory which we describe has already started to be employed or referred to in a number of independent studies of some of these matters.[4]

The second chapter in Part I tackles a set of issues which are almost as fundamental: namely, the general effects of 'professionalism' in the design of organization.

Study of these issues with regard to social work in particular is of course no new matter and a sizeable literature already exists.[5] Over the past decade or so we at Brunel have been in the fortunate position to be able to explore them in a wider variety of actual work situations, involving a whole range of other professionals in the general field of health and social services as well as social workers: doctors, nurses, home helps, paramedical workers, and so on. Some of this experience was tapped in *Social Services Departments*. There, for example, we drew attention to the very different assumptions which underlay typical present-day medical organization and typical social work organization, and went on to discuss the reality of any widespread shift in social work towards the medical model.[6]

Now however, by drawing more deeply on the material and find-

[4] See, for example, British Association of Social Workers' (1977) *The Social Work Task*, 'The Role of the Social Work Assistant', A Report by Members of Cambridgeshire Social Services Training Workshop, *Social Work Today*, vol. 7, no. 9, 22 July 1976; and, Social Services Liaison Group (1978), *Residential Care, Staffing and Training*.

[5] Blau, P. and Scott, W. (1963), *Formal Organizations*, Chapter 3 and Appendix; Toren, N. (1969), 'Semi-Professionalism and Social Work: A Theoretical Perspective' in Etzioni, A. (ed.), *The Semi-Professions and their Organization*; Smith, G. (1970) op. cit.; Forder, A. (1974), *Concepts in Social Administration*, Chapter 7; Hill, M. (1976), *The State, Administration, and the Individual*, Chapter 5; and, Wareham, J. (1977), *An Open Case, The Organizational Context of Social Work*; Heraud, B. J. (1970), *Sociology and Social Work*.

[6] See *Social Services Departments*, Appendix B.

ings which have accumulated over the years, we are able to offer in Chapter 2 a more general set of formulations and models. We discuss for health and welfare professionals as a whole, how various forms and characteristics of developed professional practice affect appropriate management arrangements; what they imply in terms of 'professional autonomy'; and also what they imply in terms of relations between different types of professionals.

Both the chapters in Part I touch then on deep theoretical issues. Together they illustrate a prominent feature of the social analytic method described in the Preface. In both, the theories have grown in the first instance from specific pieces of action-research directed to helping members of social services and health services to cope with immediate practical problems. In both, the theories have turned out to have applications not only to the immediate problems from which they derived, but to a far wider range of other problems and issues as well. So social theory may be developed which both grows from practice and at the same time strengthens and enriches it.[7]

[7] See further discussion of this idea in *Social Analysis*, Chapter 8.

1   The Stratification of Work and Organizational Design[1]

by Ralph Rowbottom and David Billis

What is the hierarchy of management levels in organizations *about?* In keeping with the spirit of their age, the earliest writers on management, the so-called 'classical' school – the Fayols, Taylors and Urwicks – simply took them for granted. These people were not so much concerned with why management levels were there, as how to strengthen them and improve their efficiency. In a different way the subsequent Human Relations writers also took them for granted, in their case by largely ignoring the 'formal' system in the pursuit of supportive, participatory processes. It was not until the advent of the later, more sociology-minded and systems-minded researchers, that managerial systems as such came under stern and critical review. Generalizing very broadly, two models were identified. The first was a conventional or traditional model variously described as 'hierarchical', 'bureaucratic', 'mechanistic', and 'authoritarian'. The second was a new, emerging model, by implication more suited to the turbulent social environment of the 20th century, and variously described as 'nonhierarchical', 'antibureaucratic', 'organic', 'responsive' and 'democratic'.[2] But a whole host of other names could be added to the founders of, and subscribers to, this now-dominant ideology – Argyris, Bennis, Blake and Mouton, Katz and Kahn, Lawrence and Lorsch, etc.

However, in spite of the generally enthusiastic espousal of the second vision, not only by the academics and commentators but by many of the more lively and forward-looking of managers themselves, strong

[1] Reprinted (with minor alterations) from *Human Relations*, vol. 30, no. 1, 1977.

[2] We might take as key works here those of McGregor, D. (1960), *The Human Side of Enterprise*; Burns, T. and Stalker, G. M. (1961), *The Management of Innovation*; and Emery, F. E. and Trist, E. L. (1965), 'The Causal Texture of Organizational Environments'.

elements of hierarchical structure still manifestly and stubbornly abound in most real-life organizations, public as well as private. The men at the top (or more modishly, the 'centre') still seem to carry significant extra increments of power and authority, not to speak of pay and status.

In this chapter we shall be examining a detailed thesis which serves to explain this persistence of hierarchical structure on the general grounds that there are different kinds of work to be carried out in organizations which can quite reasonably be described as 'higher' and 'lower'. Although we shall not be concerned with how these different kinds of work might justify differences in pay or status, we shall be very much concerned with what they imply in terms of authority. We shall also be concerned with the question of how the existence of work at a variety of levels is related to differing capacities amongst organization members and, more especially, to the way in which the capacity of any one individual member may develop through time. Here we may note the considerable influence on the ideas expressed in this paper of the theories and findings of Elliott Jaques on these same subjects.[3] We may also note, without further pursuing, the links at this point with more general issues of social stratification.[4]

[3] See Jaques, E. (1965). 'Preliminary Sketch of a General Structure of Executive Strata', and 'Speculations Concerning Level of Capacity'; (1967), *Equitable Payment* (2nd ed.); *A General Theory of Bureaucracy*, op. cit. His own initial conception of the stratification of work was based on empirical observations of a natural spacing of managerial tiers in terms of 'time-span' measures of levels of work ('Preliminary Sketch of a General Structure of Executive Strata', op. cit.). If the two approaches – his and the one described here – are consistent (as it is assumed they are) then his critical time-span boundaries between strata – 3 months, 1 year, 2 years, 5 years, and 10 years – will correspond to the boundaries between successive strata of work identified in the qualitative terms used below. In the various descriptions of work-strata offered below the links may also be noted with the idea of the 'perceptual-concrete' nature of the lowest stratum of human capacity; the 'imaginal-concrete' nature of the second stratum; and the 'conceptual-concrete' nature of the third stratum ('Speculations Concerning Level of Capacity', op. cit.).

[4] For the general terms of the social-stratification discussion, see the Davis and Moore versus Tumin debate (Bendix, R. and Lipset, S. M. (eds.) (1953), *Class, Status and Power*), and also Dahrendorf, R. (1968), 'On the Origin of Inequality Among Men'. Specifically, the issue may be noted of how far in general, differences in power, status and wealth in society may be explained or justified either in terms of the need to have a variety of different social functions carried out (which bears an obvious relation to the present discussion of *Work Strata*), or in terms of the existence of a given 'natural' distribution of human abilities (which bears an obvious relation to Jaques' notion of 'capacity').

Origin of the Work Stratum model

The ideas to be described arose from an action-research programme which has been in progress since 1969 in the new social services departments in local authorities.[5] In the course of work with a number of these departments one of the recurrent problems noted was that of the precise role within the hierarchy of certain particular groups of senior staff. Time and again in field or seminar discussion members of departments would spontaneously refer to the difficult organizational position of social work team leaders or seniors, in relation to the members of their teams; or of homes advisers in relation to the heads of the various residential homes for children that they were expected to supervise; or of specialist advisers, principal officers and the like at headquarters in relation to teams of social workers at area offices; or of deputy directors in relation to assistant directors.

Although each of these groups of staff were shown 'higher' on the charts than their counterparts, and were often indeed in more highly-graded posts, analysis often revealed considerable uncertainties or disagreements about the extent of their managerial authority. There would be doubt as to how far they had the right to set policies or general authoritative guides for work which were binding on their counterparts, or to make authoritative appraisals of their performance, their suitability for promotion, etc. There would be doubt as to how far it would be right to describe them as accountable for the work of their counterparts.

By contrast, none of these same doubts would usually exist to any significant extent for certain other posts in the hierarchy – area officers in relation to team leaders; heads of homes in relation to the staff of the home; assistant directors in relation to principal officers; or indeed directors of departments in relation to any or all other staff.

The attempt to probe further into why these distinctions should arise (and the answer was obviously more general than that of the personal strengths or weaknesses of particular individuals) led to a general consideration of the *kinds* of work carried out in these various positions, and whether any significant stratification in the work itself might be observable. Clearly these 'kinds' of work would be perceived as not just different, but themselves as 'higher' or 'lower' in responsibility. However, there would be no need to deny as well the presence of some continuing scale of responsibility within each discrete kind or category. Hence, what we should be seeking to identify would

[5] See *Social Services Departments.*

be a series of discrete, qualitatively different *strata* of work, super-imposed on a continuous scale of work of increasing responsibility from bottom to top of the organization.

In the attempt to identify these various work strata some immediate observations appeared relevant. Ignoring the manifest hierarchy of authority and grades it was noteworthy:

(*a*) that certain social workers talked of 'their' caseload, and apparently carried a full measure of responsibility for each case within it;

(*b*) that others – students, trainees and assistants, for example – did not talk in quite the same way and apparently did not carry full case responsibility, but carried out work under the close supervision and direction of some of the first group of staff; and

(*c*) that there were others again – more senior social workers, area officers, and specialist advisers, for example – who often spoke with regret about being unable at this stage of their careers to carry a personal caseload, and who seemed to be more concerned with general systems of provision and general procedures for work, training, administration, etc., than getting involved in particular cases.

Gradually from these beginnings a general thesis grew; and as it grew it seemed that it might be applicable not only to SSDs but to a much wider range of organizations. In essence the thesis was this:

(*a*) that the work to be done in organizations falls into a hierarchy of discrete strata in which the range of the ends or objectives to be achieved and the range of environmental circumstances to be taken into account both broadens and changes in quality at successive steps;

(*b*) that the work at successively higher strata is judged to be more responsible, but that significant differences of responsibility are also felt to arise *within* strata; that is, that these qualitative strata form stages within a continuous scale of increasing levels of work or responsibility;

(*c*) that at least five such possible strata can be precisely identified in qualitative terms; in successive order and starting from the lowest: *prescribed output, situational response, systematic service provision, comprehensive service provision* and *comprehensive field coverage*;

(*d*) that these strata form a natural chain for delegating work and hence provide the basis for constructing an effective chain of successive managerial levels within the organization; and

(*e*) that the understanding of these strata can also provide a practical guide to designing new organizations (or part-organizations) accord-ing to the kind and level of organizational response required in relation to the social and physical environment in which the organization is to operate.

One important proviso needs to be added to the fourth point just made. It is assumed there (and for the rest of this chapter) that managerial relationships are not for any reason inappropriate in principle. It should be noted that there are some situations in which the development of full managerial relationships (in the precise sense in which 'managerial' is defined later in the chapter) appears for good reasons to be specifically excluded – as, for example, in the organization of medical consultants.[6] However, even in these situations the questions of the various levels or kinds of work to be done still remains, as well as the question of who is expected to carry them out.

Table 1.1 Summary of work strata

Work stratum	Description of work	Upper boundary
1	*Prescribed output* – working towards objectives which can be completely specified (as far as is significant) beforehand, according to defined circumstances which may present themselves.	Not expected to make any significant judgements on what output to aim for or under what circumstances to aim for it.
2	*Systematic service provision* – making where the precise objectives to be pursued have to be judged according to the needs of each specific concrete situation which presents itself.	Not expected to make any decisions, i.e., commitments, on how future possible situations are to be dealt with.
3	*Systematic service provision* – making systematic provision of services of some given kinds shaped to the needs of a continuous sequence of concrete situations which present themselves.	Not expected to make any decisions on the re-allocation of resources to meet as yet unmanifested needs (for the given kinds of services) within some given territorial or organizational society.
4	*Comprehensive service provision* – making comprehensive provision of services of some given kinds according to the total and continuing needs for them throughout some given territorial or organizational society.	Not expected to make any decisions on the re-allocation of resources to meet needs for services of different or new kinds.
5	*Comprehensive field coverage* – making comprehensive provision of services within some general field of need throughout some given territorial or organizational society.	Not expected to make any decisions on the re-allocation of resources to provide services outside the given field of need.

[6] See Rowbottom, R. W. (1973), 'Organizing Social Services, Hierarchy or...?'

This descriptive model of the natural hierarchy of work in organizations outlined above has been tested and developed over the year or so since its first formulation in a series of seminar discussions with groups of senior staff from social services throughout the country. More specifically it has been employed in a series of exploratory projects during this period (some of which are described below) undertaken within specific social services departments, and has already been absorbed into executive action in several of these projects.

The main features of each stratum of work in the model are summarized in Table 1.1 and elaborated one by one below. Illustrative examples are taken from the project work described in social services, but since the thesis is in such general terms, tentative illustrations have been offered as well drawing upon recent work in the field of health services,[7] and certain other material from the authors' combined experience. In addition precise definitions of the boundary between strata are given in clearcut terms of the kinds of decisions which the worker at any level is or is not expected to make in the course of his work. (These boundary definitions provide the ultimate test in practice in classifying the kind of work required in specific given jobs.)

Stratum 1 – prescribed output

At the lowest stratum of work the output required of the worker is completely prescribed or prescribable, as are the specific circumstances in which this or that task should be pursued. If he is in doubt as to which task to pursue, it is prescribed that he take the matter up with his immediate superior. Work consists of such things as rendering given services, collecting given information, making prescribed checks or tests, producing predetermined products. What is to be done, in terms of the kind or form of results to be achieved, does not have to be decided. This will (either) have been specifically prescribed for the occasion or (frequently) have been communicated during the process of induction to the job as the sorts of response required when certain stimuli are experienced. If there is any doubt about the result required it can be dispelled by further description or demonstration to the point where more detailed discrimination becomes irrelevant to the quality of result required. What does need to be decided – and this may not necessarily be at all straightforward – is just how to produce the results required, that is, by

[7] See Rowbottom, R. W. *et al.* (1973), *Hospital Organization*.

what method and also with what priority. Thus, greater or lesser exercise of discretion is necessary – the work is far from being prescribed in totality.

The personal qualities called for within this stratum include possession of knowledge of the range of demands to be expected in daily work, knowledge of the proper responses called for, skills in carrying out these various responses and, not least, appropriate attitudes to the work in question and the people to be dealt with.

And so within this stratum we have the typical work of those in SSDs described as social work assistants, care assistants, cleaners, cooks, drivers and clerks. More generally, it may be assumed that most artisans and craftsmen work within this stratum, and also those professional trainees and apprentices destined for work at higher levels who are as yet in some early and preparatory stages of their career.

Stratum 2 – situational response

Within the second stratum the ends to be pursued are again in the form of results required in specific situations, but here the output required can be partially, and only partially, specified beforehand. The appropriate results or output must now depend to a significant degree on assessments of the social or physical nature of the situation which presents itself and in which the task is to be carried out. The work is such that it is impossible in principle to demonstrate fully beforehand just what the final outcome should look like – this could only be established by actually going through the task concerned. However, by way of limit, no decisions, that is no commitments to future action, are called for in respect to possible future situations which may arise. The work is still concerned with the concrete and the particular.

Rather than collecting given information, or making prescribed tests or checks as in Stratum 1, the task would now be redefined in Stratum 2 in the more general form of producing an appraisal or making an assessment. Rather than rendering a prescribed service or making a prescribed product, the task would now be redefined as producing a service or product of a certain kind but shaped according to the judged needs of the particular situation. The 'judged needs' might, for example, be those of a person in distress (social services), or a child at school (education), or a customer (commerce). Within this stratum 'demands' can never be taken at their face value: there is always an implicit requirement to explore and assess what the 'real' needs of the situation are.

Thus in addition to the technical skills of the Stratum 1 worker, the worker in Stratum 2 must have the ability to penetrate to the underlying nature of the specific situations with which he finds himself in contact. Indeed it is this latter ability, based on some body of explicit theoretical knowledge, which perhaps distinguishes the true 'professional' in his particular field from the craftsman or technician who is only equipped to work within the first stratum described above.[8] However, this is not to imply that only members of the acknowledged professions may work at this stratum or higher ones. The ability itself is the thing in question, not any body of explicit theory.

Within this stratum the sort of managerial roles can be expected to emerge which carry full accountability for the work of Stratum 1 workers and duties of assessing their needs and capabilities in allocating work and promoting their personal development. (In contrast, what might be called 'supervisory' roles may exist in the upper reaches of Stratum 1, but those in them will not be expected to make rounded appraisals of the ability and need of subordinate staff, but rather to carry out such prescribed tasks as instructing staff in their work, allocating specific jobs and dealing with specific queries.) However, it is not at all necessary to assume that all roles within this stratum have a managerial content, and indeed the kind of definitions proposed here and below surmount the problem of being forced to describe higher-than-basic strata of work in a way which automatically links them to the carrying of managerial or supervisory responsibility. The example of the experienced social worker who takes full responsibility for cases but works without subordinates has already been cited.

Stratum 3 – systematic service provision

At Stratum 3 it is required to go beyond responding to specific situations case by case, however adequately. It is required to envisage

---

[8] The introduction of ideas of discrete work-strata into theories of occupation and profession presents intriguing prospects. Apart from the possible distinction of 'craftsmen' and 'technicians' from 'professionals' just described, it also draws attention to the likely presence of many different strata or levels within any one occupational group – or, putting it another way, of finding social workers, teachers, doctors, etc. within any one of Strata 2, 3, 4, etc. This stratification within occupational groups is usually obscured by a sociological habit of treating each group as if its members had one unique status or prestige level – treating the house-surgeon as identical with the President of the Royal College of Surgeons, for example.

the needs of a continuing sequence of situations, some as yet in the future and unmaterialized, in terms of the patterns of response which may be established. Relationships of one situation to another and the characteristics of the sequence as a whole are crucial. In order to design appropriate responses some general specifications of the *kinds* of services which are required must be available.

Thus in SSDs an example of Stratum 3 work would be the development of intake and assessment procedures for all those clients who apply to, or are referred to, a particular area office; or the development of standard assessment procedures for the range of children being referred by existing fieldwork services for residential care. In health services an example might be the development of systematic accident and emergency services in a particular hospital. In education, it might be the development of a general curriculum for all the infants who present themselves at a particular school for primary education. In manufacturing, it might be developing a system for handling orders for a particular kind of product.

Within this stratum, however, work is confined to dealing with some particular flow or sequence of situations which naturally arises from the given organizational provision. The work does not extend to considering and dealing with various situations of need that do not, without further investments of resource, yet manifest themselves in any particular organizational or territorial society – for example, needs for social work that might be manifested were additional local offices to be opened in new districts. Although staff working within Stratum 3 may draw attention to the possibilities of such new investments, they will not be expected to make any *decisions* about them.

Stratum 3 work is essentially concerned with developing systems and procedures which prescribe the way future situational-response work is to be carried out. There is seemingly similar work in Stratum 2 which consists of laying down general rules, methods or standards. However, this, if it is indeed within Stratum 2, will be pitched in terms of the totally prescribed responses required in completely specifiable circumstances. Thus at Stratum 3 the first genuine policy making type work emerges: that is, the laying down of general prescriptions which guide, without precisely specifying. In using the word 'system' here we are referring to prescriptions of this general type. Characteristically, the work involves initial discussions and negotiations with a number of fellow workers and co-ordinating with them the introduction of new schemes. Necessarily, it involves some use of conceptualization, both of types of situations likely to be faced and of appropriate kinds of response.

Within SSDs it has become clear that many specialist advisers and development officers work at this level; and also the area officers in charge of large local offices containing several teams of social workers and ancillary staff.

Stratum 4 – comprehensive service provision

At Stratum 4 the definition of the aims of work and the environmental situation to be encompassed takes a decisive jump again. No longer is it sufficient to stay passively within the bounds of the succession of situations with which contact arises in the normal course of things. Now further initiative is required. It is required to take account systematically of the need for service as it exists and wherever it exists in some given society, territorially or organizationally defined. However, within this stratum the identification of the need to be met is still limited by a particular conception of the kinds of service which the organization is understood to be legitimately providing. Let us elaborate this last point.

At Stratum 2 the identification of need which can be met is limited both by the existence of certain given systems and procedures and the existence (or non-existence) of substantive organizational resources with which to carry out work at a given point in the broader society concerned. At Stratum 3 the former constraint disappears but the latter remains. But at Stratum 4 both these constraints disappear. The only constraint on developing new services or proposals for new services is the constraint of given policy, explicit or understood, on the particular kind of services which will be regarded as well-established, sanctioned, and legitimated.

The starting question at Stratum 4 is: what is the extent of the need for services of these kinds throughout the given territorial or organizational society? New information about the various ranges of past situations encountered is not enough. More information must be fed in, of the kind that can often only be discovered by systematic survey or deliberate 'intelligence' work.

Thus, in social services the starting point may be all those in a given county or borough, known or unknown, needing advice or material aid or other specific services because of their physical disabilities; or all those who could benefit, for one reason or another from, say, meals on wheels or home help services. In commerce, it might be all those in some given regional, national, or international territory who would be potential customers for certain established ranges of product or service. Within any given organizational society, it might be the internal needs for facilities to carry out various kinds of personnel, administrative or financial work.

At Stratum 4 then, the essence of the work is concerned with developing comprehensive provision of services or products of a specified kind throughout some defined society. Financial investment in plant and buildings and, in general, recruitment and training programmes are a natural concomitant. Since new capital investment of any significant size is always a sensitive matter, the final sanction for it may often rest at higher organization levels, or indeed within governing bodies of various kinds. Organization members within Stratum 4 may not themselves have authority to make the final decision on investment therefore, but at least they will need some degree of authority to reallocate existing resources so as to cope with emerging or as yet untapped areas of need within the society concerned.

Within this stratum are to be found in SSDs various assistant directors and divisional directors. In health services it is presumed that most of the new community physicians, the chief nurses, and the administrators at area and district level are also working within this stratum. It appears unlikely that any people within this fourth stratum can carry out their work without assistance; all appear to need access to subordinate or ancillary staff.

Stratum 5 – comprehensive field coverage

At Stratum 5 need has to be considered again in its complete incidence throughout some given territorial or organizational society, but the scope is broadened by moving from a framework of accepted, specified, and sanctioned kinds of service on offer to a framework which simply defines some general field of need. The work consists essentially of developing whatever comprehensive provision may be required within this given general field. Thus, in SSDs, in moving from Stratum 4 to Stratum 5, the focus changes from things like needs for homes for the elderly, casework with problem families, provision of home help, to the general question 'how can social distress in this district, in all its forms, best be prevented or alleviated?' In health services the question changes from 'what sorts of hospital, general practice, and public health services are needed throughout this district?' (with the meanings that these terms already attract) to 'what are the basic health needs of this district, group by group, and how they may best be met in any combination of old or new services?' Other general fields of need in the public sector whose nature would imply potential Stratum 5 work would include education, leisure, housing, physical environment, transportation, etc., where similar questions might be posed. In industry, needs in Stratum 4 terms for things like overcoats, telephones, or calculators would presumably become redefined as needs for 'clothing', 'communication systems', and 'data processing', respectively, in Stratum 5 terms.

Thus there is an important distinction to be observed here between what we have called *particular kinds of service* and *general fields of need*. As we are using it, the phrase 'particular kinds of service' is one which at a given point of cultural development would conjure up a precise picture of what the services comprised and what kinds of physical facilities and staff were needed to provide them. On the other hand, a field-of-need description would convey no such precise image. (Presumably, in the normal course of social development many terms, which initially imply little more than fields of possible need, later acquire much more concrete connotations. Think, for example, of the now-specific connotations of such phrases as 'general medical practice' or 'social casework' or 'television services' or 'life insurance' compared with their imprecise significance at earlier points of social history.)

Work within this stratum involves much interaction with directing and sponsoring bodies of various kinds – boards of directors or other governing bodies, financial bodies, trusts, public authorities, and the like. Inevitably, staff within this stratum spend much time 'outside' the immediate operational zone of the organization.

Within this stratum then, we should expect to find the chief officers of at least the major departments in local authorities, some senior executive posts (as yet not altogether clear) in the new health authorities, and the chief executives of many large commercial operating organizations, freestanding or part of larger financial groupings.

Possible higher strata
So far we have described five discrete strata of work but there seems no necessary reason to stop here. Jaques for example, has assumed on the basis of his own observations of viable managerial structures in a number of varied organizational settings that at least seven distinct levels can be identified.[9] There is evidently further work above the fifth stratum concerned with the interaction of many fields of need at local, regional, national, or even international levels. There is the

[9] 'Preliminary Sketch of a General Structure of Executive Strata', op. cit.

need within local authorities to produce plans which intermesh the whole range of public services – education, social services, planning, leisure, etc. – provided at local level. The same intermeshing of various broad fields of public service, together with nationalized industries, arises at national level. In the private sector there is the increasing growth of national or multinational conglomerates bringing together operating divisions or subsidiaries in many broad fields. For the moment the existence of such higher level work is noted, but no definite classification can be advanced.

'Zooming' and 'transitional phases'

Before passing on, however, two important elaborations of the thesis which have been developed in discussions of its applicability to SSDs must be mentioned. The first is the idea of 'zooming'; the second what might be called the 'transitional phase'.

It is evident that staff at Stratum 3 and upward are not able to spend, and do not spend, all their time simply considering extended ranges of work and needs, as it were, in abstraction. Stratum 5 staff will frequently get involved in discussions of the comprehensive provision of existing kinds of services, the establishment of specific systems, or the correct handling of the specific and perhaps quite crucial cases; Stratum 4 staff will quite frequently get involved with particular systems or they too with particular cases; and so on. Such phenomena may be described as 'zooming'.[10] There may be a variety of causes: direct externally given requirements, such as insistence by the governing body that the head or director of a public agency looks into a particular case; or the need to help some subordinate in difficulty; or a laudable aim to get the 'feel' of lower level and more concrete realities, from time to time; or even perhaps the occasional attempted flight from higher demands!

Does this mean that more senior people commonly act at several different levels of work, concurrently or in rapid succession? To assume this would in fact be to assume that they experienced rapid expansion and contraction of personal capacity, one moment only capable of seeing aims and situations in a narrow context, and the next far more broadly – which seems implausible. On the contrary, it is readily observable that when people capable of operating at high levels get involved in work which is at *apparently* lower levels, that they tackle them in crucially different ways, ways which constantly exhibit the

[10] See Evans, J. S. (1970), 'Managerial Accountability – Chief Officers, Consultants and Boards'.

characteristics of the higher level approach. Where people with Stratum 3 capacity become involved in concrete situations needing their attention, these specific situations are rapidly seized on as illustrative instances of a general problem demanding a more systematic response. Where Stratum 4 people become involved with particular ailing systems or procedures their interventions inevitably lead to considerations of how the benefits might be extended comprehensively throughout the organization concerned.

An actual illustration of this process which has come to our notice is that of the industrial chief executive who asked his secretary to prepare and keep up-to-date an organization chart of his company for the wall of his office. Given the written, highly explicit accounts of jobs and organization which were current in this particular company, this task would appear to have been straightforward enough, but nevertheless the chief executive found himself dissatisfied in this instance with the results of his secretary's work. As anyone knows who has tried to draw charts of the detailed and complex relationships, however well-established, in large organizations, the sheer job of charting itself is not so simple as it might seem. The chief executive grappled with it for several hours – indeed all evening. What he began to devise was not simply an answer to his immediate problem (Stratum 2) but the outlines of a general system of organizational charting (Stratum 3). Moreover, having devised such a system he proceeded to think about, and later to act upon, the possibility of its useful employment throughout the company (Stratum 4). (Whether he proceeded to any further action which indicated a Stratum 5 or higher outlook is not known; however, the point is made.)

What this suggests then is that 'zooming' is a normal or proper part of executive work, and must be thought of as not simply a 'zoom down' into a lower stratum of work (leaving apart, that is, the case where the person concerned is not in fact capable of operating at the higher stratum) but also properly a subsequent zoom *up*, or return, the total sweep in fact providing valuable concrete experience for the more abstract work to be carried out.

The second phenomenon which must be taken into account is that of the *transitional phase*, which is to do with the observable development in people's abilities as they approach the points in their careers where they are ready to take on work at the next higher stratum. Now it is possible, as described above, to define a completely sharp boundary between strata in terms of certain kinds of decisions which may or may not be made, but it is not easy to believe that human capacity develops in the same completely discontinuous way. One does not go to bed one night unable to think beyond the case in hand and wake up next morning unable to do other than see cases as illustrative of whole ranges of work to be tackled accordingly. There is evidence that personal capacity to do work at various levels develops in a continuous pattern over time though at different rates for different people – as A, B and C in Figure 1.1.[11] Moreover, for those like A

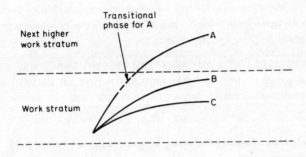

Figure 1.1   Differing patterns of development of personal capacity

who are on their way to achieving not merely a higher ability within a given stratum, but ability of a different and higher kind (and only for those people), observation now suggests that they begin to show evidences of this higher ability in a nascent form well before it has reached its fully realized state. The one- or two-year practical post-qualification experience in 'responsible positions' required by many professional bodies, before full-professional registration is awarded, is no doubt a particular recognition of this phenomenon at the Stratum 1–2 boundary.

The organizational consequences of this phenomenon are as follows. Whereas the manager with the next higher stratum, say, for example, the *systematic service provision* stratum, Stratum 3, may involve A, B and C, who are all at this moment of their careers in Stratum 2, in discussion about new policies (say, the introduction of new systems or procedures) he is likely, it seems, to get contributions of a different quality from A than from B or C. Such discussion may help to train A for his forthcoming leap. Indeed, he may be asked to do such things as chairing working parties to produce ideas for new policies, though at this stage of his career he will not be judged quite ready to take full responsibility for the final formulation of such policies or responsibility for their implementation following approval.

[11] Jaques, E. (1967), op. cit.

Applications of the model

Having now laid out the model, at least in its present stage of development, the remainder of the chapter is devoted to the uses to which it can be put. We shall consider:

(*a*) how the ideas can be used to clarify roles and organizational structure within existing organization; and
(*b*) how the ideas may help to design new organizations considered as total systems from which a particular quality of response is required in relation to their environment.

Illustrations of both applications will be given from actual developmental project work that has been carried out in particular social services departments.

The clarification of existing organizational roles and structure

As has been noted, the theory under discussion grew out of observations of the equivocal position of certain apparently managerial posts in many SSDs. Such posts seemed regularly to attract conflicts about their status and authority in a way not true of other posts within the hierarchy. Earlier studies in manufacturing and nursing organizations had revealed similar phenomena.[12] Generalizing, it seems that if a hierarchy is set up in any organization on the basis of all the various different grades of post which may exist or be required in the given organization, then not all of them will turn out in practice to carry the same relationship to those beneath them. Moreover, to the extent that this phenomenon is denied officially, or by those in the particular posts concerned, certain inevitable and quite painful stresses and conflicts will result.

Let us start with a definition. Let us describe the strongest, most secure, most authoritative posts in the hierarchy as 'fully managerial' or simply 'managerial'. We shall associate these with unquestioned rights to set or sanction general aims and guides for subordinates, and with rights to appraise their performance and capacity in practice and to assign or reassign work to them accordingly. Then we may pose a simple proposition: that no more than one of these managerial posts can be sustained in any one stratum of work (as here defined) within the hierarchy. Thus, knowing the range of strata of work to

[12] See Brown, W. (1960), *Exploration in Management*, and Rowbottom, R. W. *et al.* (1973), op. cit.

be carried out within any organization, we can readily compute the maximum number of viable managerial posts in the hierarchy. In the case of SSDs for example, assuming the desire to carry out work at all five of the strata identified above, there would only be room for four such managerial posts in any strand of the hierarchy.

However, as it happens, there are something of the order of ten or twelve main *grades* of post in SSDs, and indeed it seems quite usual for organizations to generate many more steps in their grading hierarchies than can be justified in terms of the basic managerial hierarchy required. What is the position of the people in all these other posts? Judging from project work in various fields that has been quoted, the answer, it appears, is that they will in reality tend to carry roles which are less than, and crucially different from, full managerial roles as they have just been described. At least four possible alternative roles have been identified in these various fields of project work – *co-ordinating roles*, *monitoring roles*, *staff-officer roles* and *supervisory roles*.[13] Each has its distinct qualities, but in general none of these types of role carries authority to set general aims and guides for those in posts of lower grade, or to appraise their performance and capacity, or to assign or reassign work accordingly.

In other words, these other people will not naturally and readily be identified as 'the boss'. It will be more natural and satisfactory to have a boss who is (and is capable of) working at the next higher stratum of work, and one who is therefore able to make a radical adjustment to the whole *setting* within which work is carried out when major problems loom. What is unsatisfactory and a constant source of tension is a supposed boss who goes through some motions of appraising performance and setting general aims and guides, even though in reality he is only carrying out work of essentially the same kind himself, and therefore needs to refer any major difficulties requiring radical readjustments in work or circumstance to some further point still in the hierarchy. This is indeed bureaucracy with a vengeance!

Some examples from social services

Let us briefly illustrate how this idea of linking managerial roles with different strata of work has been applied in actual projects in SSDs.

One project (still in hand) is concerned with the managerial structure of an area social work office and in particular with the role

[13] Brown, W. (1960), op. cit.; Rowbottom, R. W. *et al.* (1973), op. cit.; *Social Services Departments*.

of the team leader, which has been felt in this department as elsewhere to raise considerable problems. There are four teams in this particular office and each team leader is 'in charge of' a team of up to a dozen or so people. Manifestly, the hierarchy is as shown in Figure 1.2(a). On the surface it appears that all members of the team are managed, directly or indirectly, by the team leader. Collaborative analyses, using these ideas of discrete strata of work and managerial and other roles, have revealed a very different situation, one much closer to the model of Figure 1.2(b), which, now it has been made explicit, seems to command considerable approval. In reality it appears that team leaders, senior social workers, and certain of the more experienced basic grade workers are all working within the same *situational response* stratum – they are all carrying full 'professional' responsibility for their cases, drawing only on voluntary consultation with colleagues as and when they require it. Moreover, when large issues appear on the scene, they all tend to look directly to the area officer for guidance rather than the team leader. In respect of the other workers at this second stratum then, the team leader has essentially a *co-ordinative* role – co-ordinating the daily flow of work, co-ordinating duty arrangements, chairing team meetings, etc. – though in addition he provides advice to his colleagues, when asked. In contrast, the social work assistants, the trainees and students, and other of the basic grade social workers, both unqualified and newly qualified, are still working in Stratum 1, although many of them, particularly the students and newly qualified social workers, may be expected to be within the transitional phase leading to Stratum 2. This latter group clearly requires special treatment. However, since none of these people have actually realized a Stratum 2 capability, they can all be expected to find it acceptable to see the team leader (or perhaps one of the other Stratum 2 workers to whom they may be attached for training purposes in the case of students) in a managerial role – in conventional social work terminology as a realistic and accepted 'supervisor'.[14] Thus, what could easily be seen and interpreted (or misinterpreted) as a long, complex hierarchy within the area office can now be seen in a much clearer, simpler, and more functional form, with only one intermediate management level, and that not applying to all staff within the office.

[14] It may be noted that the term 'supervisor' as used in social work practice implies in fact a range of authority and accountability commensurate with a 'managerial' role, as defined above. However, the term 'supervisor' in the Glacier Project (Brown, W., (1960), op. cit.) and later work was used, in keeping with industrial and certain other practice, to define a role with precisely *less* than full managerial characteristics.

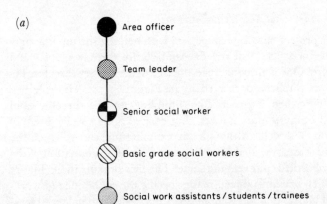

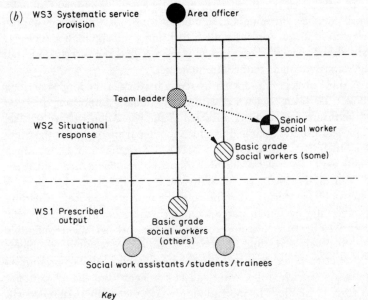

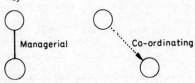

Figure 1.2   Organization of an area social work team
   (a)   Manifest organization
   (b)   Requisite organization shown in terms of work strata roles

Another project has been concerned with helping the top management group of an SSD to redefine and clarify their own roles and relationships. One issue concerned the role of the deputy director. His position was publicly portrayed as in Figure 1.3(a). His role was generally described in terms like 'doubling for the director' and 'dealing with day-to-day matters', but carried some specific areas of responsibility as well. Although on examination the roles of the assistant directors revealed clear Stratum 4 work, examination of the deputy's role failed to reveal the same. The new organization (Figure 1.3(b)) which was introduced made specific use of the idea of work-strata, and failing to find room for any intermediate managerial level between the work of the director (Stratum 5) and his assistant directors (Stratum 4), the deputy was assigned a senior Stratum 4 post, with responsibility in this case for the comprehensive provision of all field-work services. Although a significant co-ordinative role was also recognized in relation to his other Stratum 4 colleagues, it was clearly established that all these people were to regard the director and not the deputy as their immediate manager.

A third project (supported by seminar work of the kind described above) has been concerned with the nationally important question of the future role and organization of the education welfare service, at present usually attached to education departments but with strong links to SSDs. The distinction between Stratum 1 and Stratum 2 definition of the role of the education welfare officer turns out to be of central significance. In a Stratum 1 conception, his work is describable in terms like enforcing school attendance, providing specific information to parents and providing or arranging specific material aids. In a Stratum 2 conception his work becomes redefinable in terms such as dealing in a flexible, responsive way with problems of non-attendance and their social causes, with a view to promoting a situation in which the child can best benefit from the educational facilities available. The indications are that the strong preference will be for the second definition of the role – a decision with profound implications for the training and deployment of staff – with perhaps recognition of the need for the provision of ancillary staff at Stratum 1 as well.

Other projects have applied similar analyses to the kind of work required of heads of homes in residential social work – whether it should be at Stratum 1 or 2;[15] to the kind of work required of so-called 'training officers' – whether it should be at Stratum 2 or 3; and to the kind of work required of those developing new types of

[15] See Chapter 5.

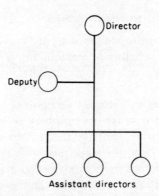

(a)

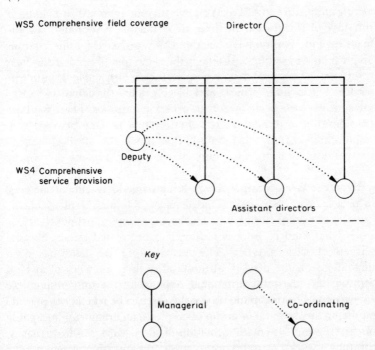

Figure 1.3 Top management structure of a social services department
   (a) Manifest organization
   (b) Requisite organization shown in terms of work strata roles

social work with disturbed adolescents known as 'intermediate treatment' – again, whether at Stratum 2 or 3.[16]

Designing new organizational structure

The examples quoted so far have all been of situations where staff and organization already exist and the problem is to clarify the levels of work to be done, and the consequent managerial and other role structure called for. In a more fundamental application, the theory can also be applied to the design and establishment of new organizations by posing the question: what strata of work is the organization as a whole required to encompass?

A current example from our own project work is that of the setting up, or rather re-establishment, of hospital social work organization following the recent transfer of hospital social workers en bloc from health authorities to SSDs. We have become involved in helping in this task of integration in three departments. Nationally, the difficulties of integration have been much exacerbated by uncertainties about relative gradings. Although the same sort of grade-titles have traditionally been used in both hospital social work and local authority services – 'principal', 'senior', and 'basic' grade – the actual associated salary scales have been lower for workers in hospitals. There has been considerable argument as to whether this in fact betokens less responsibility, grade-title for grade-title; or whether it simply reflects the continuous history of comparative underpayment of hospital workers.

Here, the Work Stratum theory has provided a useful cutting edge in project work. Separating and leaving aside for the moment any questions of grade and pay, it has been possible to expose the basic issue: what kind of work is required to be carried out in hospital settings of various types? The answer from the field has been unanimous on the need in all hospital settings for work of at least Stratum 2 – the total situational response of the fully responsible caseworker. The remaining issue is then seen to be whether to provide on site, in any hospital or group of hospitals, an organization capable of carrying out systematic provision of social work services (that is, Stratum 3 work), or to leave the on-site organization as one merely capable of co-ordinated Stratum 2 work, the necessary higher level work being done by others not specifically associated with the particular hospitals concerned.

Given this analysis, the three project departments concerned are

[16] See Chapter 9.

now in the process of making explicit choices, and seem in fact to be opting for full Stratum 3 organizations in the larger hospitals or hospital groups, and Stratum 2 individual posts or teams in the smaller hospitals. Questions of appropriate grading can properly follow, starting with the question of whether there could be any justification for lower grades for the same stratum of work in one setting or the other.

Thus, the Work Stratum theory appears to offer a new way, not only of deciding the design of extensions to existing organizations, but of designing organizations from new. It is a way which starts from the question of the *kind* of impact which is required on some given social and physical environment. At the same time it is a way which does not seek to deny the fundamental reality of the stratification of authority in many situations. Such stratification is justified in defensible terms of higher and lower kinds of work to be performed, rather than in such crude arguments as the inevitability of having those who direct and those who obey.

It may be stressed that the quality of organizational impact on, or response to, its environment can be a matter of *choice*. As Silverman and Child separately observe, organizations are the creation of conscious decision-taking actors, not simply a product of a 'causal' environment.[17] Much has been written about the correlations between various kinds of organizational structure and organizational environment, but not a lot has been said about the precise mechanisms by which managers might create so-called 'organic' or 'mechanistic' organizations. Apart from some of the Tavistock work on detailed systems design, using ideas of 'primary tasks' and 'sentient groups' (see, for example, Miller and Rice), the literature is content for the most part to rest at broad descriptive or ideological levels; or to observe empirical correlation in certain organizational and environmental characteristics.[18] But the levers of change are rarely revealed.

The work stratum model, as described here, offers one very concrete way in which organizations may be designed to react in various ways, or various degrees of depth, to their environment. Thus, a Stratum 3 system will respond in quite a different and perhaps more 'organic' way than a Stratum 2 system. Conversely, the model also offers a precise way of categorizing the various possible stages of evolution of any given organization from the Stratum 1 solitary-jobber type of organization, capable only of a prescribed response to its environ-

[17] Silverman, D. (1970), *The Theory of Organizations*, and Child, J. (1972), 'Organizational Structure, Environment and Performance: The Role of Strategic Choice'.

[18] Miller, E. J. and Rice, A. K. (1967), *Systems of Organization*.

ment, right through to the fully mature Stratum 5 type of organization. (This may be compared with other published descriptions of
organizational evolution such as those of Chandler, Jaques,
Greiner.)[19]

From this viewpoint the Stratum 5 organization with its fully
realized capability for self-development emerges as the system of
special interest. It appears to offer one concrete answer to the general
problem posed by Schon of how society is to produce organizations,
both public and private, capable of coping with the demands of an
increasingly unstable world.[20] The increasing establishment of
Stratum 5 organizations at the 'periphery' (in Schon's term) seems
to offer a means of getting away from a society dominated by the
exclusive development of new ideas at the 'centre', and their diffusion
on a 'centre periphery' model, with all the attendant problems he
so ably identifies. It offers a means of retaining coherent organizational
structure. At the same time it does not exclude the possibility of basic
political and legal control from the centre. Thus, to stick to the
examples quoted extensively in this chapter, the current establishment
in Britain of new organizations at local level in the fields of both
social services and health services, capable of working to the most
general, i.e., Stratum 5 terms of reference, while still subject to the
overall legal–political control of central government, seems a
development to be welcomed.

At this point the thesis leaves us with some large questions: Are
there other public services which could benefit from establishment
in Stratum 5 organizations, either by extension or reduction of their
present structure? What is the justification for the many large national
public services which presumably require more than four-level
executive structures, but with a brief which suggests only a Stratum
4 definition of need, such as providing comprehensive national rail
services or a national supply of coal? What is the social justification
for the existence of larger-than-Stratum-5 industrial and commercial
organizations? How far might we see the proliferation of these as
symptomatic of a society over-obsessed with advantages of the
economy of size and scale, and neglectful of the needs for more convivial
institutions in which men can live and work?

---

[19] Chandler, A. D. (1963), *Strategy and Structure*; Jaques, E. (1965b)
'Preliminary Sketch of a General Structure of Executive Strata; Greiner, E. L. (1972),
'Evolution and Revolution as Organizations Grow'.
[20] Schon, D. A. (1971), *Beyond the Stable State*.

2 Professionals in Health and Social Services Organizations[1]

by Ralph Rowbottom

Introduction

Action-research[2] at BIOSS since the late 1960s in the health and social services field has provided a rich opportunity to study many basic questions about the way in which professions may be organized. Work has been undertaken with a wide range of medical specialists, with general practitioners, nurses and midwives, remedial therapists, social workers, pharmacists, engineers and technicians, and a whole host of members of other paramedical and ancillary professions employed in the NHS or in local authority social services departments.

Some of the issues that have been encountered are to do with how far the external management or direction of professional work is appropriate or possible. Can doctors, nurses, social workers, engineers, and so on, be managed by their employers and, if so, in what sense of the word? Can they appropriately be put under the control of some senior lay administrator, some 'general manager'? How far can even the employing authorities themselves (the governing bodies that is, as distinct from their officers) properly guide or direct the work of their professional employees?

A second set of issues are to do generally with organizational relationships within particular professional groups. Put baldly, can even doctors appropriately manage other doctors, or nurses other nurses, or social workers other social workers, without improper interference with the exercise of professional judgement?

A third set are to do with relationships between professional or occupational groups as a whole. Some professions or occupations are

[1] An earlier version of the material to be presented was published jointly by the two Research Units in the form of a Working Paper 'Professionals in Health and Social Services Organisations' (1976).

[2] See *Social Analysis*.

(for whatever reason) manifestly of higher status than others. Does this higher status automatically confer authority in dealings with others of lower status? If doctors, for example, have authority over nurses or paramedical staff, how far does it extend, and what justifies it? Are doctors also justified in assuming authority over social workers or psychologists?

In general the question might be put: how much autonomy, how much independence, is it appropriate for the members of any given profession to have where they are employed by public authorities or other bodies? Are there different answers for different types of profession or occupation, or for professions or occupations at different stages of development, or for different practice situations; and if so, from what do these differences spring?

In exploring these questions over the years it has become clear that there is no one definite set of answers which applies equally to all the various occupational groups under consideration. It turns out that there are a number of different characteristics which basically distinguish the practice of one occupational group from another. Each of these characteristics where it arises carries its own particular and specific consequences for what is organizationally possible and appropriate. In brief, these four characteristics are:

(*a*) *degree of professional development* – whether the occupational group possesses its own specific body of theory and practice which has moved beyond the stage where non-members can be expected to appreciate emerging possibilities for extension and further development;

(*b*) *the practice assumption* – whether the assumptions, explicit or otherwise, of the nature of the practice in any given situation are consistent with what may be called 'agency service', or whether they demand what may be called 'independent practice' for the individual practitioner;

(*c*) *existence of an 'encompassing' profession* – whether or not another occupation or profession exists which is regarded as having a deeper or more encompassing view of practice in the field concerned;

(*d*) *primacy* – whether or not its members are recognized as automatically carrying prime responsibility where members of other occupational groups regularly work together with them on the same cases or projects.

The specific organizational consequences of these various characteristics are summarized in Table 2.1. As will be demonstrated, not all these characteristics by any means are inimical in principle to the development of straightforward hierarchical organization built upon extended lines of managerial relationships. It is only one of the characteristics here identified – the existence of practice-assumptions which demand 'independent practice', or the 'independent practitioner' – which is absolutely at odds with managerial relationships (in the precise definition of this term which we shall use). Thus, our general conclusion will be that it is not professionalism as such that is inimical to managerial organization, but only one and by no means universally occurring aspect of it.[3] However, all the characteristics described will be shown to have implications for organization, more or less radical, even where managerial structure is in general possible.

The four characteristics listed and their various organizational implications are discussed one by one in the sections that follow. First, some consideration will be given to the idea of 'profession' – a word which (naturally enough) figures prominently in discussions.

The attempt to define 'profession'

When particular occupational groups in health or social services are pressing for greater independence, or defending existing situations of independence, it is common for them to place much weight on their claimed 'professional status' in arguing their case. Even before the validity of such arguments can be assessed there is of course a prior problem of pinning an exact meaning to this phrase, and of finding a definition which will provide an unambiguous and generally acceptable means of deciding whether a particular claim of professional status is in fact justified.

[3] Care must be taken here to avoid any too ready equation of 'managerial organization' with 'bureaucracy'. From the time of Weber onwards, the conception of bureaucracy has carried ambivalent, if not outrightly pejorative, overtones. If 'bureaucracy' is taken to imply rule-bound organization, the removal of all discretion and freedom, a machine-like impersonality, rigidity of structure, identification with narrow cost-scraping aims, etc., it will be little surprise if professionals (amongst others) find bureaucratic environments highly uncongenial!

Again, within any given organization, bureaucratic or other, the particular *ethos* that has developed may or may not be in conflict with the prevailing ethos of any given professional group at any time. (An accountant, a doctor, and a physicist, for example, may find themselves feeling very differently about employment in a highly profit-conscious commercial company as opposed to a public service or voluntary organization. It should be stressed that what is being considered in this paper are any implicit conflicts in authority structures – whether anyone may properly have *authority* to direct certain kinds of professionals, assess their work, reallocate it, etc., whatever the particular objects of the organization in question, its prevailing ethos, or the rigidity or flexibility of its structure.

Table 2.1   *Various characteristics of occupational groups and their*
organizational consequences

Occupational characteristic	Organizational consequence
1. Existence of an advanced degree of professional development.	– *management* by non-members of the occupational group becomes increasingly inappropriate.
2. Practice assumptions adopted in any situation:	
(*a*) are compatible with *agency service*	– possibility of *managerial* organization.
(*b*) demand *independent practice* (*independent practitioners*).	– impossibility of *managerial* organization (trainees apart even within the same occupational group, but possibility of *monitoring* and *co-ordinating* roles.
3. Existence of a profession with a deeper or more encompassing knowledge-base in the field.	– possibility of members in the encompassing profession carrying *prescribing* authority
4. Existence of primacy, i.e. members of the occupational group or sub-group automatically take prime responsibility in work with other groups or sub-groups in the same field.	– leads to *co-ordinating* roles for those carrying primacy.

The considerable sociological literature on professions is filled with attempts to find an adequate definition. Things such as possession of a body of particular and specialized knowledge, adoption of a service ethic, existence of a professional association, control of training and testing of competence, public registration, length of training and many other factors have been given due weight by various commentators.[4] Others again claim that the whole attempt to find a rational definition is misguided: that professions are simply those occupational groups who have been lucky or clever enough to negotiate themselves into a situation of high status and power.[5]

It is our own belief that there is some significant and useful definition of 'profession' to be discovered. Clearly, the word has everyday currency, and as it is used conveys something over and beyond the more general term 'occupation'. A theory developed from this same research programme on the subject of the stratification of organized

[4] See Wilensky, H. L. (1964) 'The Professionalisation of Everyone?'; Goode, W. J. (1969), 'The Theoretical Limits of Professionalisation'; and Hickson, D. J. and Thomas, M. W. (1969), 'Professionalisation in Britain, A Preliminary Measurement'.

[5] See Johnson, T. J. (1972), *Professions and Power*.

work offers one lead. In brief, this theory distinguishes a number of distinguishable bands or strata of work in all organizations. In the first stratum the outputs desired can be specifically prescribed before work commences and demands can be taken as they stand. The second and higher strata have in common the requirement to exercise judgement in assessing the precise needs of a situation, and hence judgement in constructing the necessary responses.[6] It seems likely that one element lurking in everyday usage of 'profession' is the idea of ability to work somewhere within these higher strata: of ability, that is, to penetrate from demands-as-given to underlying needs. (Of course, this alone does not define professional work, just as there are many who might not qualify on other counts as 'professionals' who nevertheless show ability to do work at such levels.)

There is surely also in everyday usage an implication that being a professional means being able to bring specific theoretical knowledge and insight to bear which non-professionals do not have, or have in lower degree. Further still, there is an implicit expectation that the true professional practitioner will exercise his own judgement in particular cases as impartially and objectively as possible. In other words, there is an implication of some kind of accompanying *ethic*.

In the remainder of this chapter where the word 'professional' is used, it will be used then in this broad sense: of a person capable of applying special theoretical knowledge or insight in cases where objective and impartial judgement of both needs and appropriate responses is called for.[7] Now, this still does not amount to an exact definition, or at least one that could act as a precise criterion in contentious situations, but the propositions or arguments which follow do not depend on the existence of an exact definition of 'profession' for their validity.

Degree of professional development

As has already been noted, a question which regularly arises in health and welfare organizations is, how far it is possible or appropriate for so-called 'senior administrators' or 'general managers' to control doctors, nurses, paramedics, engineers, social workers, or members of various other professions or occupational groups.

The issue here is not whether such *generalists* could actually do with equal proficiency all the work of those of various specific professions

[6] See Chapter 1.
[7] Compare Goode's two 'central generating qualities' of profession as (1) a basic body of abstract knowledge, and (2) the ideal of service (Goode, W. J. (1969), op. cit.).

or crafts of whom they are in charge. Nor is it whether they could give detailed 'technical' instructions to such; for where even a moderate level of special knowledge or competence is called for this is readily conceded to be difficult if not impossible for non-members. The real issue is whether they could be expected to understand enough about the work and the specific needs which it has to meet, to *manage* the performers of that work.

Here of course, we are obliged to clarity what is meant by 'manage'. The word is, in fact, commonly employed in a whole range of somewhat different circumstances. We ourselves start from the specific notion of a manager as one who is accountable for his subordinates' work in all its aspects; who is able to assess the quality and effectiveness of his subordinates' work as it is done, and who has the authority to make any further prescriptions or re-assignments of work which he may judge to be necessary. Beyond this there is an implication that an effective manager, at any rate one who is capable of working at Stratum 3 or higher,[8] is able to lead his subordinates in new developments in approach and practice. There is also the implication that he must understand the needs and characteristics of developing practice thoroughly enough to be able to represent their ideas and views adequately in external discussion and negotiation.

Clearly, the more developed an occupational or professional group becomes, the more difficult it is for a non-member, however generally capable, to perform these managerial functions adequately. Where a so-called manager cannot really help his subordinates with technical problems encountered, where he cannot really judge the all-round competence of his subordinates in any precise degree, and where he lacks any feel for emerging possibilities of general developments in practice, it is necessary to question in exactly what sense the word 'manager' is being used.

The following situation may illuminate these points further. In our earlier project work in health services we frequently came across senior hospital 'lay' administrators who were willing to assert (privately, if not publicly) their collective competence to 'manage' doctors or members of any other professions deployed in hospitals, however specialized or advanced the nature of their work. However, further exploration would invariably demonstrate that these same administrators did not mean by this that they would feel able, for example, to assign particular clinical cases to doctors, or to make effective assessments of their clinical as well as general abilities. Nor would they feel able to carry full accountability for all aspects of the work

[8] See Chapter 1. See also Chapter 5 for detailed discussion.

of doctors, or indeed of many other professionals, in the same way that they would quite naturally do for the work of their own immediate assistants. Nor would they feel competent to guide doctors in important developments in medical practice.

However, these same senior administrators were clearly carrying some relationship of control or guidance, even if not managerial, with respect to doctors and other professionals employed in the hospital. Two further distinct kinds of relationship were identified and described by the terms 'monitoring' and 'co-ordinating', respectively.[9] What neither relationship includes is either the right to issue final or binding prescriptions in the face of strongly conflicting views, or the right to make or act upon fine assessments of performance of personal competence, as is expected in the managerial relationship. Thus, hospital administrators might take action where one of the doctors had gone sharply off the rails; but they had no rights to instruct him in such matters of judgement as exact choice of treatment methods, or where expensive drugs were to be used and where not, or at what rate to clear beds by discharging patients from hospital, for example.[10]

Generalizing, it can be seen that as any profession develops an increasing body of specific knowledge, ideas, and practice of its own, it will be natural for a number of things to follow. First, it will be natural for members to seek to interact with one another through specifically-formed professional associations in order to forward the development of their common practice and knowledge. (This is over and above any desire to associate in order to protect their collective interests, a desire which they may share with less well-developed occupational groups.) Second, it will be natural for them to begin to take an increasing interest in training and the setting of qualification for practice. Thirdly, they will tend to want control of their own practice development in specific organizations where they are employed in large numbers, and they will look to the establishment

[9] A *monitoring* relationship involves checking, or keeping informed of, the effects of others' activity in some given area; warning of sustained or significant deficiencies; and advising corrective action. It does not imply authority either to give instruction or to appraise personal ability or performance. A *co-ordinating* relationship involves preparing and issuing detailed plans and programmes to forward agreed objectives, keeping informed of actual progress, and attempting to overcome obstacles and setbacks. It implies authority to obtain information of progress and to decide what shall be done in situations of uncertainty. It does not imply authority to set new directions, to override sustained disagreements, or to appraise personal performance or ability.

[10] See Rowbottom, R. W. *et al.* (1973), op. cit.

of management posts to be filled by their own members, and the direct access of such members to policy forming bodies. (This leaves aside for the moment the special case to be discussed below where managerial relationships are prohibited even within the profession.)

Of course, there are many cases where there is no suggestion that the specialized knowledge and practice of an occupational group has got to a stage where management by a non-member is impossible in principle. To extend the example considered above, it appears to be accepted that health service administrators may readily manage personnel and supplies specialists, or catering and cleaning staff, notwithstanding any special skills and expertise which the latter might be expected to possess. It has not, however, been generally accepted that the same administrators may manage engineering and building staff, or nurses, or members of the paramedical occupations. In a different field the gathering together in recent years of all social workers in separate social services departments, headed by directors who are increasingly chosen from the ranks of qualified social workers themselves, suggests recognition that social workers, too, have reached a stage of professional development which prohibits effective management by non-members.

Binding standards

As an occupational group or profession evolves it develops not only an underlying body of knowledge but also certain very specific standards and norms of behaviour. Certain things are invariably (and therefore 'properly') done this way; other things should always be avoided. What is of particular interest from the organizational point of view are any standards or conditions which are regarded at any time as absolute and binding; standards which are not to be abandoned in deference to the judgement of some superior, however highly placed, capable or better qualified. Thus, engineers will not be expected to install plant which is unsafe, however badly needed; pharmacists will not be expected to supply certain dangerous combinations of drugs; accountants will not be expected to cook the books in order to help cover overspending or to prove a case for more investment; nurses will not be expected to undertake certain clinical procedures which are reckoned to be beyond nursing competence.

Where (as in all the cases quoted) professional associations already exist, they will serve as a source of potential external support should excessive pressures be applied to change or ignore such standards. Where, as in the case of many professions in the health field, there is public registration as well, then the threat of being struck off the register for 'unprofessional conduct' will act as a further reinforcement.

The organizational effect of such binding standards where they occur is thus to impose certain *limits* on possible direction by superior officers or bodies. They can be added to other more general limits which exist for all employees, professional or not, such as not being required to carry out illegal actions or acts which go beyond the bounds of what is considered to be decent and acceptable human behaviour. It may be noted that the existence of any such binding professional standards do not in themselves prohibit in principle the establishment of managerial or any other directive relationships, either by other members of the same profession or by non-members. However, it will usually be the case that the emergence of various constraints which are universal and binding reflects a general degree of professional development that already makes effective management by non-members difficult if not impossible (as discussed above).

Agency service and independent practice

In terms of possibilities for managerial organization the occupational characteristics described so far have significant but not radical implications. They condition, but they do not prohibit, managerial forms. Either the occupational group or profession concerned can be incorporated into pre-existing managerial hierarchies (Figure 2.1(a)), or they may need the creation of an independent managerial hierarchy of their own under the employing authority (Figure 2.1(b)). 'Bureaucratic organization' (using the term neutrally) is thus still, in a general sense, possible.

The next characteristic to be discussed raises more profound issues. It is best expressed in terms of the distinction between two kinds of practice assumptions: those compatible with what may be called 'agency service' and those demanding 'independent practice'. The distinction may be illustrated sharply in relation to the different position of hospital doctors and nurses. When a patient arrives in hospital he expects both medical care and nursing. As far as nursing is concerned, although he sees, and no doubt identifies with, a number of individual nurses, he is nevertheless in the hands of the local nursing service as a whole. It is up to the senior nurse and, ultimately, to the employing body to see that the patient gets the nursing that he needs around the clock, whatever the immediate changes in nursing

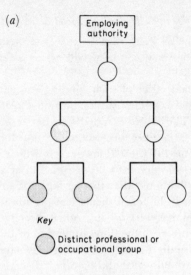

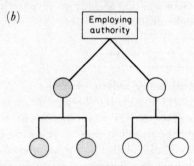

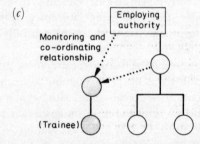

Figure 2.1   *Three ways of organizing a distinct professional or occupational group*
    (a) *Integrated into pre-existing managerial hierarchy*
    (b) *As a separate managerial hierarchy*
    (c) *In independent practice*

staff due to absence, shift-working, or transfers. In this situation any particular nurse is acting not as an independent professional practitioner but as an agent of the employing authority. He or she is providing what may be called *agency service*.

On the other hand, the patient arriving in hospital finds his medical care in the hands of a particular and identified consultant – Dr X. The referral to Dr X as an identified person may well have been advised after careful thought by the general medical practitioner who first dealt with the patient. He is now described as 'Dr X's patient'; he is in 'Dr X's beds'; dealt with by 'Dr X's house officer', or 'Dr X's registrar'. Moreover, he hopes and expects to be examined or attended to at some point (in anything but the most trivial cases) by Dr X in person. The exact choice and quality of medical service which he gets will (within the limits of what is available) be entirely determined by Dr X, or his assistants who are understood to be acting on Dr X's behalf. Dr X will not think of himself as employed to execute the specific policies and programmes of the employing authority. He will think of himself as an independent practitioner, enjoying 'clinical autonomy', employed to pursue his professional practice as he thinks best within the broad terms of his contract.

In most situations where doctors work, a very high value is set upon the quality of the therapeutic relationship established with the individual patient. Such a relationship obviously revolves upon individual trust, and the more confident the patient that his physician has complete freedom (within certain broad limits) to diagnose, treat, and make prognosis as he personally judges best, the more likely is such trust to develop. Thus, independent practice is linked in this particular case to the requirement to establish a strong therapeutic relationship. This is turn implies the possibility of choice; the ability of the patient to choose or change his doctors, and indeed, the ability of the doctor to transfer his patient where a minimal necessary level of trust and co-operation cannot be established.

What then is the justification for establishing doctors in independent practice where there is no effective choice – where as often happens, one psychiatrist or one geriatrician automatically deals with all cases arising in one predetermined geographical sector? What is the justification for establishing, say, pathologists, radiologists, or anaesthetists in independent practice, who rarely if ever have patients of their own, and where patient-choice is again usually non-existent? Are biochemists, physicists and other clinical scientists to be thought of as in independent practice? So far, we have found no general answers to these questions. We have only been able to establish the one firm ground for independent practice. This is acceptance of a pre-eminent need to establish a voluntarily-maintained relationship of trust and co-operation between a specifically-identified professional practitioner and a specifically-identified patient or client.[11] However, it may be that there are other good grounds for establishing situations of independent practice. Perhaps, for example, the requirement of the academic to have 'academic freedom' to teach and think what he will, is another and quite different ground in certain situations. Perhaps the freedom of the judge to pursue justice in individual cases before him irrespective of governmental policy or intervention is another again.[12]

The implications of independent practice

Where independent practice arises, whatever the justification for it, the organizational implications are, as we have said, profound. Not only is one talking about the inapplicability of management by non-members of the profession concerned, but also by other members too. For should a manager be appointed, either from within the professional group or from outside, the reality of independent practice could no longer be sustained. No longer could the user or the hirer of the service see only a professional acting in his own name and entirely at the dictates of his own skill and conscience; but behind him a figure, or whole line of figures, each with power to direct, adjust, or override. Where many professionals work together in independent practice then, however unequal their individual capabilities or personal reputation, in the organizational sense all must be equal colleagues; none subordinate to another. Here, and in this particular

[11] It is for this reason that what we are now calling 'independent practice' was in earlier work described by us as 'personalized service' – implying both the personal identification of the service-giver in the eyes of the client, and client-choice. It now seems better, however, to regard 'personalized service' (see the definition in the (1977) Working Paper 'Organization of Physiotherapy and Occupational Therapy in the NHS') as one only of a possible range of situations which may demand 'independent practice'.

[12] The supposition that it is the 'service ethic' of professionals which makes it impossible to assimilate them fully into bureaucracies, a position sometimes adopted in the sociological literature, seems far too sweeping. To state the obvious point again, the service ethic of the professional need not necessarily conflict with either the avowed aims, or the actual and existing ethos, of the employing organization. Far more specific reasons are required to explain, or justify, the granting of what we are specifically defining here as *independent practitioner* status.

circumstance only, is the true peer-group, true collegiate organization.[13]

Two important provisos must be made however. The first is that there are naturally limits to freedom even in independent practice. 'Limitless freedom' is a meaningless conception. In fact, the limits and the sanctions which may be brought to bear if they are infringed, for example in medicine, can be quite readily and explicitly drawn out. They include the constraints of common and criminal law; the limits of acceptable professional practice; and, in the case of those employed, the limits explicit or implicit within particular employment contracts.

The second proviso is that although established practitioners will be allowed a wide scope for free and unreviewed action in this situation, those on the way up – the trainees, acolytes and apprentices – will be very much subject to the review and prescription of their masters. (Hierarchic authority will be present in this particular respect then, which may broadly be described as managerial even though it partakes something of the flavour of an older 'master-apprentice' quality.) Furthermore, where practitioners are in crucial positions to affect the future life and happiness of their clientele – as is clearly the case in medicine – there will be predictable social pressures for there to be a prolonged period of learning for apprentices, and for the proof of accredited qualifications at the end of it.

Indeed, if the *Work Stratum* theory is considered, a further proposition about the requisite level of work for independent practice may be posed. If the practitioner is to be given complete freedom to work on his own it seems reasonable to require not only that he is able to cope with work at the *situational response* level (i.e. Stratum 2), but also with work at the *systematic service provision* level (Stratum 3). In other words, it seems reasonable to require that such practitioners should have the ability to be developing continually for themselves (and in conjunction with their colleagues) better general methods, procedures and frameworks for the application of their skills in particular cases. If this point is valid it implies, for example, that both medical consultants and general medical practitioners should be capable of Stratum 3 work at minimum. It has the same

[13] We must of course avoid the error – see for example Blau, P. M. and Scott, W. R. (1963), op. cit., Chapter 3 – of confusing *professional associations*, that is associations formed to protect and forward the interests of members themselves, with the various organizations in which professionals are actually *employed*. The former, like all prime associations, are non-hierarchic in form. The real issue is under what circumstances the *employment* organization of professionals needs to be non-hierarchic.

implications for those social workers, psychologists and psycho-therapists who aspire to independent practice in fields such as child guidance, or for physiotherapists and occupational therapists with similar aspirations.[14]

Various arrangements for independent practice

With the exception of the case of trainees then, managerial relationships as we have defined them, or indeed other prescriptive relationships, are inconsistent with independent practice. What comes in as it were to fill the vacuum where independent practitioners work together, or with others, are two different kinds of relationships which have already been identified – the *monitoring* relationship and the *co-ordinating* relationship (see Figure 2.1c). For, in the first place, although fully-fledged practitioners cannot in these circumstances be managed, there is nevertheless the possibility of – and arguably from a broader social view, the necessity for – monitoring their adherence to the kinds of limits described above. And again, though their work cannot be managed, there is nevertheless the need to see that it is co-ordinated and integrated with other contingent work and developments.

One ready way of achieving independent practice is by setting up in private practice. Frequently in this situation mutual support and protection without loss of autonomy can be secured through the device of the partnership-in-law. Such is found, for example, in medical practice, or in law, or in accountancy. Where *senior* partners emerge this title implies not a *managerial* role but rather a *monitoring* and co-ordinating one (as each of these terms has been defined here) carrying a limited authority within, and only within, the general terms of any policies or practices adopted by the partnership as a whole.

For professionals intent on staying in independent practice however, there are many obvious advantages to working in a larger organization. There are a number of ways of arranging this. Some will take the legal form of 'contract *for* services'. Others will be situations of straightforward salaried employment, i.e. 'contract *of* service'. In this latter case the professional finds himself working alongside other fellow-professionals, some of whom may be more senior or eminent; but again, if independent practice is truly required, this is inimical to the establishment of managerial relationships. Even the employing body itself will have no right to impose particular rules or policies, or to demand that specific tasks be accomplished, or that specific methods be followed, unless each or any of these have been

[14] See *Health Services,* Chapters 9 and 10.

the subject of specific contract negotiation. If there is any system of discretionary pay awards, it is likely to be applied in effect by the profession itself rather than the employing authority.

Thus, general medical practitioners, dentists, or ophthalmic opticians, all of whom have contracts-for-services within the NHS, recognize no right on the part of their sponsoring bodies, the Family Practitioner Committees, to tell them how to diagnose or treat, or what priorities to give to patients, or how to organize their work. Also, although medical consultants are actually in the salaried employment of Health Authorities who provide their premises, supporting staff, equipment and materials, they too recognize no constraints on work that are not the subject of specific agreement. Any change in work arises by a kind of continuous negotiation and re-negotiation of the employment contract.[15] (Nevertheless, the point must be noted that the employing bodies in this and the previous case obviously have ultimate rights to set limits – unilaterally if necessary – on the availability and use of resources.) Merit payments for medical consultants in the NHS are determined by a National Distinction Awards Committee appointed by the Secretary of State but composed of doctors, that is fellow-professionals.

Sometimes the professional practitioner in such situations will be grouped with his fellows in 'divisions', 'departments', and 'firms', or the like, and it will be usual for one of the most senior chosen by the group itself to act both as spokesman to the external world and as a co-ordinator within the group; acting always within the framework of agreed policies and practices. However, the role of such elected representatives has its limits, and in no way can they be held accountable by the employing authority. In addition then, there will need to be certain designated senior staff, not necessarily of the same professional group, who act unequivocally as agents or officers of the employing authority, with the job of carrying out such additional and broader-focused co-ordination as is necessary, as well as monitoring adherence to contract conditions.

Where a number of distinct specialties exist, that is a number of sub-groups within the main profession, questions will arise about how many of them have their own separate representatives to speak and negotiate on their behalf. For example in medicine there are questions of how many specialties are banded together in each 'cogwheel'

---

[15] The exact legal situation of employing and contracting authorities as far as their responsibility for the work of doctors is concerned is complex, and indeed in some respects debatable. However, so far as we are aware, nothing in the present legal situation contradicts the propositions just advanced.

division, and which specialties are directly represented in negotiations with health authorities and their officers.[16] The basic problem here has already been mentioned – the difficulty of non-members of any distinct professional group (or sub-profession) having adequate understanding of the specific needs and possibilities for new developments in order to act as effective spokesmen.

Where independent practice is appropriate

It has been noted that it is not the existence of a medical qualification, but the need for the establishment of strong one-to-one therapeutic relationships which argues for independent practice in medicine. In situations where doctors are employed outside clinical work with individuals (as in epidemiological work or medical administration), or in clinical work where the same emphasis does not fall on the establishment of individual therapeutic links (as in large-scale screening or immunization programmes), the same arguments do not apply, whatever others may be brought to bear.

Moreover, the case for independent practice is not specific to medicine in the health field. Considerable work with child psychotherapists has revealed their explicit preference for this mode. Educational psychologists and social workers employed in child guidance work, school psychological services or child psychiatric clinics, lean towards it as well.[17]

By contrast, it has been confirmed over the years that the bulk of social workers employed in local authority SSDs see themselves in fact as working in agency service.[18] This, of course, does not rule out any possibility of seeing social workers as true professionals, certainly not in the meaning of the term established earlier.[19] The main problem for the moment appears to be how much delegated

[16] See First and Second Reports of the Joint Working Party on the *Organization of Medical Work in Hospitals*, ('Cogwheel'), DHSS, (1967 and 1972).

[17] See *Health Services*, Chapter 10.

[18] See *Social Services Departments*.

[19] The dangers can be noted here of making the choice of organizational forms turn upon some attempted distinction of 'professionals' from 'semi-professionals' and 'non-professionals'. See Etzioni, A. (1964), *Modern Organization*, and Etzioni, A. (ed.) (1969), op. cit. The main thesis of this paper is that much more specific determinants than these can be found; and whilst those who on virtually any grounds would be judged true 'professionals' may well be fitted with perfect adequacy into managerial hierarchies in some situation, others, whose claim to general 'professional' status is far more arguable, may nevertheless clearly require to be acknowledged as independent practitioners.

discretion social workers should carry at various stages of career development.[20] However, tendencies towards independent practice can be observed strongly in those parts of social work that approach psychotherapy. They can also be observed in community work and it may be that the model of the free-floating, independent 'change-agent' who helps community groups to look after themselves and fight for themselves, is absolutely inconsistent with the idea of agency service-type employment, given the strong fiduciary bond with the client that is implicit in such work.

Existence of encompassing professions

We turn now to the third characteristic identified at the start of this chapter – the idea of 'encompassing professions'. It is a commonplace observation that members of certain occupations carry more status, influence or power than others, but it is rarely enquired what legitimate *authority* might exist in them. Once attention is turned to this feature, the striking point emerges that certain professions or occupations do in fact carry quite clear-cut authority in relation to others. Our own research has revealed for example, as a clear social fact acted upon universally, the right of doctors to prescribe specific medical treatment to be carried out by nurses, or by remedial therapists.[21] (The personal attitudes and styles adopted in interaction is of course another matter again. Having authority does not necessarily mean behaving in an authoritarian way. Encouraging participation in decision-making does not necessarily mean relinquishing authority.)

On the other hand, our own research has shown that no prescriptive rights exist between doctor and doctor, other than where the second doctor is in training or specifically employed as an assistant.[22] This applies even where prescription might at first sight have been expected, for example between surgeons and anaesthetists, or physicians and pathologists. It has also highlighted, for example, the strong move for social work to establish itself as a profession independent

---

[20] See Chapter 3.

[21] This statement applies at any rate to the administration of drugs and other physical treatments or procedures, where clear and explicit prescriptions can readily be given. In other matters, our own research has revealed that the authority of doctors in relation to nurses may be much more problematic – for example in respect of the general regime in psychiatric hospitals. See Rowbottom, R. W. *et al.* (1973), op. cit., Chapters 5 and 7. See also Strauss, A. *et al.* (1963), 'The Hospital and its Negotiated Order'.

[22] Rowbottom, R. W. *et al.* (1973), op. cit.

of medicine, even where the two professions work closely together as they do in the hospital setting. It has observed a state of some tension in fields such as psychotherapy, psychology and other clinical sciences where many practitioners would also wish to establish a clear independence of doctors, but are not sure whether they have it at the moment.

Where any state of authority exists or is claimed to exist between any two professional groups, what then legitimates the claim? It is suggested that any justifications must turn, and can only turn, again on questions of knowledge or competence. For it seems reasonable to suggest that one occupational or professional group should have prescriptive rights over the work of another if, and only if, the first is generally accepted as having a better or broader competence to assess the *real* needs or problems in the field concerned. Thus, the right of doctors to prescribe to nurses can only be rationally supported if it can be shown that medical education gives better grounds for diagnosing disease and physical malfunction, and deciding what is best done about it, than a nursing education.

Clearly, where any contrast arises between those we might think of as craftsmen or technicians on the one hand, and those we might readily think of as higher professionals in the same field on the other, there is always likely, according to this argument, to be an authoritative relationship between the two. For whereas 'craft' or 'technical skill' implies no more than special competence in the execution of certain kinds of tasks, 'profession' here implies a deeper understanding of the nature of the field, and an accepted competence in exploring complex problems and penetrating to fundamental needs. For example, in the health field, the laboratory technician will always be subordinate in technical matters to the qualified pathologist or biochemist; the orthoptist will be subordinate to the qualified ophthalmologist; the audiometrician to the audiologist; the radiographer to the radiologist – and so it turns out in practice.[23]

But beyond this there are cases where a group which is itself naturally thought of as a profession in its own right rather than a craft, is nevertheless subject to at least a certain level of prescription from members of another professional group. Physiotherapy provides a good case in point. Trained physiotherapists with whom discussions have been held have laid claims not only to competence in executing certain therapeutic procedures but also in making judgements, in some degree at least, about their patients' physical condition, problems, and capabilities. and in deciding which particular set of therapeutic

[23] Rowbottom, R. W. *et al.* (1973), op. cit.

procedures to apply. By this criterion, as has been suggested, they justify a 'professional' rather than a 'craft' label. Nevertheless, it appears in this situation not only that prime responsibility (a concept which will be explored later) for the patient usually rests with a doctor rather with the physiotherapist, it also appears that the doctor carries an accepted right to determine what treatment objectives and boundaries should be set in any case, even though he may on many occasions do no more than invite, either directly or by implication, standard therapeutic treatment for the condition concerned.[24]

We may recognize then, that there are certain crafts or professions which may in principle be subject to prescriptions from some other profession with a deeper or more embracing knowledge in the same field of endeavour. The words 'in principle' have to be added to cover the point just made. There is no need to assume that members of the first group of crafts or professions operate only upon receipt of prescriptions. Much of the nurses' work, like seeing to the comfort, general care, and cleanliness of patients for example, arises at their own initiative, though always with the assumption that what is done would not run counter to any obvious medical prescription likely to be issued.

Where such encompassing professions exist then, there is always an underlying authority-base which would allow the prescription of certain specific actions – what has been identified in our own research as a *prescribing* relationship.[25] Indeed certain (though not necessarily all) of the pre-conditions discussed above for establishing full *managerial* relationships, are already met by definition. In general, a number of more or less complex organizational arrangements may follow. For example:

(*a*) members of the profession or craft in question can be organized in a separate managerial hierarchy, subject to specific prescriptions in its lower reaches from members of the encompassing profession – as for example in hospital nursing;

(*b*) members of the profession or craft in question, though themselves hierarchically organized if employed in sufficient numbers, can be organized directly under the managerial control of a member of the encompassing profession, as where medical pathologists directly manage a group of laboratory technicians, or manage a chief

[24] See *Health Services*, Chapter 9.
[25] A *prescribing* relationship implies the right to set specific tasks to be carried out, and the right to check results, but no other right to manage, supervise or direct.

technician who himself manages a group of such technicians;
(*c*) specific members of the profession or craft in question can be attached to specific members or groups of the encompassing profession to work permanently under their direction, but whilst still retaining a superior manager in their own profession. This sometimes arises in physiotherapy for example.[26]

In general, it may be taken that models of the second kind (*b*) will only be appropriate where the prime profession or occupation concerned is at a relatively low level of professional development. In other cases all the arguments already explored will apply. Although members of the profession concerned will be willing to accept prescriptions on specific pieces of work referred to them, they will be looking to the establishment of managerial posts at Stratum 3 or higher in their own profession to give the lead in the general development of professional practice. Moreover, they will be wanting such senior managers to have direct access to resource-allocating groups and, indeed in the ultimate, to the employing authority itself.

Prime responsibility
Finally we come to the fourth feature identified at the start of this chapter – the idea of 'primacy', and (what it springs from) that of 'prime responsibility'. One of the most noted features of social and health services in advanced societies is the increasing variety of professionals who may be called upon to contribute to some personal or social problem posed by an individual. The illness which was formerly dealt with by the all-purpose doctor may now involve, besides the general practitioner, the work of half a dozen or more different kinds of medical specialists, clinical scientists, ancillary therapists and technicians. The social distress once dealt with by a charitable visitor might now involve several different social workers, a 'home help', a volunteer delivering 'meals on wheels', and perhaps an occupational therapist as well. In situations such as those to be found in child guidance clinics, psychiatric hospitals, or special schools, even more complex combinations of professionals are called for, drawn not just from one but from several separate fields of work – health, education, and social welfare.

In our experience such situations are invariably seen as more or less problematic by those within them. Immediate expressions of anxiety are often accompanied by strong statements of the need for greater team spirit, but further exploration nearly always reveals

[26] See *Health Services*, Chapter 9.

structural problems. For a start there is frequently doubt as to the state of relative authority or independence of the particular professional groups involved. In the mental health field for example, there is often doubt as to whether the psychotherapist, or the psychologist, or the social worker, or the psychiatric nurse, is really independent of the psychiatrist's prescription.[27]

Even where there is clear understanding that no prescriptive authority exists between one professional group and another, there is frequently an uncertainty about who is 'in charge' of the case. Who is meant to be seeing that as many different specialists are involved in any case as are required, that their work is co-ordinated, and that necessary actions or decisions are taken in situations of ambiguity or uncertainty? Who is meant to be seeing that the underlying needs of the case or person in question do not pass undealt with through any holes or gaps in the system?

What is at issue here can be described more precisely as *prime responsibility*. When fully spelt out this appears to involve the person who carries it in the following duties:

(*a*) making a personal assessment of the general needs of the case at the time of assumption of prime responsibility;

(*b*) undertaking personally any action needed in consequence, or initiating such action through subordinate or ancillary staff;

(*c*) referring as necessary to colleagues and other independent agencies for collaboration in further assessment or action, or for action in parallel;

(*d*) keeping continuous awareness of the progress of the case, and taking further initiative as necessary.[28]

The exercise of these functions above implies what has already been defined as co-ordinative authority. Again, it may be noted that such authority does not include either the right to issue final or binding prescriptions in the face of strongly conflicting views, or the right to make assessments of overall performance or personal competence of other workers involved, as arises in the managerial relationship. It

---

[27] See *Health Services*, Chapter 10.

[28] Previous versions of this definition have added a fifth possible element, namely the right of the person carrying prime responsibility to terminate action in any case, and more particularly to terminate the activities of any collaborating colleagues working in the same case. In the light of further discussion however, it now appears more plausible perhaps to think of the right of termination as an additional feature of the distinct notion of *primacy*, which is introduced below, rather than a feature of 'prime responsibility'.

does not, therefore, cut at the roots of the independent professional practice of any other members of the team concerned.

Primacy

The desirability of having prime responsibility clearly identified and clearly assigned to one particular professional practitioner in each particular case can easily be argued. The deeper issues which arise however, are not just to do with individual cases, but whether there are any valid generalizations about the particular professional groups or sub-groups who most appropriately carry prime responsibility where several work together; and if so, about the boundaries of the kinds of work to which the claim is valid.

It seems, for example in the health field, that there are certain sorts of doctors who regularly carry prime responsibility as defined above, and others who do not. The first includes all those who are in a position to talk about *their* patients – general practitioners, surgeons, physicians, psychiatrists, and so on. On the other hand, anaesthetists and radiologists (in contrast to radiotherapists) are not likely in the nature of things to carry prime responsibility. Neither are clinical scientists like biologists or physicists, who are not medically qualified, even though they may act independently of medical prescription. Nor do nurses or members of paramedical professions carry primacy. By and large, there appears to be a very well-developed etiquette in medicine itself as to who carries prime responsibility in any case, and at what point it transfers. However, even in this highly-developed professional field there are still significant pockets of doubt, for example as our own researches have shown in transactions between consultants and general practitioners in relation to patients in 'cottage' hospitals.[29]

In the social services field, project work has frequently revealed different concepts of the location of prime responsibility in particular cases, and of whether any automatic primacy exists. For example, there is often confusion where residential staff and field social workers are continuously concerned with the same child in care, or where home help organizers, specialist workers with the handicapped and field social workers are concerned with the same handicapped person living at home.

On the second issue, the extent and limit of the area within which prime responsibility is carried, it now seems likely in the kinds of situation we have been examining that important boundaries are to

[29] See Rowbottom, R. W. *et al.* (1973), op. cit., Chapter 5.

be discerned between the health field and the field of social welfare (and perhaps between both of these and the field of education). It appears, for example, that though hospital doctors of certain kinds may carry prime responsibility for the health care of their 'patients', to the extent that these same people are seen as 'clients' for social aid, responsibility for co-ordinating arrangements for their welfare has to be understood as resting with the hospital social workers. Conversely, where 'clients' of social services are in residential care, once a doctor has been called in to deal with clear symptoms of 'illness' of some kind, prime responsibility for medical treatment thereafter (in contrast to social welfare) will rest with him. In both situations doctors may find themselves co-ordinating members of other groups of health professionals, whilst social workers simultaneously co-ordinate the work of various ancillary welfare workers.

Thus, if it is desired to establish the existence of primacy, that is the automatic allocation of prime responsibility (as defined) to one particular occupational group or sub-group where several work together, it is apparent that such a concept must always be limited to some particular field of work. One may properly and usefully talk about carrying prime responsibility for the health care of a person, or his social well-being, or his educational well-being; but not about prime responsibility for all aspects of a person's life or activity. (Again, special problems may be noted in a field of psychiatry, where it is often debatable whether it is 'illness' that is at issue, 'social rehabilitation', or 'personal re-education'. Issues of the limits of prime responsibility are correspondingly debatable as well.)

Summary and conclusion

We started with a statement of some of the problems encountered over the years in health and social services in relation to the situation of professionals who work there. In its most general form, the issue could be said to be that of how much independence professionals should have when they are employed in organizations.

In effect, we have seen that there is no general answer to this question. There are a number of different characteristics of professional or occupational groups, which bear on the issue of appropriate organizational accommodation. Each of these characteristics poses definite and specific organizational requirements. We have seen:

(a) that where the work assumptions of the occupational group in certain situations demand independent practice (such as in many branches of medicine, or in psychotherapy, for example), that this is absolutely inconsistent with managerial hierarchy or technical direction; and that the appropriate organizational form will be collegial, strengthened and interwoven with co-ordinating and monitoring relationships at various points;

(*b*) that where the specific body of knowledge, ideas and practice of an occupational group has developed beyond a certain stage (as is the case in nursing, social work, clinical science, and physiotherapy, for example) there will be strong arguments for management by members of the profession only (assuming that the practice assumptions allow any extended managerial structure) with the direct access of the senior manager to policy-making bodies and to the employing authority;

(*c*) that over and above this, certain intrinsic relationships may exist between various professional or occupational groups – the intrinsic 'prescribing' authority of one to the other as far as specific action is concerned, or the 'primacy' of one of two or more professions who regularly work together in the same field – and that these will have particular organizational consequences which can be built into a variety of organizational forms, either basically hierarchical or basically collegial.

These specific propositions, it may be suggested, provide the key to many organizational issues in the health and social services field. They offer some answer, for example, to the question of why such complex organization arises in health services, given its wide range of developed professions and its mixture of independent practice and agency service. They provide clues to some of the tensions emerging in SSDs, given social workers who are pulled by the contradictory practice assumptions of counselling, psychotherapeutic, or community work approaches on the one hand, and agency service needs on the other. They provide insights into some of the increasing problems of multidisciplinary teamwork in and across various public agencies, given the complex mixture of developed and developing professions often to be discovered there. Over and above this, they offer definite statements about the conditions under which any professional may be assimilated into bureaucratic organization, and the *specific* circumstances in which radically different organizational arrangements become necessary – an area in which it is all too easy to contemplate the broad generalities of 'ideological conflict' and 'ideal types' without considering concrete propositions.

PART II

Fieldwork

Introduction

by Anthea Hey

In the early days of SSDs, fieldwork and social work were synonymous terms. Social workers were the professional group working in the field; that is, with people in their own homes. In the last six years, the view that not all fieldwork activity is properly construed as requiring a social work response as such, has gathered considerable support.[1] Similarly, social work takes place other than in the 'field', for instance in some residential and day centres.

New ways of perceiving the causes of social need, coupled with heavy bombardment of new referrals and insufficient numbers of trained social workers have had significant effects on the concept of fieldwork.

First, a variety of other workers as well as social workers now work in the field. Some workers, like home help organizers, were transferred to the SSD in 1971; others, like occupational therapists, have been recruited since. In addition, SSDs have created new roles like social services officers and social work assistants.

Secondly, these factors have disturbed another key assumption about the way social services work would be approached. 'The need for services, intended to be of universal access was to be determined by the exercise of professional judgement rather than by fixed criteria embodied in a rulebook.'[2] Demographic changes, poor housing, inflation and new legislation have increased the rate of referral for help with practical aspects of daily living. It is as a response to these practical aspects that non-social work staff have been recruited[3] and it is in relation to these practical services that criteria of eligibility have come to be established.

[1] See, for example, DHSS (1976), 'Report of the Working Party on Manpower and Training for the Social Services' (the Birch Report); Cypher, J. (1977), *Personal Social Services, Manpower and Training*; BASW (1977), op. cit.; and various CCETSW Discussion Documents which have analysed work to be done by various staff groups prior to advancing training proposals.

[2] Cooper, J., (1978), 'The Collective and the Personal – A Decade of Tension'.

[3] See Goldberg, E. M. *et al.*, (1978). 'Towards Accountability in Social Work: Long Term Social Work in an Area Office'.

Social workers have accepted the recruitment of other professional and occupational groups because they do not wish to collude with a system in which 'a number of citizens have to convert themselves into clients in order to receive, at the discretion of social workers, services which should be theirs by right'.[4] However, there is still much confusion about the boundaries between social work and other kinds of work and about the status, training and organization of non-social work staff. Which of these non-social work staff are to be regarded as professionals in their own right, working in parallel with social workers, carrying accountability for cases and exercising discretion to model their responses to meet the specific needs of clients? Which of these other workers are best regarded as ancillary or assistant staff?

The two chapters in Part II examine, in turn, two kinds of work, Social Work and Basic Services Work.[5] Social work is seen as the particular activity of developing and maintaining the personal and social functioning capacities of individuals, families and communities. Social functioning is here used in the sense of self-actualization or self-realization.[6] This is not to suggest a training for some behaviour regarded as the norm. Social workers attempt to facilitate the processes of social learning, social adjustment and social change, using the techniques of casework, groupwork and community work, as Goldstein has pointed out.[7]

By *basic services* work is meant here that work which is directed towards seeing that clients have all those basic things everyone needs in order to sustain life and, therefore, to securing or, in some cases, providing them for those clients who cannot obtain them entirely on their own initiative. They include accommodation, food, money, goods, help with personal and home care, transport (to prevent social isolation), and recreational opportunity.

---

[4] Thomas, J., (1978), 'Which Way for Social Work?'.

[5] A third kind of work, Supplementary Services, was identified in our first book. Supplementary Services included a number of social services provided by SSDs particularly to the physically and mentally handicapped, for example social training, communications and mobility training and aids and adaptations. This area of work was given scant attention in the first book though the inadequacy of general terms such as day care and domiciliary services was pointed out. Although there has been some additional research opportunity both within SSDs and with staff of the NHS whose work is concerned with physically handicapped persons and there is work in progress in relation to the provision of services for the mentally handicapped, this work is not yet sufficiently complete to include in this book.

[6] BASW (1975), 'A Code of Ethics'.

[7] See Goldstein, H. (1973), 'Social Work Practice'.

Chapter 3 considers *social work* roles and organization in area teams. The chapter re-examines much of the material contained in the chapter on Organization of Fieldwork in the first book. It does so first by reconsidering the issues of independence or management of practice in the light of more research experience in this and related spheres, drawing on the ideas about levels of work in Part I. It looks in detail at the expectations held of main grade social workers, social work assistants, beginning social workers, career graded or senior practitioners, team leaders and area officers.

While career progression, in a general sense, has improved beyond the expectations of all but the most recently recruited social workers, many have become resentful that this progression has been accompanied by an apparent devaluation of practitioner skills, higher pay and status being reserved for executive work. 'Industrial action' by social workers in 1978–9 in part reflects these longer term dissatisfactions as well as more immediate concerns with current pay and negotiating rights. At present, career progression for practitioners is limited and where it exists has, in any case, tended to beg the consequent questions about organization, accountability and autonomy to which career progression gives rise. The analysis and models in this chapter offer a base for developing further practitioner progression.

The changes that have taken place in demands and responses have meant that social workers have come to be, at least numerically, a small element in SSDs.[8]

It is galling for many non-social work staff to see the social worker element consuming a disproportionate amount of attention, given the relative numbers of staff and clients served by social workers, in contrast to the large numbers of clients and staff involved, for example in the home help service. In the first book it was not possible, because of the lack of research experience in the field at that time, to give more than cursory mention to the home help or other domiciliary services. This gap has been in part rectified by more recent work and it is now clear that there are many critical issues concerning both provision and organization in the basic services field.

Home help organizers are left wondering what is best for them and their clients. There is widespread dissatisfaction in the service with conditions of work, high workloads, lack of professional and admini-

[8] This is demonstrated by staffing figures published for the largest UK authority, Strathclyde Social Work Department, in the *Health and Social Services Journal*, 22 October 1976, p. 1892: 2400 fieldworkers, managers and administrators; 8000 supervisory, care and domestic staff (in homes and centres); 8000 home helps.

strative assistance, lack of career progression opportunity and disagreement about appropriate training.

Chapter 3, therefore, considers the growing importance of basic services work and differing assumptions about its relationships to social work. The trend to establish more encompassing professional roles in basic services work is noted and alternative ways of achieving this are analysed. The first way is through extension of the home help organizer role; the second is through establishing new roles such as social services officer, whilst leaving the home help service much as it is today.

3 Social Work – Careers, Practice and Organization in Area Teams[1]

by Anthea Hey

Introduction

Some of the issues and conflicts surrounding the practice and organization of social work in SSDs were outlined in the introduction to this part of the book. In spite of the many concerted attempts to find solutions to the difficulties, consensus is elusive about the nature of social work and the proper arrangements for its practice. However, every department is having to make choices about how best to organize its social workers and each social worker has to decide under what organizational conditions they can best practise. This chapter seeks to make a contribution to the continuing debate about these critical organizational and professional concerns.

The main issue considered in the first instance is whether social workers should or can be managed and under what conditions they might have a realistic claim to be considered as independent practitioners. In the second part of the chapter propositions are made about six kinds of roles – main grade practitioners, social work assistants, beginning social workers, career graded and senior practitioners, team leaders, and area officers.

The models of roles offered within this chapter relate to the context of field social work based on area offices.[2] This is not to imply

---

[1] An earlier version of this appeared in October 1978 as a Working Paper.

[2] The analyses and models developed here derive from several field projects conducted in the last five years. This work built in turn on earlier projects which were reported in our first book (Chapter 5). Some projects have been concerned generally with the organization of area teams or of teams of social workers in health care settings. Three projects were focused on particular aspects of social work organization: on the role of team leaders, on specialization, and on the particular position of a group of highly trained and experienced social workers who were expected to develop practice theory

that area offices are the only, or the most important, location of social work practice. Some of the models developed can be applied to social workers wherever they work, in day or residential settings, in hospitals, general practices or schools. Additional features are relevant in such situations, some of which have been considered elsewhere.[3] Indeed, the issue of independent or managed practice is particularly relevant in some of these other locations where some colleagues enjoy considerably more independence in their practice than do social workers.

Independent or managed practitioners?

Social workers frequently point to the professional autonomy base of other professionals, particularly doctors, as a desirable mode of organization, though there are other elements of these professions they do not wish to emulate. Doctors are seen to have a degree of independence in determining the content and methods of their work with their patients and a larger say in how scarce resources should be utilized. It is useful to contrast two concepts of organization – *Agency Service* and *Independent Practice* – explored in Chapter 2, but repeated here in brief to make the argument clear.

(*a*) *Agency Service* – a situation where the professional practitioner (or other worker) is employed to act as the agent of the employing authority, to carry out its specific policies and programmes as these develop. In this situation managerial relationships are not precluded, at least within single professions.

(*b*) *Independent Practice* – is a situation where though the professional practitioner may be employed, he has complete freedom to pursue his professional practice as his thinks best (with available resources) provided he stays within certain broad limits of professional ethics, contract, and accepted norms of behaviour. In this situation, after the training period, managerial relationships are specifically ruled out, even within the same profession.

It is frequently assumed that simply being a registered doctor conveys

---

and teach others as well as engage in direct practice. The models derived from all these projects have been widely discussed in research conferences. Two conferences held in conjunction with the BIOSS Measurement of Capacity Unit specifically focused on careers and organization in social work.

[3] See Chapter 5; also Chapters 10 and 17 in *Health Services*; and Rowbottom, R. W. and Hey, A. M. (1978), 'Organization of Services for the Mentally Ill'.

clinical autonomy. This is patently not the case as is explored else-where.[4] It is useful to note that it is only in two situations that doctors are accorded this independence – as general practitioners and as consultants. This pattern is regarded as requisite where patients have regard to their free choice of clinician and desire to have a personal (in a non-legal sense) contract with him. Developments in health services, such as sectorization in psychiatric medicine and the growth of health centres may, it is claimed, reduce this freedom of choice, but the principle is, nonetheless, sought by patients and clinicians alike. Other more junior clinicians are, however, managed by their senior colleagues, the consultants.

Despite sideways glances of envy, local authority social workers, it seems, assume that local authorities are organized on an agency service model. This means that the professional practitioner is employed to act as the agent of the employing authority, to carry out its specific policies and programmes as these develop. Managerial relationships are constructed to ensure that work is carried out accordingly.

Those who support the agency service model argue that it is the requisite model for social services organization because it is, poten-tially, the most effective system for dealing with the allocation of resources and securing accountability for action in particular cases. From this it is concluded that no matter how highly trained and experienced they are, social workers can be managed at least by a more senior member of the same discipline.

By contrast, in the independent practice model applying to some doctors, the relationship with patients is regarded as paramount and therefore their professional practice has to be independent, that is, free from interference and prescription by a manager. Many social workers would argue that their relationship with clients should be regarded as equally paramount.

Our research work now suggests that society applies two conditions before 'independent practitioner' status is granted. Independent practitioners must demonstrate their capacity to handle individual case situations appropriately (Work Stratum 2),[5] and also their capacity to develop their own modes of practice, evaluating them and making consequential systematic changes in the way in which

[4] See *Health Services*, Chapter 4.
[5] Reference may be made to Chapter 1 for full exposition of *Work Strata Theory* – which will be referred to extensively throughout this chapter without further explana-tion.

they deal with a continuous sequence of demand from cases of particular kinds (Work Stratum 3). The competence of doctors is secured through the prolonged education and training, formal and on the job, which they receive; and tested in the basic and fellowship qualification examinations.

Consultant appointments are not usually obtained before the doctor reaches his thirties. While this may be in part dictated by the limited number of posts available, it is worth noting the prolonged period of formal study involved, as well as the apprenticeship in practice. It is possible to become an independent practitioner in general practice rather earlier. However, recent trends indicate the recognition of the need for further formal training (post registration) to prepare doctors in general practice and by the creation of more explicit apprenticeship posts as assistants in general practice, which carry the implication of being extantly managed by the Principals to whom they are attached. There are few opportunities currently provided in SSDs for social workers to be employed as practitioners beyond Work Stratum 2. Only 54 per cent of those employed as social workers possess the CQSW qualification (CQSW – Certificate of Qualification in Social Work awarded by the Central Council for Education and Training in Social Work). Most CQSW programmes compare unfavourably in breadth, depth and time scales with medical qualifications.[6]

It is no doubt an indication of public concern about the competence of social workers that they have been called to account for their actions in numerous cases, particularly in non-accidental injury incidents being brought to enquiry. Insofar as social workers at this stage in the profession's development cannot offer the same assurances about training, competence, ethieal and professional practices as the medical profession, such public enquiries may be seen as appropriate. They may also be seen as important opportunities for the future development of the profession as they place pressure on social workers to explicate their objectives, which in turn will lead to greater clarity about the boundaries of social work.

There are a number of current developments which indicate that systematic attempts are being mounted to improve the quality of practice. Recent CCETSW policies to facilitate and validate post-qualifying training are one example, but it is ironic that these

---

[6] Perhaps only those entrants who follow degrees in the Social Sciences with two-year graduate CQSW programmes could be said to study to a similar level as medical students. However, there is a move to prolong social work training to a minimum of four years. CCETSW *Consultation Papers* 1, 2 and 3 on CQSW training, 1976/77/78.

opportunities are running somewhat ahead of departments' facilities to use and pay for more competent practitioners. It would probably be helpful if a sharper distinction could be made in post-qualifying studies to distinguish between those studies which are designed to increase competence within Work Stratum 2 and those which seek to move people towards Work Stratum 3 responses.

It seems reasonable to interpret the Birch Report[7] recommendations within this framework – the suggestion that all workers should have further opportunity equal to a period of three months' study in every five years as being an expression of concern with updating. On the other hand, the suggestion that ten per cent of staff should have the opportunity for one year's study could be interpreted as the recognition of a need to equip a sufficient number of staff to move to higher level work. Perhaps at some point these longer courses will attract an advanced qualification which will clarify their purpose.

BASW has also tackled a number of related issues. Most interesting in this regard is the document 'Accredited in Social Work'. In this document the explicit assumption is that social workers should be 'self-regulating practitioners' and operate 'autonomously within the limits of operational accountability'.[8] However, discussions to date would suggest that in the current context of formal training, most workers starting out from a CQSW programme will need two years further on-the-job training before they achieve even a Work Stratum 2 competence. Perhaps this would be the point to implement registration. It will take considerably longer, say minimally a further five years, to establish levels of competence consistent with the notion of self-regulation to which a system of accreditation might properly apply.

It is an open question as to whether if social workers of higher calibre are developed, they could continue to be managed. The question involves issues of principle as well as structure. In this connection it is worth drawing attention to two methods of social work where both questions might arise. Interestingly, these lie at the opposite ends of a continuum of possible social work interventions. At one end of the spectrum is systematic psychotherapeutic work; at the other end is community action. Both seem to require that the client or client group has the right to freedom of choice in his social worker if the work processes are to be satisfactory. Tasks must also be mutually agreed between worker and client(s) and clients cease

[7] DHSS (1976), op. cit.

[8] BASW (1976), 'Accredited in Social Work', a Report of the Professional Development and Practice Committee.

to engage in collaborative work if they are not satisified with what is occurring.

Many workers currently using these methods find their activities constrained and inhibited by the prevailing agency service assumption that they must be managed in the same way as every other employee. Such modes of work rest on continuing relationship and sanction between worker and clientele, and managerial prescriptions which may run counter to client/worker agreements seem inappropriate.

If such work is to be regarded as the business of SSDs then it seems that different organizational relationships will be needed for the workers involved.[9] It will be necessary to ensure that sufficient workers are trained and developed to be capable of being independent practitioners. Different employment contracts, salary grading mechanisms and systems of work will be needed.

Pursuing the analysis, the question can be raised as to whether psychotherapy and community action are really significantly different in assumptions about level and practice from what should apply to social work generally. The more significant distinction may not be within social work, but between social work and other social services work.

The urgent requirement in most SSDs is for more social workers to operate comfortably at Work Stratum 2. It is arguable that the development of some social workers is held back by the requirement to be personally involved in arranging the delivery of (and not just the assessment for) basic and supplementary services. This distracts them from concentrating on in-depth work in which other elements of their practice skills could develop.

In the longer term it is a debatable point as to whether one profession can hold together workers whose levels of practice are pitched at different work strata. If the balance is not corrected it may be that other more distinctive specialisms, like psychotherapy and community work, may split off and form new professions. The tendencies are already apparent.[10]

It is worth noting that there seems no reason, in principle, why one employment system should be based wholly on either indepen-

[9] Amongst psychotherapists and community workers are some who originally trained as social workers as well as those who were trained in other professions, e.g. psychologists and teachers. To some degree the 'multi'-disciplinary nature of these developing professions suggests that they might be usefully employed in a variety of agencies and SSDs must surely be one of them.

[10] Tavistock Centre (1978), 'Statutory Registration of Psychotherapists'.

dent or managed practitioners. The NHS encompasses both types of employment contracts. Local authorities, however, have little or no experience of independent practitioners, apart from former health departments who employed some clinicians (usually on a sessional basis) in the maternity and child welfare clinics. The other professionals they employ (like lawyers and architects), who do practice independently in other contexts, are serving other local authority departments or the local authority itself – not establishing working relationships with members of the public as are social workers.

Most social workers as described earlier would require further, advanced, training and personal development before they might reasonably press for recognition as independent practitioners. However, the foregoing analysis at least raises the question as to how far the development of individual social workers, and thereby the ultimate development of social work as a socially sanctioned profession, is being inhibited by present assumptions about the nature of social work, its allocation and management.

It is likely to take some time to establish whether there is a need in SSDs for the independent practice model. However, it is not too early to accrue evidence about different organizational forms, and to explore the types of safeguards necessary to protect clients, as well as professional and public interests, should such a form be considered feasible.[11]

The models which follow about work and organization at least open up the possibility of a more considered system which could ultimately lead to establishing a firmer base for higher level social work practice than is presently the case.

Roles in area teams

Main grade social workers
Before it is possible to model the work and interactions of several roles it is necessary to establish some bench marks from which such role differentiation may rationally flow. The obvious role around which to frame some propositions would appear to be the main grade social

[11] Indicative of the widespread concern with this matter is the following resolution passed at the AGM, BASW, September 1978, 'That this Annual General Meeting considers that the present organization structure of local authority SSDs is harmful to the practice of social work and urges those concerned to give detailed consideration to alternative structures more compatible with the nature of social work and to exert its influence for change'.

worker. This term is used to apply to qualified social workers with minimally two years' post-qualification experience and not to any particular pay grade. What follows are some propositions about the way a main grade social worker should work.

The following suggestions derive from discussions with workers in the field. They are not comprehensive across all areas of performance but they do provide a framework within which the less tangible aspects of a social worker's performance might be judged. Rather than describing the attributes of the worker an attempt has been made to translate the generalized notion of situational response work (Stratum 2) to the expectations on social workers. By inference, only workers of a certain competence will be able to tackle this work.

Suggested appropriate work responses for main grade social workers

(*a*) The tasks naturally arising from case work allocation require assessment and planning by the worker concerned. The worker can only respond by applying systematic knowledge and skills.

(*b*) The worker's tasks are aimed at producing changes in the state of the case (i.e. aimed at self-realization and improved social functioning, and may include changes in the social environment). The tasks are clearly identified, contracted with the client(s), have a systematic programme of activity attaching to them and an explicit time scale.

(*c*) Time scales may be variable, from hours up to say one year. But, as shorter tasks could have the same complexity as longer tasks in the variables to be handled, decisions to be made, and knowledge and skills to be applied, the same quality of response is observable in all tasks.

(*d*) The tasks are appropriate to the client's state and his capacities to engage in collaborative work. They take account of the worker's own skills and time commitments and the availability of any other services which might be needed to facilitate the agreed changes, i.e. the tasks are reality based.

(*e*) The worker, in judging and planning his work, recognizes his own need for further information, advice and support.

It would, of course be preferable if the above quality of response could be expected at qualification point. To achieve this, however, would require both extended and deeper education and training than is currently available to the majority of entrants to the service. Failing this, at the present time a considerable responsibility devolves on both beginning workers and their employing agencies to fill the gaps in knowledge, but particularly skills.[12]

These proposals have a congruence with the British Association of Social Workers' proposals for accreditation referred to earlier. However, it seems more reasonable to use the term registration to match this stage of development and to reserve the term accreditation for some later stage of development, based perhaps on further study and assessment, which would accredit genuine senior status and provide employers and clients alike with credible evidence to trust the granting of independent practitioner status, or at least high discretion to workers of proven distinctive competence. Competence, if it is to mean anything, must convey some expectations which do not simply reflect the internal state of the profession but mean something to colleague professionals and the general public.

Main grade workers can be expected to be case accountable, and it follows from this that they should have appropriate delegated discretion. At present there are anomalies in the delegation of discretion. Often social workers have discretion to make the weightiest decisions which affect civil liberties and also commit departmental resources in the long term, for example receiving children into care. By contrast, they do not have the discretion to authorize quite minor amounts of direct expenditure.

Similarly, little difference is noticeable in the way in which they are supervised or managed, from beginning workers or students, either in frequency of reviews of work, or in who conducts them. In short, they are often constrained by departmental procedures and organization from developing a personal professional sense of responsibility for their own work.

In the light of the analysis offered earlier it is not suggested that main grade social workers should be regarded as independent practitioners, or even as what might be meant as 'semi-autonomous'. However, it is argued that they should have increased discretion and that appropriate mechanisms are established to review their use of discretion. It is also expected that main grade workers will continue to need planned development opportunity consistent with the career paths they wish to pursue (i.e. as practitioners or executives). In short, they will need a manager, though the nature and style of the

[1] Kassels, M. (1973), 'Guidelines for the Design of Career Systems', writes of the problem of 'overqualifying employees in terms of their general and professional education, while at the same time failing to improve the actual skills needed to serve clients effectively'.

relationship will be different from that of beginning workers. The team leader role as presently construed does not provide a suitable manager for main grade workers.

It is appropriate at this point to share some assumptions about the optimum conditions of managerial relationships. Two propositions follow as a result of research experience over many years.[13]

First, any chain of accountability will only work effectively when successive managers are expected and able to work at the next higher work stratum from those they manage. Second, individuals needing authoritative guidance and support instinctively refer themselves (whatever the manifest statement of accountability) to a person whom they feel can give them what they need, whose judgements they trust. When their choice cuts out the person next in the manifest chain this is called bypassing, a familiar phenomenon.

Returning to the organizational propositions made above, it can be demonstrated that these conditions will not be met in the case of main grade workers whose work and capacities fall firmly within Work Stratum 2, when the team leaders' own work and capacities as presently structured fall within the same stratum.

In most departments it would be required that main grade workers are organized as members of teams alongside beginning workers and social work assistants. Many departments are currently wrestling with this dilemma. The answer lies in recognizing the difference in need for closeness of managerial review, support and staff development and to locate the managerial relationship of main grade workers with the area officer. Extantly this is probably where it is effected anyway – more competent workers relating directly to the area officer on a variety of matters.

However, if main grade workers are to be part of teams then, of course, their work and the work of other team members has to fit and make a coherent whole. Team leaders may then be given co-ordinating authority in respect of general team organization, for example use of office services, duty and allocation systems and monitoring authority in respect of adherence to the boundaries of policy, practice and budget allocations. However, this does not convey authority to make and act on judgements on the professional discretion of main grade workers; this would rest with the area officer. Similarly, the area officer would need to arbitrate on sustained disagreements about matters of general team practice which were not acceptable to main grade workers. Discussion on cases would in-

[13] See *A General Theory of Bureaucracy.*

evitably occur but it would be clear that this is of the order of colleague advice and not authoritative.

It is main grade workers who would probably be making the biggest demand on post-qualifying study opportunities. They will need to both extend and deepen their ability to work with particular kinds of problems and extend their range of skills. In so far as they start to specialize they will need opportunities which are not even within the scope of their managers, the area officers, who are by definition generalists. They will need access to other higher level specialists. Some of these will be available in the department in other locations at headquarters in the form of consultants/advisers/development officers,[14] and in the form of principal social workers in hospitals and clinics, and indeed other professionals outside SSDs, for example psychiatrists.

Having proposed a base line for the work, competence and organization of main grade practitioners, it is possible to make limited proposals about the other roles and their relationships.

Social Work Assistants
This group of workers might be expected to demonstrate the most marked departure from this base line. The present picture is often blurred. Irrespective of capacities, current bombardments require an 'all hands to the pump' response. Social work assistants are often allocated cases which arguably call for a situational response mode and the systematic application of social work knowledge and skills if they are to be handled requisitely. Some departments are opposed to social work assistants having caseloads but many acquire them by default or because they demonstrate a capacity to do more responsible work.

It appears that the bulk of social work assistants' work is with the elderly and physically handicapped where the social services being provided are mostly what has been described earlier as basic or supplementary services. Sometimes they function as family aides and sometimes undertake tasks which are framed by a social worker.

In the early days many of the younger people recruited as social work assistants rapidly demonstrated their potential and were encouraged to apply for social work training (CQSW). With hindsight, it might have been better to regard these appointees as trainee social workers. More recently there has been a trend to employ rather older people, normally women. They often have families, may have personal experience of the problems of the elderly and handicapped,

[14] See Chapter 8.

and generally have life experience which is greater than that of younger social workers. Often these older recruits do not consider undertaking professional training for psychological, age, or practical reasons.

Many of these social work assistants have appropriate personal qualities and capacities to undertake the situational response work, irrespective of previous educational experience. They lack the specific knowledge and skills of social work and cannot acquire them without undertaking training. In some real sense they may be underemployed relative to their potential, yet cannot be employed at higher levels in social work without qualifications, though in departments where qualified social workers are in short supply they may get promoted into (unqualified) social worker posts.

There would appear to be two possibilities for dealing more rationally with the anomalies which have developed.

(*a*) Where it is genuinely felt that some clients do not require the intervention of a social worker and it is clear that there is a need to bring to bear a situational response to the framing of basic services, then the new role of social service officer might be established and graded appropriately.

(*b*) Where it is felt that some tasks with clients of social workers (or social service officers) can be delegated there is a case for retaining a role of 'assistant to ...'.

In the first role – the social service officer – the expectation would be that such workers would be accountable for assessing all the potential basic services needs of clients and not simply responding to presenting requests for concrete services. In the second role – the social work or service assistant – the assessment would be made by the Work Stratum 2 officer, and the work of assistants would be allocated in the form of tasks. Case accountability would rest with the social worker who would also be held to account for the way they delegated tasks and reviewed and supported the assistants.

The genuine assistant work, it is suggested, should consist of relatively concrete tasks whose ends and means can be described in quite a detailed way. The boundaries of the tasks should be capable of being quite clearly defined so that it is possible to specify events which would make the continuing pursuit of the allocated task inappropriate, requiring reference back for further instruction. This work lies in Stratum 1, being described as *prescribed output*.

It could be that there needs to be more than one grade available to mark the difference in ability between experienced and inexperienced assistants, and that the complexity of the tasks allocated could vary. However, the exceptionally able (i.e. capable of progression to the next work stratum) would only be appointed as social workers if obtaining a CQSW, and as social service officers if obtaining a Certificate in Social Service (CSS).

As for training, whilst the CSS was proposed as a relevant form of training for social work assistants, as this has developed it seems that it is being directed at persons with Work Stratum 2 potential. It might best be regarded as suitable for those social work assistants who fit the social service officer model developed above. The demands of the training probably puts it beyond the scope of workers whose capacity best fits prescribed output work. (From the point of view of employers the cost of this full-time training probably only makes it a feasible investment for genuine Work Stratum 2 workers.)

This is not to say that genuine 'assistants to' do not require training, but this might best be provided on a day release and part-time basis, either by the internal efforts of the department or on some extended version of current In-service Study courses.

Three alternative models seem to exist for organizing genuine assistants:

(*a*) The continuation of the prevailing model – social work assistants belong to social work teams, led by a senior social worker (team leader) who is seen as the accountable manager of the social work assistants. This model might continue as long as there are proportionately fewer social work assistants than social workers. As far as intake teams undertaking brief focal work exist, then there presumably would be a continuing case for the presence of genuine assistants.

(*b*) An alternative model would be for each main grade (and senior social work practitioner and social service officer) to have their own assistant(s). This would be appropriate if at some future point there were more competent experienced social workers than there are at present.

(*c*) A third alternative is for social work assistants to be organized as a group (team) in a service-giving relationship to social workers/social service officers. Such a team might be managed by a CSS holder who had taken a management option.

Beginning social workers

The view has been expressed earlier that most social workers in the first two years or so after completing CQSW training are still less than fully-fledged. In practice, then, they are to be viewed as still in training.

Amongst the group will be people of exceptional potential who will be future leaders of the profession, as well as those whose careers will be more modest. They will include people of various ages. They will encompass a wide range of life experiences, different educational experiences and abilities to progress at different rates. This is the degree of heterogeneity found among beginning workers at present.

The performance of the many who are less than fully-fledged professionally will be variable. They will be able to respond to some situations in much the same way as a fully-fledged worker. In other situations which present a new experience or which challenge their emotions and ideologies, they will need considerable support and guidance if they are to learn to make systematic responses and not unconsciously shy away from the real nature of the problems and thus make superficial or narrow responses.

Well-trained beginning social workers may have an additional problem. They may be able to make assessments of the real needs in the situation, but unable to construct and sustain the subsequent intervention tasks.[15]

In particular they are likely to feel overwhelmed by cases which are sensitive among the lay public – cases of ill-treatment or social disturbance, when decisions have to be made for the protection of individuals and/or society at large.

It is necessary to state such widely accepted propositions explicitly so that the consequences can be analysed in context. For example, should less than fully-fledged social workers be assumed to be accountable for cases allocated to them, or should case accountability only rest with fully-fledged workers? What mixes and quantities of work should be allocated? How should this be negotiated? If these beginning workers are not wholly accountable, who is?

The major issue for the beginning worker is whether his own developmental needs are met as well as the needs of his clientele. If our theories are valid, the two go hand in hand. If workers are not capable of the work they are expected to do, then clients, workers

[15] Kassels, M. (1973) op. cit., writes about graduates being 'well equipped with the conceptual armour of the human behaviourist. However, they are ordinarily short-handed in interactive skills and unprepared to deal with ... (e.g. many situations given). A frequent result is a flowering of diagnostic prose which fills out many a case record. On the other hand, there is seldom a comparable achievement of work towards solving the problems identified in diagnostic workups'.

and departments are all vulnerable, as many recent enquiries demonstrate only too painfully.

The BASW paper on accreditation deals with the basic requirements of beginning workers: 'a realistic workload, including experience with a wide range of client groups, experience in different methods of intervention and opportunity to work in depth over an extended period with a few clients'. It is also stressed that this work should be supervised by someone, it is inferred, who is not only accredited but has further consolidated their own practice before undertaking supervisory work. The analysis here would strongly support these propositions.

Many of our research discussions about the functions and roles of beginning social workers seem to concentrate on issues about how to train them. Systematic short part-time courses may well be needed to supplement on-job training, to meet both gaps in earlier full-time training and to meet worker interests. Short courses and conferences on various topics are readily available if financial sponsorship is earmarked in departmental budgets. However, perhaps there is a need for more planned use of short courses within an explicit staff development contract. More substantial part-time training is becoming available under CCETSW accredited post-qualifying courses, but these are usually only available for staff with two years' experience.

Beginning workers will be best considered as accountable to a specific manager who is capable of helping them to develop their skills in a systematic way. Workers at this stage are perhaps the equivalent of pre-registration junior doctors. They will work with limited discretion, their use of which should be regularly and systematically reviewed and further experiences planned in consequence. The present (Work Stratum 2) concept of the team leader role should be capable of meeting the needs of accountability and it should be clear that full managerial authority attaches to the role in respect of beginning workers.

Career-graded and senior practitioners

As research discussions have developed and deepened, it has become clear that many present so-called career grade schemes are only really taking care of main grade social workers as defined in this chapter and not catering for significant advanced or senior practice. This arises both because of problems of supply, anomalies in grading systems and inadequate definition of differentiated quality of work. Where the caseloads of career graded workers do not change it is likely to be difficult, if not impossible, because of pay codes, to pay higher salaries when it is not demonstrable that greater responsibilities are assumed on re-grading. It is, of course, possible to get round this by stipulating that certain kinds of cases or types of work (for example non-accidental injury or compulsory admissions of any kind or all intake work) will only be undertaken by senior workers. It would be possible to use additional delegated discretion in the same way, for example, authority to spend money or to institute court proceedings, but this has rarely occurred. This is probably because of fear of disturbing existing organizational assumptions that career graded and senior practitioners should continue to be managed by team leaders and should not therefore enjoy the same discretion as their managers.

Career grade schemes fall into two main types. Some schemes allow for automatic accelerated progression to a higher grade on the basis of a specified number of years experience, usually two or three years. Other schemes are based on evaluation of performance before accelerated progression is allowed. In neither case is there necessarily any expectation that the work expected of the individual progressed worker will change.[16]

By contrast our research shows that some departments have, in addition to (or instead of) career grade schemes, established a limited number of posts for senior social workers which are advertised when they become vacant and applied for in the normal way. The grades may be the same or higher than those offered to career graded workers. However, in this situation the appointee almost certainly changes his job as the department will have attached some particular, usually 'specialist', functions to these posts.

However, where the expectations of the work change in either complexity or quality, and a genuine notion of seniority emerges, then there is surely a case for some evaluation process. It seems somewhat anomalous to many staff at the moment, that internal progression through assessment is a far more rigorous process than the normal appointment system to senior practitioner posts, or to any others for that matter.

The use of time limitations for eligibility might be entirely justified for progressing beginning workers into the main grades. This is consistent with notions of probation and registration. Such time scales should be appropriate for the vast majority of beginning workers and not too long to be grossly unfair to the exceptionally able. Thereafter, however, it may be that differences in the ultimate potential, and thereby rates of growth, of individuals may be more apparent. At

[16] Devon County Council (1975), *Career Grade – A National Study.*

the point of delineating senior practitioners, whether through career grade mechanisms or specific posts, it is competence which is of the essence and not length of experience. Undue emphasis on the latter, particularly when supply falls short of need, may bring career grades into disrepute. The differentiation on which notions of senior skills are based may become blurred. A sense of more or less automatic progression may be created with consequent dissatisfactions all round when some individual who has 'served his time' is not promoted.

It is stressed then that if an evaluation based scheme is the model of choice, the basis of that evaluation should strongly relate to actual performance. It is also necessary to be clear about the nature of the required competence of workers in order to ensure appropriate allocation of work and to justify why some clients have the benefit of services from these senior practitioners. A number of other questions need to be considered.

What particular skills are needed by a particular department to facilitate more effective service? What skills does a department wish to foster and what skills does it wish to play down in terms of its objectives? What skills is the particular worker interested in cultivating? It is, for example, no use a worker cultivating his skills in adoption work, where the department already has a highly competent group of adoption workers, and the priority need in the department is for workers with advanced skills in work with the mentally handicapped. The logic of pursuing the answers would seem to be that departments will need to develop both career grade schemes, based on evaluation processes to identify and reward senior workers, and to establish senior posts to take forward developments in key areas where no spontaneous interest has emerged from existing staff. It would seem reasonable to expect that selection processes for senior practitioner posts should not be less rigorous than those for progressing existing workers.

It must not be assumed either that senior workers will always specialize in a narrow field of work. Effective client service in remote and sparsely populated areas of the United Kingdom may be dependent on departments cultivating modes of work, ensuring not only that workers are reasonably equipped to work with a wide range of clients and problems but also competent in the main methods of casework, group work and community work. This approach is needed so that one competent social worker can relate to the needs of a specific geographical patch which it would be uneconomic to have many social workers traversing.

On the other hand, in compact urban areas there is the possibility of high degrees of specialization among both main grade and senior social workers, based on client groups or problems and related locations of work, or on the use of particular techniques, task centred work, conjoint family therapy, small groups or community action.

The main issue at the moment, both nationally and for each department, is to ensure that development opportunities are available to staff with potential in order to meet the needs for both a sufficiency of managers and trainers and a sufficiency of practitioners.

What are some of the possible outcomes of the current trends to give more emphasis to developing opportunities for senior social workers? As noted earlier, even the most generous schemes rarely allow for progression as a practitioner beyond Stratum 2. In a limited number of situations, for example, principal social workers in hospitals and clinics have been assimilated into SSDs at Work Stratum 3. These posts usually allow opportunities for practice with other duties of a managerial, co-ordinating and/or training nature. It is for the latter element that the higher grade is usually paid. There is otherwise advancement for specialists in executive, but non-managerial roles as consultants, advisers, development officers. Rarely, however, do the occupants of such roles have duties in direct service to clients. The nature of all the foregoing roles in general work strata terms, we suggest, is always requisitely pitched at organizational level 3, being concerned with systematic service provision.

It seems reasonable to suppose that if more opportunities are provided for competent practitioners to remain in direct service, then as the more able of these workers develop a capacity for higher level work, some of them at least are going to be equally motivated and committed to continuing to apply their capabilities mainly in practice rather than management. The argument that such advanced practitioners should be allowed to do just that will be even more cogent.[17]

It has already been suggested that certain kinds of psychotherapeutic and community action work may require social workers of Work Stratum 3 capacity, able to be entrusted with the independent practitioner mode of organization that those particular work methods demand. Let us now take a forward look at those workers whose interests lead them to steer clear of either psychotherapy or community action. Do we need highly competent social workers? If we do, will there be continuing opportunities for progression which takes account of their advanced practitioner skills and interests and which allows them to spend the bulk of their time on direct service work? If so, how might they be organized? Will the degree of specialization they

---

[17] See Chapter 8 for comments on consultant practitioners.

carry make it impossible for them to be organized in a managed agency system? Will they too need to be organized as independent practitioners?

In the short term, such highly capable practitioners are likely to be in such short supply that their capacities are almost certainly required to contribute to training, consultation and development work. They may often be required to spend the major part of their time on such activities so that their expertise can be directly injected into the ongoing social work and social services system.

In the longer term, it seems possible that SSDs will need to extend the progression channels for practitioners beyond the modest level of Work Stratum 2, even perhaps beyond Work Stratum 3, to higher strata. This is certainly a need, if there is to be any opportunity for the development of new practice theory which is derived from actual practice. If this happens, social work, as medicine already does, will offer a wide range of career progression paths for its most able recruits. The social work profession will wish to ensure that the activities of any independent practitioners are clearly harnessed to social needs, and that they in no way form an elite corps, unsusceptible to changes in demand or in normative professional values. Practitioner oriented courses should be available for those who wish to progress their careers in this direction, and other courses concerned with social planning, research, managerial and educational work for others who wish to pursue alternative career paths.

All the points made already in respect of main grade practitioners naturally apply to the organization of senior practitioners. They need extended discretion. If managerial roles are required, the managers should be located at the next higher work stratum, and monitoring and co-ordinating roles can be used to weld together the work of various groups and types of workers. The managerial role would continue to be needed at least in respect of those workers located at top Stratum 2 and would rest with the area officer – augmented as necessary with formal consultation arrangements with other specialists.

If society wants social workers who can work at Work Stratum 3, then the issue is whether they can be managed or not, taking account of the required nature of the worker relationship with clients as one line of analysis. The other question is whether these social workers will be so highly specialized that it is unlikely that any one other person can encompass their work adequately enough to be held to account. There is, of course, no reason why independent practitioners could not have 'junior' staff attached for training purposes.

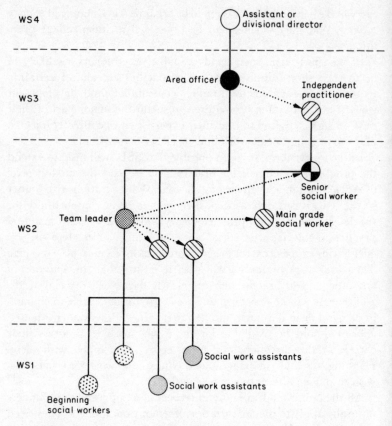

Figure 3.1 Four work strata of social workers and social work assistants

The organization of the various levels of social workers and social work assistants is illustrated in Figure 3.1. It shows a team composed of one independent practitioner with one 'attached' senior and main grade worker, two main grade social workers managed by the area officer, two beginning workers managed by the team leader and two social work assistants. The team leader co-ordinates the work of all the team, an issue we shall explore in the next section.

The team leader
It is not surprising in the light of the foregoing analysis that the team leader role is often said to be one of the most difficult to sustain. It is felt to be a buffer between two sets of demands. On the one hand, there are the demands of the external world and, as matters stand,

the relatively junior and inexperienced staff who work in that world. On the other hand, there are the rather different demands of more senior staff who are often criticized as having 'forgotten what a client is'.

The recommendations of the BASW paper are that accredited workers (in their terms) or main grade workers (in the terms of this analysis) should undergo a consolidation period after registration before any further move is made to be a manager, teacher, or senior practitioner.[18] Just as it was observed earlier that many social workers are moving into senior social worker positions at this point, so are many moving immediately to become team leaders. Clearly this situation is self-defeating, since they will be unready to accept the onerous responsibility of the role.

The general expectations on team leaders can be modelled as follows. Team leaders are accountable for managing assistants and beginning social workers, and for co-ordinating the work of the whole team which may include main grade and senior social workers. They are expected to maintain services according to statutory and departmental prescription, review service provision, develop the skills of their subordinates and co-ordinate the work of their team with others, both within and outside the public sector. Additionally, they may, subject to negotiation, carry small caseloads and often are directly accountable for the fieldwork training of students attached to their teams.

This model derives from identifying the expectations currently made on a wide cross-section of team leaders. Arguably there are only three optional items, the last ones on the list. Fieldwork teaching is often the business of specialist fieldwork teachers. Probably team leaders for their own development needs will want to take up opportunities to take part in departmental working parties or in experimental projects. This leaves the matter of whether team leaders should have small caseloads of their own. This is a matter for continuing debate.[19]

Clients present special kinds of priorities and cannot be ignored. By responding to their own clients the team leaders may act to the detriment of other workers and their clients. On balance, however, it is almost certainly desirable for team leaders to have some practice opportunities. Not only does this help them to keep their hand in, or establish their credibility, both of which are important, but it also provides them with opportunities to extend their own skills as new

[18] BASW, (1976), op. cit.
[19] See Pettes, D. E. (1967), *Supervision in Social Work*.

social policies are brought in or new modes of intervention are taught to the new generation of workers.

Team leader posts seem to be largely awarded in recognition of experience. In my experience in former years groups of social workers were quite small, sometimes just a senior and a couple of main grade workers. The need for new knowledge and skills was not so obvious. Most 'seniors' had experience of supervising students and had opportunities provided by the social work courses to learn something of the techniques of supervision, which they could use appropriately with staff.

The job meanwhile has changed beyond recognition in range and scope, and the size of teams has grown apace. Yet most people are still appointed on the basis of being able to hold down a main grade social work job, perhaps some experience of student teaching, but with no other systematic training for it.

The analysis offered suggests that team leaders should be regarded as the managers of beginning workers and social work assistants, but that main grade and senior social workers would look elsewhere for more appropriate management and professional development. If such patterns do develop, then the numbers of team members who need close supervision and support may decrease, though the size of teams overall will not diminish.

The co-ordinating and monitoring tasks and the general leadership of teams will, however, be an increasing demand.

Following the proposition offered, it is expected that team leaders will be accountable to area officers. Confusions of accountability can occur when there are deputy area officers. Sometimes these posts are primarily themselves team leaders, often of non-social work staff, and designated to act up in the absence of the area officer. In this case lines of accountability remain tolerably clear. However, some deputies do not have teams and carry roving briefs in relation to matters which concern the whole area. It is in this situation that it happens that the deputy is assumed to constitute another managerial level between the area officer and team leaders. According to our premise, and assuming area officers are expected to work at Stratum 3, this is likely to cause difficulty, by excluding the team leader from having the guidance and feedback needed. It is also likely to distance the area officer from a sense of daily work issues, which is needed to be in touch with the job.

If beginning social workers are not fully capable of situational response work but moving towards this position are expected to find their support and development needs met by team leaders, then the relationship between team leaders and beginning workers is likely to be under some strain. In so far as team leaders are themselves only just reaching the main grade stage (and as we have seen, at the moment this is quite likely) then the relationships will be under greater strain. For neither party will have any sense of the necessary distance in capacity that research findings suggest are a pre-requisite of managerial relationships.

Where this is recognized, the importance of the area officer's managerial support to team leaders will be especially crucial. Further, both team leaders and beginning workers will need opportunities, for formal training through short courses and to have available expert consultancy in respect of complex cases.

Most important will be the way in which interactions between social workers and team leaders are structured. Where it is acknowledged that beginning workers are able to handle some cases in appropriate ways, then review and supervisory sessions will reflect this. Discussion will be concentrated on those cases which are problematic and those areas of performance which are underdeveloped. These situations will need identification. The less experienced team leaders as well as the social workers will wish to plan and prepare for their discussions together. The beginning social worker cannot reasonably be left to identify his own needs nor the inexperienced team leader expect to be able to respond appropriately off the cuff to what are acknowledged as difficult cases and limited perceptions.

Area officers

Managerial work at higher work strata is not so much about managing and guiding subordinates in individual cases, as about providing appropriate policy and procedural frameworks and resources which allow the work to be done. Of course, subordinates need to be clear about what is expected of them, to have support and development opportunity, but the frequency of direct discussions will not be so great as for more junior employees. A team leader may only need an individual session, say three-monthly, with an area officer; in turn the area officer may only need to meet individually with the assistant or divisional director annually.

It is suggested then that the work of an area officer is primarily about developing systems for getting the area's work done. They will have regard to the particular patterns of team organization which will provide an optimum match between clients' needs and his staff's stage of development. They will have to fix area priorities and systems within the guidelines provided departmentally, and will need to keep under review systems and procedures of all kinds to ensure the provision of effective and efficient services to clientele. They will have a particular responsibility to represent the department in the particular locality and to maintain effective links with counterparts in other departments and agencies. These links will not just be for public relations, important as this is, but in order to develop appropriate agreed systems for work to flow between agencies. The work is clearly of the systematic service provision kind (Work Stratum 3).

Many of the remarks about team leaders apply equally to area officers. However, in addition our research shows that there has been a decided trend to decentralize responsibility for an increasing range of social services work to areas. Areas now contain many different occupational groups providing domiciliary and community services of various kinds. In addition, some area officers have responsibilities to a wide variety of day and residential centres in their patch. Area officers are drawn almost exclusively from those trained as social workers.

It follows from this that area officers may need two different kinds of training opportunity. Firstly, specific opportunity to extend their knowledge about current developments in the aspects of operational work with which they are not already familiar.

Second, they need the opportunity to develop those managerial skills which are directly related to systems and procedure planning and implementation – priority scaling, organization design, and methods of evaluation.

The particular responsibility of area officers is to ensure that incoming work is organized in such a way as to obtain the right fit between client needs, service resources and the specific levels of competence of workers at different stages of development: the importance of the cycle of screening, intake, allocation, review and case closure processes cannot be over-stressed.[20]

Summary

Various aspects of the practice and organization of social work have been reviewed. Consideration has been given to the possible need to provide for social work practice at higher work strata than is presently the case. The possible consequences of such a development in terms of preparation and organization were considered. In particular analysis was offered of the difference between agency and independent

[20] For further exploration of this cycle, see *Social Services Departments*, Chapter 8.

practice. The conditions necessary to underpin independent practice were examined.

Models were developed for the roles of beginning, main grade, senior social workers and social work assistants, and of team leaders and area officers, and for their relationships to each other.

4 Providing Basic Services at Home[1]

by Anthea Hey

Introduction

Basic service activities are directed towards seeing that clients have all those basic things everyone needs in order to sustain life, and to securing or providing them for those who cannot obtain them entirely on their own initiative. These services include the provision of accommodation, food, money, goods, help with personal and home care, transport (to prevent social isolation), and recreational opportunity.

This group of activities might be more aptly termed social or welfare services; but the use of these terms was pre-empted by the names of present or past departments. Although in this chapter basic services will be explored in the context of staff who are working with clients living at home, the term domiciliary services is, on the one hand, too broad a term, and on the other hand too narrow a term. It is normally used to include what is described here as basic services and also some of the activities described earlier as supplementary services. It is not usually taken to include social work, though most social work probably takes place in clients' own homes. However, it must also be noted that basic services work is not simply under-taken on a domiciliary basis; many residential and day centres are primarily in business to provide for people's basic needs. Other centres which exist primarily to provide social work or supplementary services have necessarily to provide basic services while clients attend or live there.

There is a great deal of confusion in the social services field as to who should be doing what in this basic services area between agencies, between divisions within agencies and between individual

[1] The main elements of this chapter are based on papers delivered to the National Council of Home Help Services Study Day in London (5 November 1976) and to a Day Seminar 'Domiciliary Care in the 80s' organized by Central Regional Council SWD at Stirling on 6 June 1978.

workers. The basic services field is not therefore an island of stability in the midst of social services chaos as one might suppose when dealing with concrete and tangible services, but is itself subject to a number of conflicting pulls and pushes. Some workers in this field are as divided as social workers are about the proper boundaries to their work, the conditions which should apply and the kind of training and organization which is needed to deliver an effective service to clients and provide a satisfactory career. This field of work is attracting more attention and the need to rationalize and develop services is increasingly recognized.[2]

This chapter considers reasons for the growing importance of basic services work and the current arrangements for, and problems in providing, basic services to people in their own homes.

The possible need for a new professional role is then considered, first in relation to extending the role and functions of present home help organizers, and second in relation to the alternative development of social services officers.

The growing importance of basic services provision to clients at home

In the early days of the Welfare State it was expected that most people would be in a position to provide for their own basic needs. National Insurance schemes would provide adequate incomes for the retired, the sick and unemployed. Where eligibility had not been established, or had expired, supplementary benefits would cater for deficiencies and allow people to be self-sufficient financially. Education, health and housing services would be comprehensive and provide for all ages and sectors of society. Demographic changes and inflation have together resulted in a level of demand with which the universal services have been unable to keep pace.

It has become clear that there will be a continuing expansion of need and demand for basic services of various kinds to be delivered to people in their own homes. This expansion arises very directly from the demands for community care. There are numerous specific 'community care policies' in relation to the categories of clients who have tended to be the Cinderellas of health provision, and whose problems are increasingly being defined primarily in social rather than medical terms. The mentally ill, the mentally handicapped, the chronic sick and disabled, and the elderly – all have an increased life expectancy as a result of technical and social advancements. The

[2] See Goldberg, E. M. and Connelly, N. (1978), 'Reviewing Services for the Old'.

total numbers of physically and socially frail people in the population are therefore greater than formerly.

Wrapped up in trends towards community care are a number of considerations. First, there are the high capital costs in building residential institutions, whether they are called homes or hospitals, as well as the high revenue costs in running them because of high staffing ratios and the shorter working week. Secondly, there is increasing recognition of the doubtful relevance of institutional care to the nature of the problems being addressed. Thirdly, there are the peculiar problems which seem to surround the running of residential establishments, the problems arising from the particular vulnerability of the clients involved, and the insufficiency in numbers and quality of staff willing to undertake the onerous work. Fourth, the recognition that all citizens, no matter what their condition, should have maximum opportunities for choice and, in particular, the possibility of living in private households. Finally, there is the related recognition that it is technically possible to provide that opportunity, given a willingness to redirect resources and make more available. There are few professional or technical blocks to providing health and social services in private households except surgery and intensive care.

It is clearly wrong to define everything bearing the title 'community' as being the responsibility of local authorities, and everything bearing a 'health' label as being the responsibility of hospitals. But as the redefinition of problems proceeds, and as ways of coping with these problems outside of longstay institutions, both hospitals and homes, are sought, SSDs are going to be faced with demands for an increased quantity, quality and range of support services, particularly for those services which have been categorized here under the basic services heading.[3] The client groups involved are those who, for a variety of physical as well as psychological and social reasons, are the least likely to be able to manage unaided all their own daily living needs.

Alternative assumptions about basic services work

At present there are three different assumptions about the way domiciliary basic services work is organized and to some degree these are in unhelpful competition with each other. The three assumptions are: one, that basic services work is part of social work; two, that

---

[3] It is equally and critically clear that health services need to develop in tandem to provide health care services outside of hospitals; community care policies demand a development of a wide range of domiciliary and local health and social services. See *Health Services*, Chapter 17.

it is part of social work but at a lower level; three, that it is different in kind from social work.

In the first, no distinction is made between basic services and social work. It follows that social workers are those most capable of assessing clients' needs for all social services. They are expected to range across the three aspects of social services activity analysed here: social work, basic services and supplementary services.[4] Once social workers have made their assessments, other workers provide various elements of service.

This is arguably wrong. Social workers are ill-prepared by their training to assess basic service needs. By and large social workers, in dealing with basic services, are reliant on their own practical experience in everyday living matters. This may be limited and not to say inappropriate to the clients' situations. Probably the only systematic output in CQSW training which is directly relevant to basic services provision is the introduction in some courses of Welfare Rights Studies – sometimes derided by academics.

Furthermore, so long as social workers are expected to deal with basic services, they are possibly losing opportunities to develop the skills they need to do social work as analysed in the previous chapter.

In the second assumption: basic services are seen as the business of social work, but it is assumed that the practical issues involved do not require the skills of fully trained social workers. Basic services needs are regarded as less complex to understand. Lower graded staff, usually social work assistants, are allocated to assess needs and to pass requests for particular elements of service to service providers – organizers of home help, meals, transport, volunteers. In effect this assumption leads to a response based on demand rationed by eligibility criteria rather than a response which seeks to respond situationally to each request.[5]

In the previous chapter, ambiguities in roles, expectations and capacities of social work assistants were analysed in some detail. Suffice it to say here that staff who are best regarded as genuine 'assistants to' (working at Work Stratum 1), should not be expected to make open-ended assessments. They are best deployed on tasks that have been framed by workers at Work Stratum 2.

[4] In practice, this is sometimes taken to ridiculous lengths. The author came across a situation in which occupational therapists were employed as unqualified social workers expected to undertake social work. Qualified social workers meanwhile undertook assessments for aids and adaptations.

[5] In the work stratum terms analysed in Chapter 1, this leads to a Work Stratum 1 prescribed output response rather than a Work Stratum 2 situational response.

The third assumption is that not all clients needing basic services need social work, and that therefore basic services work can be defined as intrinsically different from social work. This assumption accords most closely with the analysis of kinds of work in this book. However, before exploring this in more depth, some current roles which are solely or largely concerned with basic services work are reviewed.

Current modes of providing basic services in the home and some current problems

In this section the contribution of the home help service (organizers and helps), family aides, auxiliary nurses, social work assistants and social services officers will be examined, as well as their inter-relationship. Significant problems affecting workers and clients will be identified.[6]

The home help service

Expectations of the home help service at present vary appreciably amongst departments, not surprisingly in view of the variations in the numbers of clients each home help organizer is serving. In some departments the service is still concerned with simple provision of delineated domestic work, primarily for the elderly. In other departments, home help organizers are explicitly concerned with a wider range of support in the home, often concerned with the assessment of the need for meals on wheels and for laundry services. In others a considerable range of differentiation is made among the home helps themselves serving different kinds of client needs (for example, from dirty squads to support of mothers with young children). In others the functions of the home help organizers have already been extended to be more broadly concerned with the manifold basic service needs of their clients. Often this extension is marked by a change in title to home care organizer. These creeping developments have usually occurred without systematic adjustments in grading structures, in supervisory support, to say nothing of the generally vexed question of administrative support.

[6] The analysis in this chapter derives from two specific research projects, from numerous working conferences, some specific to this topic and others concerned with patterns of organization more generally. The author is particularly grateful to Mary Hughes, Hon. Sec. of the National Council of Home Help Organizations and to Maureen Maclaine, currently President of the Institute of Home Help Organizers, who have not only contributed to working conferences and/or projects, but have patiently and generously given time to discussing the issues affecting their service with the author.

It is apparent that present confusions are adversely affecting the home help service. There is some unhappiness amongst members of the service about the way they are viewed and a sensed lack of interest given to their basic concerns. Many complain about lack of job satisfaction in the face of the large numbers of clients they have to try to cope with and in their relationship with other SSD staff. Many carry a sense of injustice about pay and lack of career progression opportunity, about the hiatus regarding appropriate training and about the particular organizational structures in which they have to operate. The service appears to be somewhat divided within itself as to which are the best strategies to pursue to improve the situation both for their clients and themselves.

As demands have changed and increased, these have been reflected in increasing differentiation among the home help group. These differentiations have not necessarily been reflected in payment grades. Three types of home help have emerged.

The mainstream group provide services mostly to elderly and infirm clients. There has been a change in the nature of the tasks being performed by these home helps. There is less emphasis on cleaning and more emphasis on personal care and social support.

Heavy duty squads of home helps, whose contact with clients is minimal, have been established in some urban areas. They clean up whole dwellings to render them fit for habitation again, or regularly undertake the cleaning of common lobbies and stairways in flats without caretaking services where there is a high occupancy by the elderly.

The third group to emerge is made up of those home helps, who because they are judged to have extra tact and flexibility, are selected to work in particularly demanding situations. They are typically those who handle clients of whatever age who are suffering from mental health problems which have to be accommodated too by the home help.

Family aides
It is now said that it is difficult to distinguish between home helps of the third type and other staff called family aides and assistants. Such staff are differentiated however, not just by title and pay grades, but organizationally as they often work as members of social work teams, rather than for home help organizers.

On the surface home helps and family aides often seem to be carrying out the same domestic tasks. However, discussion suggests that the home help is pursuing her own tasks, making whatever marginal adaptations to them as seem appropriate to changes observed in the client's situation from visit to visit.

The family aide, on the other hand, is pursuing tasks in a particular way which has been framed by a social worker in order to facilitate the social and emotional functioning of the client system in a specific way. The family aide is truly part of the social work field, where the plans for service are modelled on a discretionary rather than an eligibility basis, which tends to govern the basic services field. Family aides therefore need to be managed by a member of the social work profession who will carry accountability for the case.

Auxiliary nursing

A further type of help in the home is emerging which will again need recognition. Increasingly patients are being discharged home at earlier stages of their recovery or are being treated at home altogether. These patients need a good deal of personal assistance, lifting, washing, toileting, which are not normally part of a home help's tasks.[7] Here there is a need to differentiate between the responsibility of social and health services, for home helps' work and the work of auxiliary nurses.

There are some major issues to be debated here, not just about boundaries between agencies and workers within them, but about the extent of supervision and support and indeed training to be provided for home helps, which are requisite to the changing expectations. The common restrictions on home helps' activities implicitly recognize the potential difficulties when very personal services are provided by paid public employees. Issues of both client and employee protection arise. Working in the isolation of a private house is very different from working in the public arena of a hospital or home where one's behaviour is on view to others and where support and guidance are to hand.

Attempts are often made by those involved to determine appropriate boundaries by suggesting that home helps should be able to pursue those tasks which ordinary families or close neighbours and friends undertake for each other. This rather over-simplifies the consequences. Issues of privacy, vulnerability, touch and sexuality

[7] This points to the major difference to be found between the activities of home helps and care assistants in residential centres. The latter are predominantly concerned with care of persons; the former predominantly with care of premises and related matters to sustain clients at home, like shopping and laundry. Immediate post hospital care schemes are requiring home helps to be more like care assistants.

arise, around which most families have established their own norms and taboos, which are not necessarily apparent to or shared by strangers.

Social work assistants/social services officers
In the previous chapter differentiation was made between those social work assistants who are expected to operate at Work Stratum 2, making assessments of basic services needs and carrying case account-ability and others who are expected to work at Stratum 1, carrying out tasks prescribed by social workers. It was suggested that the first type of staff might more properly be called social service officers and it is the latter who might best be regarded as genuine 'assistants to'.

In so far as social work assistants or social service officers are expected to respond to the possible multiple basic service needs of clients, then there is clearly less scope for home help organizers to extend their functions in the same way, at least to the same clients.

The case for considering a new profession

Overview of issues
Given the way they are currently organized, too few or too many workers may be involved in providing basic services. Save in a limited number of cases where clients are on a social worker's caseload, no one worker is clearly carrying prime responsibility.[8] It is not inconceivable that the client's state may be more hindered than helped by such piecemeal responses often made in ignorance of one other. The problem is exacerbated in many cases, because many of the clients are also actively involved with a range of health services.

One of the idiosyncratic features of this field within SSDs is that there is potentially a multiplicity of workers who might each be interacting with the clients but there is no one profession which is responsible for the assessment and arrangement of basic services. Some home help organizers get very near to this, as do some social work assistants of the social services officer type, but this tends to result from *ad hoc* additions to roles or as a result of the initiatives of individual workers, rather than as the consequence of clarity about the need to develop more comprehensive responses. Piecemeal rather than integrated development has resulted.

The confusion, however, has possibly unfortunate consequences for workers and clients. Workers' actual contributions may be under-

[8] See Chapter 2 for a discussion of the concept of prime responsibility.

recognized and undervalued with deleterious effects on their career progression, training and financial rewards, to say nothing of job satisfaction. Clients may be at the risk of falling between two or more stools, for there is also an absence of the notion of case accountability which is a normal concomitant of professional activity.

If it is assumed that both clients and workers matter, then minimally there is a case for rationalizing the way basic services are provided. Earlier three different assumptions about the provision of basic services were noted. If basic services are to be considered part of social work then it should be noted that there is a need to be clear about the level of work expectations on social work assistants and to clarify where accountability for cases rests.

The case for developing a new profession rests on the belief that a real distinction can be made between social work and basic services work. It rests on the view that not all clients of SSDs need social work as such.

Evidence for this view comes from information about how clients are presently dealt with[9] and the fact that 90 per cent of clients in receipt of home help service are not known to social workers.[10] In pursuing this development of a new profession it has to be clear that current arrangements do not merely reflect the shortage of competent social workers and the priorities that departments have explicitly or implicitly, selected in the light of this. While recognizing that some 'basic services' clients need social work as well and are not receiving it, nonetheless there remains a substantial number of clients who need only basic services.

What would be the duties of a new profession? To illustrate the point, take a case of an elderly couple where support in the form of home help and meals and laundry service is already being provided. The wife is frail and increasingly immobilized by arthritis. The husband dies. At the moment such a case may rest with a HHO, with a social worker or a social work assistant, without it being clear which worker is expected to deal with which needs.

The new type worker would not only review the level of the particular services already provided, but seek to identify new or potential needs and provide help with a range of services. For example: advice on the client's income, expenditure and budgeting; applications for a special needs grant for new clothes; arranging a savings stamp scheme to meet electricity bills; commissioning volunteers on

[9] Goldberg, E. M. *et al.* (1977), 'Towards Accountability in Social Work: One Year's Intake to an Area Office'.

[10] Information supplied by HHOs in conjunction with two social analytic projects.

redecorations and gardening; laying on luncheon club–plus–transport facilities to ensure sufficient companionship for the widow; referral to occupational therapists for replanning and adaptation of domestic equipment; checking on the widow's bereavement responses to ensure that they were within normal expectations; referring on to GP and health services where necessary. If a home help is to continue then, her tasks would be set and reviewed at regular intervals. The possible needs are endless.

The professional associated with the basic services field would be expected to assess for all those needs, respond personally to those which fall in the basic services field, and refer on those which are outside his own limits. If other workers such as social worker and occupational therapist were brought in, together they would have to decide on their respective contributions and how best to keep each other informed. It would certainly be helpful if it were agreed that one of them carried prime responsibility for the case. Each profession would work minimally at Work Stratum 2, comprehending needs and responses in that sphere and being held to account for their judgements and actions – to be case accountable.

Case accountability

Case accountability is a significant concept. It can only devolve on those able to comprehend a distinctive area of human functioning, who know their own limits, together with the distinctive contributions other professionals might bring to bear. It entails that the prescribed limits to discretion have to be drawn fairly widely. It entails that the workers will be called to account for the exercise of judgement within those limits.

What seems crucial is where discretion and accountability rest for assessment. Assessment entails deciding the nature of need in any case, and how best to meet this need, given the various constraints of policy and resources. It is a different issue as to who is made accountable for providing the services, once assessment and appropriate provision have been decided.

This requirement to reach beyond the present problem or request, to see the person in a wider social context, is rather different from being asked to provide a home help or a meal. It implies a wider accountability for a case, as opposed to providing a particular element or item of service, to see things which are needed which the referrer, another worker, or indeed the client, does not necessarily comprehend. A secure base of knowledge and experience is implied by such accountability. At present it seems that some workers, notably social workers and heads of residential establishments, are held to be case accountable and some are not, and it is rarely clear which situation appertains.

Home help organizers do not seem to be held case accountable: it seems unclear whether social work assistants or indeed social services officers are either. HHOs are accountable for deciding whether specific services requested, over which they have control, are actually needed. They are accountable for supplying these services as nearly as possible in the right quantity and quality. Of course, they often feel responsible in a more general and diffuse way. Like any other employee, they are expected to apply their commonsense and report through any other needs they happen to notice. 'Happen to notice' is an appropriate description because invariably they are not expected to assess systematically for other needs.

Given the number of clients to be served and the number of home helps to be managed, it would be more than unjust to apply the 'case accountable' notion.[11] Unjust because the degree of contact required and the range of tasks to be pursued could not be sustained with such a large number of clients. Nevertheless, it not infrequently happens that a HHO happens to notice another need which she thinks is outside the limits of her job. She frequently gets a negative response when attempting to refer the matter to someone else. If not this, then she often encounters delays in the matter being taken up elsewhere, which results in uncertainty as to who will be held to account if something goes wrong meanwhile.

The situation leaves clients, organizers and departments somewhat vulnerable. Recent events have made it clear that departments are going to be called to account when something goes wrong with clients who are known to them.

In order to establish case accountability, caseloads would have to be limited – perhaps to not more than social workers' caseloads and even less if the new profession was to be expected to manage the people (home helps and night-sitters) actually providing the service.

Alternative models for developing a new profession

It was noted earlier that some departments have moved in the direction being discussed here either by extending the roles of home

[11] Nationally, actual numbers vary enormously. The range of clients to HHO in the UK varies from 239 to 485, and the number of helps to HHO from 38 to 77. National Council of Home Help Services (1978), *Home Help Services in Great Britain*.

help organizers or by establishing a new group of staff (social service officers) working alongside home help organizers. These alternative ways of pursuing the objective of a new profession will now be analysed in relation to their staffing, training and organizational implications. The relationship between the alternatives will be explored.

Extending the role of home help organizers

In order to understand better the difference which is implied in the extension of the home help organizer role and the structural consequences, the present pattern of the home help service is first discussed before pursuing the new role which will be called 'home care organizer'.

The main possibilities for the organization of the present home help service were predicted in our first book. Further research experience has confirmed the existence of four main patterns. Irrespective of how departments are organized at assistant director level, there seems to have been a steady trend for home help organizers to be based in area offices.

The alternatives can be outlined as follows. Home help organizers are accountable within the area office to a team leader or area officer, or they are 'attached' to areas by a centrally-based senior officer. Alternatively, they are in some urban areas, centrally based and accountable to a senior member of the home help service.[12]

What is generally at issue is whether home help organizers are a full part of the area and managerially accountable within the area structure or whether they are subject to a dual influence emanating from both the area and from a central office home help specialist. Many departments employ a senior centrally-based officer with responsibilities for the development of the home help service. Where HHOs are managed within areas these central specialists may carry monitoring and co-ordinating authority. In 'attachment' situations such a senior officer would carry full or shared managerial responsibility as well as general development duties.

Which of these alternatives is preferred? No systematic study has been conducted of how far any of these patterns are satisfactory. The general impression gained from many discussions, however, is that older established HHOs find problems with the decentralized models when they have previously been used to working closely together in a centralized location. Conversely, where the home help service is centralized, other area based staff may well feel that the possibilities

---

[12] See *Social Services Departments,* Chapter 7.

for developing strongly co-ordinated services based on local considerations of needs and priorities are made more difficult.

There are a number of reported difficulties in the decentralized models. First, where HHO, area officer and senior home help specialist at HQ all have to relate together, it is frequently unclear as to the respective duties and authority of the latter two people.

Secondly, even if the decentralized organizational model is clear, it may be distorted in practice because one or other party fails to fulfil their obligations. As seen from the home help service, area officers, drawn almost exclusively from the ranks of social workers, do not understand the complexities of the programming and personnel aspects of the home help organizer's job. Home help organizers tend to rely heavily for support and guidance on the central specialist. Where there are only one or two home help organizers in an area office, they may feel isolated in a predominantly social worker group.

Thirdly, where there are several organizers, perhaps equal to the number of social work teams, the organizers are often regarded as managed by or attached to the team leaders. Not only are there problems about the knowledge and interest of team leaders, but as explicated in the previous chapter, in respect of genuine Work Stratum 2 social workers, there is not usually sufficient distance between the general capacity of the home help organizers and that of the team leader for a managerial relationship between them to be viable as both roles are located in Work Stratum 2.

Fourthly, where, as is the predominant case, new referrals for home help services are immediately directed to the home help organizers to get on with, then the sense of isolation is perpetuated. There is also a fundamental difference in terms of values and ethos between social workers and HHOs: social workers tend to be more reflective and passive in approach to clients, HHOs practical and active. It is hardly surprising then that there is collaborative work in such a small percentage of cases as was indicated earlier.

Many organizers with whom the idea of an extended role has been discussed would, in principle, be willing to extend their functions to make comprehensive responses to basic service needs. They believe that to do so would not unduly extend the length of time taken on initial visits to the client. However, the feeling prevails that given the present patterns of organization and staffing levels, it is 'pie in the sky' to expect that substantial improvements could be wrought to make such an extension possible. They have felt that to personally initiate and co-ordinate all the responses and to visit frequently enough to exercise a continuing case accountability would be impossible with current workloads. Many anyway cannot keep up to date with current expectations for reviews of cases.

A further important point arises for debate. Is it practicable, even with smaller numbers of clients and helps and with supervisory assistants and adequate administrative and clerical support for home help organizers to carry case accountability and manage the home helps? This is a key question, for the model being developed is of seeing the home helps as assistants, helping organizers to get their work done with their clients. It is necessary to retain this direct control so that the services can be individually tailored to clients' need.

An argument is sometimes advanced that if the home help service is to be efficient, then the home helps have to be organized and programmed in substantial numbers, particularly in urban areas. The numbers have to be sufficient for the manipulations and short notice changes that have to be made to cover illness of helps or their own families, or at holiday times, or to accommodate new urgent cases. If the numbers of clients, and thereby of home helps, was substantially reduced to accommodate extended functions, it might be too difficult to retain this flexibility in deployment of helps. If managing helps in large numbers is felt to be imperative then the model of the home care organizer will not be considered viable. The home care organizer model rests on there being reductions in numbers of clients and workers for which each organizer is responsible, abetted by improvements in the quality of supervision and support of home helps. Such a suggestion obviously carries revenue cost implications; yet it could promote a more cost effective service overall. Improved support for home helps might reduce turnover of staff and cut the number of cases which provoke industrial relations problems which take a long time to resolve, to say nothing of the accompanying emotional stresses and strains.

Against this background what alternative models would be available for the organization of home care organizers? In the first place, organization will be affected by the numbers of home care organizers and the ratio of them to social workers. If, as a rough indicator, case-loads of 40 clients were assumed to be the norm, there could eventually be as many as six to twelve more home care organizers than there are present home help organizers.[13]

Obviously this expansion will not happen overnight. As HCOs increased in numbers the choice would arise of being organized in separate teams alongside social work teams or as members of social

[13] These figures are arrived at by dividing the present ratios of clients to home helps by 40 (see this Chapter, note 11).

service teams containing several disciplines. The problem of managing a large number of home helps can be relieved to some extent by appointing supervisory home helps. As for any profession, there would be a place for trainee home care officers.

Figure 4.1 demonstrates how in effect each home care organizer is manager of a team, and is in turn managed by an area social services organizer. The figure suggests that the home care team may be attached to a team, but that the team leader would carry only co-ordinating and not managerial authority.[14] The team may be a team of HCOs, a team of social workers, or a multi-disciplinary team composed of social workers, home care organizers and others. The possible need for a specialist (Work Stratum 3) home care co-ordinator for the division (functionally or geographically organized) is suggested.

The social services officer role
The establishment of new roles as distinct from extension to existing roles as just explored in this field is not a new concept; various authorities have established such posts although the duties and titles vary.[15] Probably the most developed model is that of the patch worker. The duties incumbent on patch workers seem to correspond very closely to the model of a comprehensive basic services worker analysed in this chapter with the important additional dimension of each worker relating to a precise geographical neighbourhood.[16] This model of the patchworker is currently the subject of a research investigation.[17]

Everything which was suggested for the client-related aspects of a comprehensive role earlier in relation to clients would transfer to the social service officer. A key element in this role would be the need for effective co-ordination of all social services and domiciliary health services. As far as the elderly infirm and physically handicapped are concerned, they may be in receipt of numerous community health services: district nursing, auxiliary nursing (for bathing), chiropody. As indicated earlier, these services, like social services, are often provided on a piecemeal rather than on an integrated basis.

The difference between this model and the extended home help

[14] For definition of 'co-ordinating relationship', see Chapter 2.
[15] Avon CC – Social Care Officers; East Sussex – Social Services Officers; Wakefield MD – Neighbourhood or Patch Workers; Nottinghamshire CC – Domiciliary Services Officers.
[16] City of Wakefield MD Social Services (1976), *Neighbourhood Social Workers*.
[17] By Professor R. Hadley, University of Lancaster, sponsored by DHSS.

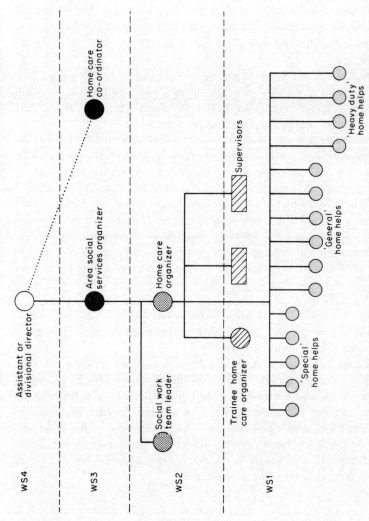

WS4 Assistant or divisional director

WS3 Area social services organizer

Home care co-ordinator

WS2 Home care organizer

Social work team leader

Supervisors

WS1 Trainee home care organizer

'Special' home helps

'General' home helps

'Heavy duty' home helps

Figure 4.1 Extended home help organizer role – the home care organizer

organizer role lies not in any interaction of worker and client but in the fact that the new professional does not manage a team of 'helps' as does the home care organizer. A social service officer or patch worker may have one or two assistants but not more. This model is in principle an alternative to the home care organizer model but would be the model of choice if home help organizers were unable (because of the problem of managing helps) or unwilling to extend their role.

Social service officers, like home care organizers, could be organized as members of social work teams, or they might be in separate teams alongside social work teams. In the case of intake teams there is clearly a case for a multi-disciplinary approach.

Social service officers working in this way at Stratum 2 would, like social workers, possibly need assistants to undertake specific tasks. Whether any assistant group would be necessarily separated by activity and organization from social work assistants is debatable.

What would be the effect on the present home help service of the development of a new professional group? The new profession would take responsibility for assessing client need across the basic services field, and for arranging service provision. The logic would be that social service officers should be equipped to make a detailed request for home helps: that is, one which delineates the tasks which need to be carried out by a home help and to determine the number of hours required. Such a prescription surely would be necessary as it could not be justified that another worker from the same field needs to undertake a personal visit.[18]

Home help organizers would be in a service-providing relationship to social service officers. They would be accountable for managing home helps, and for providing the agreed quantity of home help service, but not for assessing clients' needs nor for carrying accountability for clients. They could also be accountable in the same way for the meals and laundry services. Figure 4.2 demonstrates this model and in particular illustrates the relationship of social service officers to a more restricted home help service.

Training and career progression in basic services work
Whichever model is pursued, developments in career progression and training will be needed, opportunities for which have been singularly

[18] At the moment where social workers are referring for home help it might be reasonable that an HHO should visit on the grounds that these workers are from different fields.

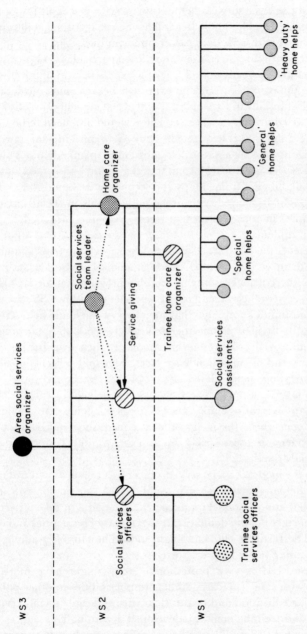

Figure 4.2 New social services officer role – alongside home help service

lacking in the basic services field. If this service is seen as important and critical, then able candidates will have to be recruited and trained and provided with adequate career opportunities.

Training structures need to mount varied curriculae and cope with recruits of various ages and of varying experiences. Some full-time training opportunities would be expected, because most professions recruit substantially from people at point of leaving school or following first further education experience. There would also need to be some part-time (and possible phased) courses to provide for current employees and older recruits. A substantial planned and guided practical experience during formal training would be assumed, as well as the availability of traineeships and secondments. Some core course content might be shared with other professionals in social services; for example, in social science degrees, or in the proposed higher education diplomas.

At present, the Certificate in Social Services represents the main attempt to meet the training needs of non-social worker staff. In principle, there is no reason why suitable programmes for HCOs or for social service officers could not be worked out within CSS schemes. This is said in full knowledge that members of the home help service are currently divided among themselves between CSS opportunities and the improved programmes promoted by their own Institute on a part-time and/or correspondence basis. This split reflects the views of those stressing client-related aspects of their work, and those who stress managerial aspects. The CSS has one element of considerable and perhaps overriding importance as far as the home care organizer model is concerned, the inclusion of planned and guided practice. Such an element must surely be a pre-requisite of any credible professional training.

Where the model of social service officer was pursued then training for home help organizers as such would concentrate on domestic and institutional and personnel management. They might take a part in the management of the domestic arrangements of residential and day centres. The Institute Diploma might indeed be suitable training for any continuing home help organizer role.

However, HHOs as a professional group might have more in common with staff who carry similar responsibilities in other public services like education and health than with colleague social services workers, and training could be developed accordingly.

As indicated earlier, if home helps are increasingly being expected to take on more personal caring functions then they will need both training and closer support than is generally available at the moment.

A modicum of training is provided by some departments to prepare the home helps not just for the client-related aspects of the job but also to understand relevant departmental systems and procedures.

Classed as manual workers, the training of home helps is not the responsibility of CCETSW but of the Local Government Training Board.[19] In the long term it is perhaps questionable as to whether this arbitrary split in responsibilities makes sense or whether a more rational distinction might be made as is attempted with higher grades of staff; the CCETSW trains operational staff and LGTB non-operational staff.

In relation to career progression and further training, one general point should be made. Whether or not those trained as social workers attain or retain primacy in the social services field in the longer term, they are likely to continue to have a monopoly on senior operational posts at team and area level in the shorter term. Remembering there is a commitment by CCETSW to develop post-qualifying studies for CSS holders as well as those with CQSW, it can be predicted that advancement to any posts at Work Stratum 3 (and beyond) will, increasingly, be associated with those workers who have undertaken such studies. It seems logical to propose that courses could be offered for CQSW and CSS holders together in such topics as management and planning.

Summary

The nature of basic services work and aspects of its current and future development were explored. Three current assumptions about basic services work were noted: that this work is an intrinsic part of social work; that it is part of social work but in some ways at a lower level; and that basic services work is intrinsically different from social work. In particular the perceived nature of present responses was reviewed, disclosing a piecemeal pattern of response in which case accountability cannot easily be established. This led to consideration of the need to develop a professional group which could encompass the basic services field as defined.

Two ways of achieving such a professional group were considered. The first way explored was through extension of the role of home help organizers to create home care organizers. The second way of achieving similar outcomes was explored through developing new roles such as social services officers or patchworkers. Social services

[19] The LGTB presently has a working party sitting to consider the training needs of home helps and other manual workers in SSDs and Wardens of Sheltered Housing.

officers would work alongside home help organizers who would continue to manage helps but have a lesser contact with and responsibility for clients.

PART III

Residential Work

Introduction

by David Billis and Geoffrey Bromley

The three chapters of this Part continue to discuss the involvement with residential care that has been a significant feature of our research. In 1974 we reported that 'a great deal of our work over the past three and a half years has been (by invitation) concerned with residential work and its organization'. This was an area which, we suggested, felt itself to be, and was often seen as, the poor relation.[1]

Two major problem areas had been presented for collaborative analysis. First, the absence of strong and clearcut lines of responsibility linking establishments and headquarters. Secondly, the vexed question of the relationship of residential with field staff. In our exploration of these problems a number of conclusions were reached. Little progress would be made, we felt, unless we first produced some list of what it was that establishments were trying to achieve. From this analysis of the work of residential homes the general conclusion was reached that many heads of establishments were also, in addition to the provision of basic and supplementary services, involved in activities which did not differ fundamentally (apart from the setting) from that of the fieldworkers 'basic social work'.[2] A further finding of the research at that time was the identification of a 'missing level' of manager above that of the head of the establishment. Both these findings had obvious and important implications for training and career development and for a wide range of organizational issues.

What has happened in the intervening period? It is probably true to say that the 'relation' still feels itself to be 'poor'. In one important sense it could hardly be different given the repeated policy declarations that community care is more desirable than residential care.[3] Residential care is – officially – a policy option of last resort.

---

[1] See *Social Services Departments*, Chapter 6.

[2] For a discussion of the 'output' functions of residential establishments, see Chapter 5. See also Introduction to Part II.

[3] See, for example, 'The DHSS Perspective', in Barnes, J. and Connelly, N. (eds.) (1978), *Social Care Research*.

But at the same time residential care dominates SSD budgets. Despite the declarations and the growing proportion of available resources going to day and support services, about 75 per cent of capital expenditure goes to the residential sector.[4] The number of residents and staff continues to rise, albeit at a slower rate.[5]

A number of substantial reports have been produced by working parties of the Personal Social Services Council (PSSC) and the Social Services Liaison Group.[6] They make a welcome and influential contribution. They go some way towards redressing the imbalance (in attention and critical discussion) between residential care and other parts of social services provision. Such reports must be seen as an essential step towards clarification and resolution of problems obstructing improvements in the quality of care for residents. A central feature of these reports, and it is an approach that can be warmly endorsed, is the clearcut link that is made between the role of staff and standards of care. For example the PSSC Report suggests that:

> The quality of life of residents is largely determined by the attitudes of staff towards that work. If their function is made clear both in general terms and in relation to individual duties, they can appreciate the part they play, think intelligently about it, and develop its scope.[7]

The Social Services Liaison Group make more detailed recommendations and demand that all posts should have written job descriptions containing lines of accountability, areas of responsibility, and extent of discretion.[8]

In our research projects and conferences, issues stemming from the residential sector still occupy a high priority. The present chapters on residential care build on earlier research. As before, they originate from real problems and have been critically discussed and evaluated by those who have to actually tackle those problems. We make no claim to make a comprehensive statement about residential care.

[4] Judge, K. (1978), *Rationing Social Services*, p. 51.

[5] DHSS (1977), *Health and Personal Social Service Statistics for England 1977*. For example, accommodation provided by or on behalf of LAs under the National Assistance Act of 1948 has risen from (about) 110000 in 1970, to 126000 in 1976; staff increases in a similar period have been from approximately 38000 to 50000. The number of children in community homes has risen from 19100 in 1974 to 22000 in 1976 with consistent staff increases.

[6] Personal Social Services Council, *Living and Working in Residential Homes*, (1975), and *Residential Care Reviewed*, (1977); Social Services Liaison Group (1978), op. cit.

[7] Personal Social Services Council (1977), op. cit.

[8] Personal Social Services Liaison Group (1978), op. cit.

We are keenly aware of issues that are not, or barely, mentioned.[9] The broadest view is provided in Chapter 5, whose title indicates the ambition to examine the nature of interaction between 'management' and 'caring'. The analytic tools that are used in this essay include a body of theory that did not appear in our first research report. Then, following the work of Elliott Jaques, one of the chronic problems was analysed as a missing managerial level. Now in this essay on the organization of residential care we utilize for the first time the new ideas of stratification in work. So in addition to (1) defining the field of work, and (2) clarifying lines of accountability, we are now able to describe the appropriate *level* of work for heads and residential group managers. Thus we can produce models which add *a third dimension* and consequently, we would claim, enable us to move ahead.

It is argued that heads of establishments must be output orientated and capable of working, at least, at Stratum 2. In turn we suggest that the residential scene will continue to stagnate without middle managers capable of working at Stratum 3 – that is to say, being occupied with patterns of service for a group or range of homes. We believe that departments that fail to employ a suitable number of capable Stratum 3 managers will not be able to develop a systematic residential service provision.

Chapter 6 continues and extends earlier research work concerned with entry into residential care, and is based on project work in Berkshire. The issues which are discussed are amongst the most important in social work. After all, if community care is the preferred policy option, the decisions that are taken at the boundary between community and residential care are of paramount importance. If – the chapter argues – interaction between field and residential workers is to be based on the assumption that they are colleagues, *then* certain procedural consequences will follow. By providing models of interaction between field and residential staff and identifying the activities that are associated with the concepts of the prime care agent, it is hoped that we begin to do justice to the magnitude of the decisions that are involved.

Chapter 7 is based on project work with two controlled status community homes. It identifies two alternative roles for managers and suggests that only by clarification of their responsibilities *vis à vis* the responsible authority can they assume the duties implied in the 1969 Act.

And what of future research into residential care? Further elabora-

[9] For example, resident participation in the running of establishments.

tion of the theory of work strata is leading to a new concept of 'basic expected work'. This has been described elsewhere as that basic stratum of production or service for which the organization was set up in the first place.[10] It is the minimum expected stratum of work of the organization, occupation, or professional group. Basic expected work is not necessarily the lowest level of work. For example, outside the context of residential care, a Stratum 2 or higher professional social worker or doctor may have assistants and trainees at a lower level, but we expect case accountability to rest with the designated professional. Basic expected work is the 'public face' of the organized group.

What then is the 'basic expected work' of various parts of residential care? What level of work do we wish to plan for, strive for, and train? What are the characteristics of the field of work boundaries in the light of the changing nature and perception of client problems? These are some of the questions that, although not reported here, are demanding current research attention. Future research, it may be expected, will continue to grapple with these and other burning problems facing those working in the residential sector.

---

[10] Billis, D., 'Organizational Responses to Social Problems' (1977), unpublished paper presented to the United Nations Social Welfare Workshop, Baden.

5 Managing to Care[1]

by David Billis

Introduction

Come the infamous 1984 there may well be more than half a million clients in residential homes.[2] What impact, if any, have the new large social services departments made upon residential work, previously described as being 'in the backwaters of the social services'?[3]

The particular area chosen for analysis is that messy middle ground where grand theories have to be translated into purposeful action. At one extreme are 'the ends', which can be in Righton's telling phrase, 'immensely respectable and dumbfoundingly vague'; at the other extreme, the blow-by-blow accounts of the daily minutiae of residential life.[4] More specifically our concern will be to examine the nature of the links between work, care, policy and organization.

The proposed examination is dangerous. In some eyes the mention of the word 'organization' is to identify the writer willy-nilly with the camp of social conservatism. It is a process of instant classification pursued strangely enough by those who in other contexts are most sensitive to the nature of stigma. There is no contradiction between care and organization *per se*. What we might discover is that it is precisely the lack of analysis, thought and interest in organizational design that contributes to unsuitable standards of care.

The analysis will utilize three sets of concepts: (a) functions or activities; (b) roles; (c) work strata.

Not by milieu alone

Two contrasting approaches to residential care can be identified.

[1] Reprinted (with minor alterations) from *Social Work Today*, vol. 6, no. 2, 1975.

[2] CCETSW (1973), *Training for Residential Work* – Discussion Document. The Discussion Document suggests the use of the word 'centre' instead of residential home or establishment. We shall use these three terms interchangeably.

[3] Beedell, C. (1970), *Residential Life with Children*.

[4] Righton, P. (1971), 'The Objectives and Methods of Residential Social Work'.

They might more accurately be thought of as opposite poles of a continuum which has been split to aid clarity of exposition. One view places its main emphasis on the milieu, the environment. Everything that happens in and around the home is potentially therapeutic. Accordingly, there is not thought to be much point in attempting to disentangle the multifarious activities of the centre. Life is seen as a continuous and bewildering interchange of work and roles. As one housemother put it, her general duty was to establish a milieu and 'once having established the milieu the unit is itself therapeutic'.[5]

The pioneering Williams report, while noting the importance of special skills and knowledge required in residential care, sees the chief work as the creation of a 'harmonious group'.[6] As other writers have commented the 'Report contains no analysis of the actual work undertaken by staff'.[7] We may all concur with enthusiasm about the need to establish harmonious groups, stable environments, a helpful atmosphere – at the same time these phrases, left at this level of generality, do indeed seem 'dumbfoundingly vague'. The 'environment', the prime therapeutic factor, is so flimsy a concept that 'care' trails in its wake as a matter of chance and individual idiosyncrasy. How can we talk of overall policies in this situation? Flair, however brilliant, is a shaky foundation upon which to build a caring system for half a million people.

An alternative approach attempts to disentangle the strands of residential work and examines the prime forces which lie beneath the concept of therapeutic environment.

In order to begin this investigation some knowledge is needed of what actually happens in and around a residential home. This knowledge must be of a particular kind. It cannot be so general and vague as to have little practical significance; similarly it should not be so detailed as to overwhelm us with its unwieldiness. We require, therefore, a middle range of functions or activities which can be used as a tool for the discussion of environment, standards of care and departmental structures. An attempt to provide such a list, abstracted from our first book, is provided below.[8]

[5] See *Brunel Project Report.*

[6] Williams, G. (Chairman) (1967), *Caring for People,* p. 28.

[7] Forder, A. (ed.) (1963), *Penelope Hall's Social Services of England and Wales,* pp. 203–4.

[8] See *Social Services Departments.* See also Hey, A. M. (1973), 'Analysis and Definition of the Function of Caring Establishments' in Ainsworth, F. (ed.), *Residential Establishments: The Evolving of Caring Systems.* The development of the concept of Basic Expected Work, described in the Introduction to this Part, may help to clarify and elaborate several issues relating to the analysis of residential functions. Are *all* residential establish-

Table 5.1   Analysis of functions to be carried out in the residential setting

Output functions	Supporting functions
Basic social work (all residential establishments) 　making or contributing to assessments of need and of appropriate response 　providing information and advice 　monitoring and supervision of residents 　helping individual residents to maintain and develop personal capacity for adequate social functioning 　arranging provision of other appropriate services for residents	**Staffing and training work** 　recruitment of domestic and other staff 　student training 　dealing with welfare problems of all staff
Basic services (all residential establishments) 　providing clothing, other goods, and money 　providing meals 　providing accommodation 　providing help in daily living (including help with personal hygiene, dressing, moving, looking after personal property, etc) 　providing recreation, social and cultural life (including the fostering of links with the local community)	**Managerial and co-ordinative work** 　selection or sharing in selection of domestic staff and care staff 　induction of new staff and prescription of work 　personal appraisal and development of staff 　dealing with problems of staff, and of staff interaction 　(in some cases) co-ordination of work of non-residential staff in relation to needs of particular residents
Supplementary services (provided as needed, and varying from establishment to establishment) 　providing aids for the physically handicapped 　providing medical or paramedical treatment 　providing formal education etc.	**Logistics, finance and secretarial work** 　ordering of supplies, replacements, and repairs 　collection and banking of incoming money 　control of petty cash 　local fund raising 　maintenance of various records and preparation of various reports 　care and security of stock and premises

The distinction between *output* and *supporting* functions is crucial to the argument since it enables us to delineate and discuss the

ments, for example, expected to provide Stratum 2 Basic Social Work (as defined in Figure 5.1)? Or, are there homes that are primarily expected to provide Basic or Supplementary Services? And at what level are these services to be provided – Stratum 1 or 2? These questions are mentioned here, rather than in the text, in order not to detract from the main argument which still stands, and is concerned with output activities as *a whole*, rather than possible sub-divisions within them.

prime orientation of residential care. The client becoming a resident may expect that his 'state of social functioning' will be maintained and developed.[9] At the very least the resident may expect that his social functioning will not deteriorate at a rate faster than it would were he not to have entered the residential establishment. The positive change or prevention of deterioration in social functioning is the output of the residential establishment.

Output activities can be distinguished from supporting activities which have no *raison d'etre* by themselves and, however vital, are means for assisting the achievement of the department's or establishment's prime function. Let us not diminish the importance of supporting functions such as finance and logistics, but at the same time we must not lose sight of the differences in one porridge of therapeutic environment. The basic premise is that some line can be drawn between these two distinct sorts of activities and not to present an inflexible list. The division between output and supporting activities may vary somewhat between types of homes, between different authorites, and over given periods of time. The contention, tested with many social services staff, is that this delineation leads to important conclusions.

Standards of care

The concept of output and supporting functions may be considered to be the first of a number of interlocking strands. For the moment, we shall leave this first strand on one side and consider the familiar phrase 'standards of care'.

How can we define standards? Of course the tangible indicators are important. Calories, financial expenditure, living space, staff ratios – all these and other hard statistical data provide essential minimum facts. But a moment's thought is sufficient to indicate the dangers in relying solely on such apparently reliable indicators. Indeed, they can be positively misleading. High expenditure on food (or on anything else for that matter) may not reflect a luxurious standard of living, but might primarily be the result of waste and inefficiency. Perhaps it could be all summed up by saying that what is missing from the data is the 'human element'. We need to know *how* people are being cared for and this of necessity demands human evaluation. Two establishments may produce almost identical indicators but to the informed and expert eye standards may be seen to

---

[9] Bartlett, Harriet, M. (1970), *The Common Base of Social Work Practice.*

vary widely. The Curtis Report commented on the same phenomenon. 'The differences between the results achieved in what would
appear to be precisely parallel conditions are often striking.' The report emphasizes that 'on the personality and skill of these workers
(matrons, superintendents) depends primarily the happiness of the
children in their care'.[10]

The second key point (the head's accountability for standards of
care) needs to be pursued beyond mere statements of idealistic
intent. This pursuit is, I believe, in the interest of all concerned
parties. It is a search, where the prize is not a rigid, mechanistic
definition of role, but a system which enables the optimum realization of community goals. We shall not, however, be able to proceed
further along this path without the introduction of two additional
concepts – role and level or stratum of work.

Role and hierarchy in the social services

Since the establishment of SSDs we have made strenuous efforts to
identify some department, somewhere, that has succeeded in abolish-
ing its hierarchical structure. We have now discussed the issue with
many hundreds of staff in conferences and project work from departments throughout the country. In this quest we must frankly admit
total failure. The quarry is as elusive as the Loch Ness Monster. On
closer inspection our new discovery turns out to be merely another
variation of that persistent organizational animal – the hierarchy.
The search goes on but, given the present state of the social work
profession and the departments' statutory obligations, we might
expect no dramatic changes in the near future. If this indeed is
the immediate prospect, then the radical critique might sound rather
hollow to the half million residents under the care of hierarchical
organizations! Simultaneously with our dreams we might ponder on
the more prosaic question – what do we really mean by hierarchy?
Perhaps if we define it we may understand and conquer undesirable
manifestations. The need for a precise definition is paramount.
Without it we remain babes in the organizational jungle.

Following previous work at Brunel we shall define hierarchy as
meaning nothing more nor less than 'a structure of successive
managerial roles'.[11] In turn a managerial role is defined as in Figure
5.1.

[10] HMSO (1969), *Report of the Care of Young Children.*
[11] See Rowbottom, R. W. (1973), op. cit., for a more detailed discussion of 'hierarchy'.

Managerial role

A managerial role arises where A is accountable for certain work and is assigned a subordinate B to assist him in this work. A is accountable for the work which B does for him.

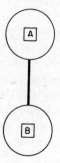

A is accountable:
  for helping to select B;
  for inducting him into his role;
  for assigning work to him and allocating resources;
  for keeping himself informed about B's work and helping him to deal with work problems;
  for appraising B's general performance and ability, and in consequence keeping B informed of his assessments, arranging or providing training, or modifying his role.

A has authority:
  to veto the selection of B for the role;
  to make an official appraisal of B's performance and ability;
  to decide if B is unsuitable for performing any of the work for which A is accountable.

Figure 5.1   The managerial role

At a stroke this definition has flattened what, in many instances, passes for 'the hierarchy'. The chart on the director's wall may portray eight or more links in the managerial chain but our research indicates that five is the maximum number of *real* managerial levels found in SSDs. (Level or rank is the distance between A and B in Figure 5.1.) To general relief not everyone, even near the top, is a manager. Within each rank there will probably be a number of grades primarily indicating differences of pay. The assumption that differences in grades (for example, senior social workers and basic grade social workers) implies some particular relationship of organizational authority is a common cause of confusion.

We must emphasize that the managerial role is only one of a range of roles that have been identified in SSDs.[12] For brevity and simplicity we shall concentrate only on this role, which, together with the theory of work strata will enable us to return to the pursuit of the main theme.

Working strata[13]

Current research has led us to the proposition that each of the five strata mentioned above involves distinct kinds of work. Once again, the test of the theory is not whether it is ideologically palatable but whether it can help us to understand reality. Will it help us to design organizations that aid, rather than hinder, the realization of community objectives? A condensed outline of the theory is presented in Table 5.2 on page 121.

Role of the head

The concepts of function, role and strata enable us to reconsider the role of the head of home with added insight. A whole range of conditions and problems begins to unfold. We are forced to consider, and perhaps more importantly reconsider, the following problems:

- What *functions* do we expect heads to be primarily performing?
- At what *stratum* of work should they be operating?
- What are the implications for the work of other members of the department concerned with residential care?
- What are the personal characteristics, abilities, capacity, that would be sought for in the various levels of residential staff?
- What are the appropriate links between the head and other members of the department?

To claim that complete 'answers' to all these questions are readily available, and even if they were, could be covered in a brief paper, would be presumptuous. The most that can be done is to outline possibilities, hint at avenues of further exploration and concentrate on a major theme.

If the earlier output-supporting classification is tenable, heads can be expected to be output orientated. It is in the area of basic social work and basic services that we should expect to find the prime focus of the head's attention. We shall be looking for people capable

---

[12] See *Social Services Departments*.

[13] See Chapter 1. This present chapter contains a few minor changes from the original paper. In particular 'stratum' replaces 'level' as a more appropriate description of work.

of understanding and assessing the real needs of residents and staff: heads who are capable of responding to various situations not merely in a routine, prescribed fashion characteristic of Stratum 1 work. It is not enough conscientiously to apply the rule-book, to present the budgets on time, to worry that the building and equipment are in an adequate state – in short, to ensure that all the tangible indicators referred to earlier are being adequately achieved. From the head is demanded all this, and more. To take a rough parallel, the situation demands that heads work (at least) at a level which would be expected of a trained, experienced social worker or senior social worker at Stratum 2. (Undoubtedly, there are homes demanding Stratum 3 or even 4 work, but to simplify the argument the writer will focus primarily on that which seems to be considered by departmental staff the broadest and most pressing issue.)

Stratum 2 workers are expected to exercise judgement about methods and attitudes to work and *real* needs in specific concrete situations. While expected to judge what *output* to aim for (implying accountability for carrying a case) they will probably not be expected to commit the organization on how future possible situations are to be dealt with.

Does this sound too remote, too idealistic? It might be argued that there are just not enough residential staff capable of working at this level. Perhaps, but first we might consider some alternative explanations to the lack of resources argument. Are the available staff being permitted to function at their optimum level? Are there heads who are forced into acting primarily as book-keepers, hotel keepers, handymen, and the like, not by personal inability, but by virtue of an absence of departmental policy and guidance? To what extent have they been given the scope to develop and implement their real abilities? In how many departments are there realistic job definitions with suitable discretion clearly delineated? And to ask an even more sensitive question, are there homes where unexploited ability is left untapped and unhelped beneath the shadow of a head who, by any objective assessment, ought not to be occupying that post? If 'standard of care' is firmly within the province of the individual head, then equally so the creation and maintenance of overall departmental standards lies somewhere else. All the questions raised earlier have not yet been tackled but it is clear that this path of analysis leads inexorably to an examination of the higher level structure of the department.

We began by reaffirming that residential 'management' is essentially about people. We continued by emphasizing the critical role of

Table 5.2   Work strata

Stratum	Kind of work	Upper boundary	Equivalent SSD grades (tentative)
1	*Prescribed output* – working towards objectives which can be completely specified (as far as is significant) beforehand according to defined circumstances which may present themselves	*Cut-off* – not expected to make any significant judgements on what output to aim for or under what circumstances to aim for it	SW aides and assistants; students, trainees, clerks, typists, etc.
2	*Situational response* – carrying out work where the precise objectives to be pursued have to be judged according to the needs of each specific concrete situation which presents itself	*Cut-off* – not expected to make any decisions, i.e. commitments on how future possible situations are to be dealt with[14]	experienced social worker, residential head, section manager, etc.
3	*Systematic service provision* – making systematic provision of services of some given kinds shaped to the needs of a continuous sequence of (concrete) situations which present themselves	*Cut-off* – not expected to make any decision on the re-allocation of resources to meet as yet unmanifested needs (for the given kinds of services) within some given territorial or organizational society	area officers, principal officers in specialist fields, residential group managers
4	*Comprehensive service provision* – making comprehensive provision of services of some given kinds according to the total and continuing needs for them throughout some given territorial or organizational society	*Cut-off* – not expected to make any decisions on the re-allocation of resources to meet needs for services of different or new kinds	assistant directors
5	*Comprehensive field coverage* – making comprehensive provision of services within some general field of need throughout some given territorial or organizational	*Cut-off* – not expected to make any decisions on the re-allocation of resources to provide services outside the given field of need	directors

[14] 'Decision' is being used 'in the full executive sense of action taken', Jaques, E. (1967), op. cit.

the head of the home. We have now reached the final strand of the argument. Departments must look hard at their own headquarters and supporting structures.

Room near the top

This article started by wondering what impact the creation of the new social services department has made on residential care. Perhaps one of the main differences between the two 'eras' (before and after integration) was summed up – with obvious feeling – by one assistant director (local authority population one million) discussing residential care with another assistant director (population 90 000), at a Brunel conference: 'What managed to pass for flexibility in the small departments can really be seen as confusion in the large authority.'

Whether this sweeping and pessimistic evaluation is valid for all large departments, can be disputed. What is hardly open to doubt is the elongation of the hierarchy. The days when the head of a residential establishment could readily contact a discernible and relatively well-known 'boss' have disappeared. The gap between the head of home and the top officer of his organization has widened considerably.

What then is the nature of the gap, not in terms of salary grades, but in terms of the work to be done? What can be said about the personal qualities of the people who need to fill that gap? What do the answers to these questions tell us about the nature of the work and the role of other headquarters staff? Given the wide variation in the numbers and types of centres in departments, any 'answers' can serve only as general guidelines.

If the head is the crucial factor in the standard of care in each home, then the search is not for someone who is managing *homes*, but for someone who is capable of managing a group of heads. Managing is used in the same distinct sense as it was when discussing the role of the head. This time the work is rather different. It remains managerial in that the *group manager* will be expected to appraise performance and ability, help to deal with work problems, arrange suitable training and so on. However, our work strata analysis points to the need for the Stratum 3 group managers to be primarily concerned with systematic service provision (see Table 5.2). They would be expected to go beyond responding to specific situations case by case. Services have to be provided which are moulded and shaped according to the needs of a continuous flow of situations. Thus, for example, a Stratum 2 head's work might be defined in terms of a given population of residents, whereas the head's Stratum 3 manager would need to be occupied with patterns of service for a range of homes. The group manager must have the personal ability to judge and respond to the comparative position in a variety of situations. How can these group managers fit in the different departmental structures?

Social services departments have chosen organizational structures which can be broadly sub-divided into two major categories:

(*a*) the functional model, primarily divided according to functions such as fieldwork, residential and day care, administration etc.;
(*b*) the geographic model, where the department is first sub-divided into a number of 'mini-departments'.

The second tier of management from the top is thus either an assistant director (residential), or a divisional director in the functional and geographic models respectively. With some few exceptions we cannot expect assistant and divisional directors to be managing heads of centres. The scope and breadth of work for both these Stratum 4 managers is such that they are now far removed from the scene of work of most heads. Yet the gap must be filled in order that the link between departmental policy and its implementation in the home shall be maintained. The gap can now be more precisely defined. The work to be done is to ensure that homes are output-orientated and that policies implemented in individual homes are subject to systematic monitoring, evaluation and support.

The role of the group manager is critical. It is certainly not to depress individual initiative, but to ensure that heads function at a level demanded by the department and by society. We cannot talk of output-orientated residential centres on a departmental basis unless we have an adequate output-orientated structure filled by capable intermediate managers. Of course, departments have created posts (between the assistant or divisional director and head of home) to fill the gap we have been describing. Many of these posts have been given titles such as 'Homes Adviser'. Whether these roles do in fact represent a genuine link in the chain can be ascertained by analysing the duties, authority and level of work of their role.

If 'advisers' are mainly concerned with functions which we have described as 'supporting', perhaps with some accountability for basic services, the basic social work aspects of output are in danger of not being filled. A vacuum is created, although valiant attempts can be .

made by departments (area liaison schemes, area adoption schemes) to pump in the missing output functions. We can state emphatically that unless support, guidance, supervision and assessment of the head's work is made in a systematic fashion by a person generally agreed to have the necessary knowledge and ability and paid at an appropriate grade, stagnation might continue to be a common feature of the residential scene.

The words 'authority' and 'assessment' appear in our image of the residential group manager. The inclusion is not accidental. It is a nettle which many practitioners and commentators seem unwilling to grasp. Indeed the Williams Report, in its brief comments on the duties of headquarters staff, is apologetic in the extreme. Large organizations, it is recognized,

> must employ people to visit the Homes in order to ensure that they are run in accordance with the policy laid down and to advise those doing the work. In one sense this might seem to be the function of an inspectorate but in practice it is very much more an advisory and consultative service.[15]

In a perfect world we could relax, no toes will be stepped on, the homes adviser could be essentially a sympathetic listener. But the Residential Services Advisory Group knows that the reality can be very different.

> ... unhappily it cannot be denied that some staff are unable to use support. They deny the need for support ... and cannot be helped to grow or make constructive progress ... because of their hardened defences and rigid attitudes they are not the best of caring people.[16]

Probably, and hopefully, only a small minority of staff fall within the advisory group's tactful description. We might also wonder to what extent the advisory group might have encountered and be describing situations wherein Stratum 2 heads were reacting to Stratum 2 advisers! Even this report, which contains much valuable material, can only suggest that 'the Adviser must *strive* to ensure that such people are not excluded ... from the common developing aims'. (Author's italics.)

For this reason, we prefer the term 'group manager' to the weaker sounding and unclear title of 'homes adviser'. The manager may need, in the interests of the residents and the community, to

---

[15] Williams, G. (Chairman) (1967), op. cit., p. 156.

[16] Residential Services Advisory Group, First Report (1973), *Staff Support and Development*.

initiate unpleasant measures. He, or she, needs the authority's sanctioning to act, as well as Stratum 3 capacity.

It is difficult to provide anything more than a guide for the number of residential group managers required to maintain an effective residential superstructure. Authorities vary widely in numbers and types of residential centres. As a rough numerical guide, and no more, let us assume that a department has sixty centres. How many heads could a group manager genuinely manage? eight? ten? twelve? If we ignore, for simplicity's sake, the possible existence of other staff who might be aiding the group manager, these are the sort of numbers we should expect to get in reply to our question. (The Residential Services Advisory Group 'sees the optimum number as one adviser to eight to ten homes, but reduced to four to five homes in respect of specialist establishment ...').[17] From here we arrive at the simple statistical position that a department of some sixty centres will require not less than six group managers. And, by looking at the highly developed fieldwork structures, we can tighten-up the picture. If, as we have already argued, heads should function at the level of experienced social workers and seniors. then the group manager slots into the comparable area officer pay and status. Having said all this, in how many departments is there still not considerable 'room near the top'?

Outline answers have been attempted for many of the questions raised earlier. Nevertheless, by concentrating on the main stream of output flowing through the department to the resident, insufficient attention has been paid to those activities we have named supporting. It is to these we must now turn.

Everyone cares

Everyone cares – and if they do not, a good case can be made out for stating that they ought to. In this sense departmental staff who have no direct contact with residents also wish to feel that their work contributes to the general well-being of clients. The image of the agency administrator as a desiccated calculating machine uninterested and unconcerned is a fiction which, as far as my own research experience is concerned, is remote from reality. For these supporting staff caring is an attitude, desirable if it can be obtained, but it is not the main focus of their work.

In contrast heads also are expected to be capable of ordering supplies, controlling petty cash funds, preparing reports and estimates,

[17] ibid.

maintaining budgets – all included in the supporting classification but in this instance we have suggested that their prime orientation should be towards the resident, i.e. output. The danger, which cannot be emphasized too strongly, is that financial, secretarial, and logistical functions are mistakenly understood to be the totality of 'residential management'.

The argument so far has been based on drawing a continuous systematic path, beginning with the social functioning of the residents, continuing to the duties of the head of the home and the position of headquarters staff. This has been designated an output-orientated path, primarily concerned with basic social work and basic services. The provision of supporting functions *to* the home has been deliberately reserved for the end of the chapter.

The output-supporting classification presented here is very different from that which appears to operate in many departments. In our model central staff primarily working in the various fields of supporting activities cannot manage residential heads and, consequently, *cannot* be held accountable for the standards of care. These staff provide essential services, monitor adherence to financial policy, and may interact with heads in a variety of non-managerial roles.

An alternative to the output-supporting pattern of residential organization might be classified as the 'fabric-casework' division. In this dichotomy 'fabric', 'bricks and mortar' or just 'management' are broadly identified with the 'hard' activities which are, in the main, supporting or basic services according to our definition. Key elements of basic social work are seen as 'professional' territory, are not precisely defined and can be frequently left in organizational limboland. We have already noted, when discussing the role of the homes adviser, some of the measures that are taken to pump professional expertise into the vacuum. Other symptoms of the confusion which can be caused by this casework-fabric bifurcation are the anxiety of heads regarding their links with headquarters, the discomfort of homes advisers regarding the true nature of their role, and the uncertainty of assistant directors in functionally organized departments, if, and where, boundaries of discretion can be drawn between professional social work and management. Where departments have moved towards the newer geographically-based organizations, the same principle would apply with the output stream leading to the divisional directors. As yet, it is too early to comment on the impact of the decentralized department on residential care.

The distinction between the two types of residential classification is illustrated in Figure 5.2.

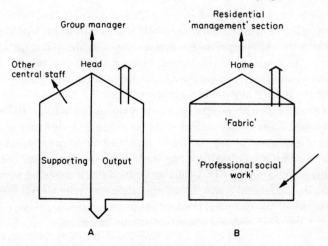

Figure 5.2 *Two contrasting patterns of residential organization*
  (*a*) *Output–supporting*
  (*b*) *Fabric–casework*

Conclusion

We have argued elsewhere that policy and organizational structure are interconnected and cannot be divorced from the notion of 'care'.[18] The existence of either one without the other leaves residential care the prisoner of whim. Aloofness from the debate is a luxury which cannot be afforded in a problem of this scope. Our concern here has been to study the nature of the interconnection and to suggest a particular analytical path.

We have proposed a list of activities carried out in the residential setting and introduced the concept of output and supporting functions in order to trace a direct line from service-delivery up through departmental structures. The role of the head is emphasized as the crucial factor in the establishment's standard of care. The creation of residential group managers is seen as fundamental to any hope of a systematic and comprehensive departmental approach to residential care. Unlike the homes adviser role often found in departments, the group manager is seen as an output-orientated person of experience and status comparable to the fieldwork area officer post. The group manager is envisaged as a role with teeth, able to act positively with regard to the support and guidance of heads and in the extreme to initiate measures to replace unsatisfactory heads.

[18] Billis, D. (1973), 'Entry into Residential Care'.

This picture of residential organization is compared with the 'fabric' pattern wherein 'management' is regarded as primarily concerned with the supporting functions (see Figure 5.1) and basic services (in contrast to the output orientation of our model). The 'fabric' model is seen to have serious deficiencies and to raise doubts about the nature of its service-delivery.

In discussions with residential workers the question has repeatedly been asked 'how do we improve the situation of residential work'? Most of the answers are naturally expressed in terms of increased resources, better pay, status, more staff, increased and newer homes, improved training etc. This chapter proposes that together with all these, organizational research can play a positive part when examining the whole panorama of residential activity, including those topics which have, perforce, been mentioned only briefly.

6 Interaction Between Field and Residential Social Workers[1]

by Geoffrey Bromley

Introduction

'Local authorities and other bodies providing residential care should state clearly the principles upon which admission is based and agree on an unambiguous process of admitting people into all homes under its control.' This recommendation from the Personal Social Services Council[2] is one with which most social workers in field or residential settings readily concur. However, to achieve genuine clarity about the process of admitting clients involves raising fundamental questions about the basis of interaction between staff in field and residential settings. Unless there is agreement about how staff should be interacting, it is difficult to obtain clarity about desired ways of admitting and working with clients.

It has long been recognized that admission into care is a time of tension. Stevenson[3] describes it as 'an action which is deeply significant for everyone involved in it'. On the question of trying to achieve constructive working relationships between field and residential social workers, Winnicott[4] describes how 'each has given something of himself to the child so there is a fundamental source of tension'. She adds that such tension can be creative if it is recognized and worked upon. Beedell[5] suggests the inherent tension between staff springs from two sources: 'A genuine but largely unacknowledged difference between the contexts in which they work and a basic uncertainty as to "whose child this is".' Tod[6] sees the two

[1] Reprinted (with minor alterations) from *British Journal of Social Work*, 7 March 1977.
[2] Personal Social Services Council, (1975), op. cit.
[3] Stevenson, O. (1963), 'Reception into Care: Its Meaning for All Concerned'.
[4] Winnicott, C. (1964), 'Casework and the Residential Treatment of Children'.
[5] Beedell, C. (1970), op. cit.
[6] Tod, R. J. N. (ed.) (1968), 'Staff Roles and Relationships in Residential Work'.

workers as creatively reflecting different parts of the child's needs; conflict may be reduced but at the price of avoiding mutual understanding and identification. Muluccio and Marlowe[7] confirm what practising social workers know only too well: that entry into residential care is traumatic for both clients and staff. In the absence of agreement about roles and functions of establishments, deception and stealth are often better tools than openness and honesty about the true characteristics of the client. Billis[8] has examined which field and residential staff should take the key decisions at the point of entry. A joint RCA/BASW report[9] has made recommendations for clarifying areas of responsibility between field and residential staff.

Origins of the project

The account which follows arises from work done with the staff of Berkshire Social Services Department between 1973 and 1975 following a request to help clarify and improve co-operation and interaction between field and residential social workers in providing a service for clients in homes. Berkshire Social Services Department used 1974 local government reorganization as an opportunity to move from a functionally organized department with residential facilities managed centrally, towards a geographic, divisionally organized structure where residential and day care facilities are managed by offices providing a full range of services for clients. Whilst the work was being done during a major reorganization of the management structure for the homes, what follows is not specific to any one organization structure.

Following consultation with the then Assistant Director for Residential Services, it was decided to work closely with a small and representative number of field and residential staff to identify ways of improving the admission and subsequent work with clients in these homes, in the hope that these findings would have application elsewhere in the department. Four establishments were selected: a home for the elderly, a hostel for the mentally handicapped, a family group home and a hostel for adolescent girls. At each, a project group was formed consisting of the senior residential staff, the

[7] Muluccio, A. N. and Marlowe, W. D. (1972), 'Residential Treatment of Emotionally Disturbed Children: A Review of the Literature'.

[8] Billis, D. (1973), op. cit.

[9] Joint RCA/BASW Report (1976), 'How Can Residential and Field Social Workers Co-operate?'

home's adviser responsible for the management of the home, the area officer concerned, and a senior and basic grade field social worker with recent experience of admitting clients into the home. Their task, in conjunction with the researcher, was to identify improved ways for field and residential staff to admit and work with clients.

Many of the issues first encountered were already well known and were probably no more serious than in many other departments. Residential staff were concerned at being insufficiently involved, and then at too late a stage, in the process of admitting clients into their home. They recognized there was often a limited choice of suitable vacancies but believed that much more discussion and consultation should occur before a client was admitted, to ensure the client's suitability for the home. They said that field staff provided them with incomplete and insufficient information about the client. Residential staff claimed they were not fully involved in decisions about whether the field staff should remain in contact with the client and what kind of contact this should be. Underlying these complaints was a conviction that they were having to operate within limitations of what work they should do with the client which were set by field staff.

On the other hand, field staff felt unreasonable demands were made upon them by residential staff to visit clients often with no very clear idea of what should be achieved by such visits. In the field staff's eyes some tasks expected of them could more appropriately be done by residential staff. Field staff felt they were not consulted sufficiently by residential staff when they took important decisions about the client. For example, although field staff recognized that a decision to initiate transfer of a mentally handicapped client from the training centre to outside employment was most appropriately taken by residential staff, they felt they should be closely involved. Underlying these complaints about the behaviour of each other was the long-standing difference in status and training between the two groups of staff. Residential staff with less training than field staff could be trusted with only a limited degree of discretion on important decisions about the client.

These were some of the issues preventing full co-operation between field and residential staff. The four project groups met regularly over some months; during this time initial hostility and confusion slowly gave way to a spirit of determination to try to effect improvements for all staff who had dealings with each of the homes. The researcher's task at each of the meetings was to offer an analysis of the issues as perceived by members of the project group which would help towards an improved method of admitting, and subsequently working with, clients.

The work of each project group can be divided into two parts. First, it was important to secure agreement about the basic principles upon which interaction should take place. Without this it was impossible to construct any model of arrangements for admitting and working with clients in the homes. Work on establishing this agreed basis was the most time-consuming part of each project and it is this part of the work which led to the principles for guiding interaction between field and residential staff (see next section). Secondly, once these principles were agreed it was possible to construct model arrangements, adapted for each home, which could be made available in writing to people outside. This model is described. The project groups recognized that not all the matters upon which they made recommendations could occur immediately. They felt, however, it was important to identify preferred ways of working which could be aimed at, and these are described here.

Principles to guide interaction

Interpersonal and organizational components of interaction
Each of the project groups recognized at an early stage that a number of extremely important interpersonal factors were influencing the process of interaction between field and residential staff. The different base of operation and working objectives meant that each worker viewed the needs of any client from a different standpoint. Such important factors as age, previous life experience, practical experience of the other's work and training, influenced the quality of the interaction between staff. When frames of reference were not shared interaction was difficult and likely to lead to conflict. Behind this lay the recognition that improvements in the quality of interaction would occur if there were a greater degree of equality in the training and status of the two parties concerned. This line of thought led each project group to feel initially that in the long run an improvement in training, particularly of residential staff, would make the greatest contribution to the quality of collaborative interaction.

However, the project groups were trying to effect improvements in interaction that would have a more immediate impact. They felt it was unsatisfactory simply to say that nothing could be achieved until there was genuine training and status equality between the two parties. Having recognized this, they turned to an examination of the organizational factors which were contributing to poor inter-action. It is these organizational components of interaction that are examined in this paper, not because they are necessarily more im-portant, but because they were thought to be more accessible to change.

Case accountability for work with clients
At an early stage in the life of each project group it was necessary to be explicit as to who among field and residential staff should be regarded as responsible for work with individual clients, or be case accountable. Among field social workers, both social work assistants and social workers were involved in admitting clients, and often seniors attended reviews on children. Among residential social workers, a variety of staff, including care assistants, were involved in taking decisions about clients, as well as the head of each home.

The project groups recognized that any arrangements they de-vised for improving interaction would have to work within existing staff and training constraints. Nevertheless, they found it necessary to clarify who was the most desirable person to take critical decisions about clients. It was agreed that in the long run this should be the trained and experienced social work staff on both sides who would be regarded as the case-accountable member of staff. In the project groups this was identified as a trained and experienced field social worker and the head of the home; staff of this kind are described here as field or residential social workers. Although there would be other staff such as social work assistants, trainees and care assistants involved with clients, the project groups' recommendation was that the case-accountable workers would take the major decisions about the care programme for the client. For example, the project group in the home for the elderly decided that in the long run it was in-appropriate for social work assistants alone to make recommenda-tions for admission.[10]

With more complex residential establishments, such as an observa-tion and assessment centre, staff below the head of the home could perhaps be held to be case accountable, but this was not the case in the establishments in this project. The ideas discussed here show a strong similarity to the criteria for the use of professionally quali-fied social workers set out in the report *Manpower and Training for*

[10] This is a reflection of the thinking in Chapters 1 and 2 where the notion of case accountability is suggested as emerging only at Work Stratum 2 and beyond.

the Social Services,[11] where the involvement of such staff is suggested when important decisions about clients are being taken.

Models of interaction between field and residential staff

Analysis of how staff saw themselves interacting with colleagues in different settings indicated there were two different models of staff behaviour. In the *prescriptive model* of interaction, field staff believed that they should determine which client entered a home, the kind of treatment and social care provided and the point at which the client should return home. Residential staff would be working within limits prescribed[12] by field staff. Although each were part of a separate organization hierarchy the prescriptive model meant field staff set the context within which residential staff worked. This model was most prevalent in work with children where the social worker remained in contact with the client but it also occurred in work with adult clients. In defence of such a model, field staff argued that it arose from disparities of skill which existed between themselves and their residential colleagues. Whatever the causes, the prescriptive model was thought to be widespread. It resulted in an arrangement where, although a goal of partnership might be stated as the aim, the field social worker took all the major decisions and the residential social worker took the small ones.

In contrast, in the *collateral model* discussed by Rowbottom, Hey and Billis,[13] each worker is again part of a separate management hierarchy, but no prescriptive authority exists between the field and residential social worker. Instead agreement has to be reached on which client is admitted, the overall care and treatment strategy, and when clients should return home. The basis for their interaction is discussion, compromise and agreement; neither can impose their decisions on the other.

Each of the project groups took an explicit decision to adopt the collateral model as the desirable basis of interaction. This, rather than the prescriptive model, was thought to reflect the realities of work with clients where both parties have separate areas of work for which they must each be held accountable to their manager. Only the collateral model was thought to adequately reflect this reality. The project groups recognized it was going to be easier to

[11] See Department of Health and Social Security (1976), op. cit., particularly Chapter 5, paras. 5.13–5.26; and Chapter 6, paras. 6.7–6.16.

[12] See *Social Services Departments*, p. 264, for a full definition of a *prescribing relationship*.

[13] See *Social Services Departments*, p. 264, for a full definition of this relationship. See particularly pp. 157 and 254.

work towards achieving the collateral model of interaction where there was genuine equality of training and status of the parties concerned, but this was not the situation at present, nor was it likely to be for the foreseeable future. However, they set about developing policy statements to guide interaction which incorporated the collateral model of interaction, the plan of which is described on page 140 (Figure 6.1).

This recognition of the collateral model led the project groups to identify a number of associated implications for the future. First, where field and residential staff are both working with a client, they are doing so jointly and responsibility is shared. Secondly, the process of admission into care involves an initial decision about the client's possible suitability for the home. This is a decision for field staff. There is a further decision as to the home's suitability for the client, which is a decision for residential staff. Ideally these two decisions should be made in face-to-face discussions between the field and residential staff. Subsequent work with the client must arise out of agreement between the field and residential social workers. Although this must occur continuously, the process needs to be formalized for all kinds of clients by regular case conferences.

Thirdly, field staff are already subject to regular supervision and review of their work with clients; the collateral model assumes the need for the same facility for residential staff. The project groups recognized that logically they too would have to receive regular supervision relating to individual clients and the needs of the whole establishment from their manager. To some extent this could occur in review conferences on clients but would have to take place beyond this, particularly where no other social worker is involved and residential staff are the sole accountable staff. Just as field staff keep records on clients as an integral part of their responsibility towards the clients, so also should residential staff. This implication of the collateral model was the subject of considerable debate, particularly covering the extent to which records should be available to each other. The project groups recognized, however, that full exchange of information and case records, and regular supervision of residential staff was a goal at which to aim.

Prime care agent
The project group also found it necessary to take account of field and residential staff's changing contribution to work with clients. The realities of interaction are complex, and different stages in the client's contact with the home place field and residential staff in a

fundamentally different position. Before admission to a home the field social worker usually knows more about the client and is naturally turned to for help as the client prepares for transfer from one environment to another. During negotiations for admission, the field social worker is the focus for the work undertaken.

Once admission has taken place, the situation is likely to change. Assuming that the field social worker is still involved, it is now the residential social worker who is the focus for work. If in difficulty, the client will turn to the residential social worker, even though the field social worker may also have to be consulted. After admission it is the residential social worker who knows most about the client's immediate needs and ideally ought to be in the best position to make a major contribution to planning work with the client.

After clients have returned to the community, conventional wisdom has it that the clients' main contact is the field social worker. During discussions this was questioned, particularly by the staff of the hostel for the mentally handicapped, and to some extent by the staff of the adolescent girls' hostel. They argued that their expertise with this client group, and the kind of relationships they developed, made them better equipped to remain in contact with many clients after they left the home. In the hostel for the mentally handicapped it was decided that a separate decision would be taken each time a client left the home on whether the field or residential social worker should undertake this task. The decision would be made by both groups of staff examining the needs of the client.

The project groups recognized that at different stages in the client's contact with homes there would be shifts between field and residential staff as to who was the key worker or, as the project group termed it, the prime care agent. The activities identified as being associated with the prime care agent included:

(a) having responsibility for ensuring that the appropriate care or treatment plan is devised with the support of the field and residential staff concerned;

(b) being the person who knows most about the client's needs and in consequence has *prime responsibility*[14] for ensuring the implementation of the care or treatment plan;

(c) having overall responsibility for ensuring the suitability of the care or treatment plan and where necessary proposing alterations to it;

[14] See Chapter 2.

(*d*) taking decisions, particularly in an emergency, on behalf of others engaged in helping the client when the others cannot be involved and subsequently calling a review to examine the new situation;

(*e*) keeping all parties informed of action and progress in the case, particularly where a decision has been taken by the prime care agent which affects work which has already been agreed to be the responsibility of some other worker;

(*f*) helping to overcome problems encountered by colleagues;

(*g*) being responsible for carrying out a task for a client when no agreement has been reached (or no policy exists) that the task should be carried out by another worker.

The notion of a designated prime care agent is not new. It is similar to the idea of a case co-ordinator[15] although the prime care agent was considered by the project groups always to be someone who is in direct contact with the client and who is the case-accountable worker. It is similar to the key or focal worker identified by departments in their procedures for dealing with non-accidental injury cases. Its application to the residential field represents a new idea which the project groups believed would contribute to improved patterns of interaction. In discussion, use of the term, with no assumption of the field social worker being designated the prime care agent, lent credibility to the decision to implement the collateral model of interaction. In addition, the procedures for negotiating work between staff laid down that tasks for the prime care agent should be identified and agreed. It is important to note that the concept of a prime care agent does not conflict with the collateral model. It is simply a recognition of the realities of life; the worker who has most to do with a client at any one moment and is in predominant contact with him on a day-to-day basis attracts a range of tasks identified with the prime care agent. This, as the definition offered implies, is likely to extend to interpreting agreed plans about the client and taking the initiative in dealing with emergencies where plans seem to conflict with the current situation.

Division of responsibility between field and residential staff
The absence of agreed tasks or areas of responsibility inevitably causes confusion about the proper activities of the field and residential staff in any case. Some clear areas of distinct responsibility are dictated by the different physical location of each worker. But there

---

[15] See *Social Services Departments*, pp. 206–8.

are also areas of potential overlap where negotiation, influenced by each worker's view of the world, is necessary; indeed, where staff work with the prescriptive model any so called negotiations are almost entirely on terms laid down by the field social worker. In this situation lack of clarity is inevitable. Questions raised by project groups included: who should normally arrange for alternative schooling for children in the family group home? Who should find employment for children when they leave the home? What part, if any, should field social workers have in arranging a move from an adult training centre to normal employment for a resident in the hostel for the mentally handicapped? Where it had been agreed that the field social worker should remain in contact with a resident in a home for the elderly, who should act as the link between relatives and the resident?

During discussions, in an effort to identify tasks of the field and residential staff, attempts were made by the staff in the old people's home and the hostel for the mentally handicapped to delineate which activities would be expected of the two parties in situations not self-evidently clear. Task statements of what is expected of either the field or residential staff were produced, with the proviso that each could be modified by the client's particular circumstances and the quality of relationship with different staff. The production of the task statements was an attempt to increase clarity about activities of each member of staff.

However, this approach did not significantly lessen the areas of disagreement. The task statements were taken as a guide; they would not remove the conflict. Every new case situation was seen as unique, so clarity of respective tasks would only set the boundaries within which negotiation and discussion could occur. It was a recognition of this that led the project groups to concentrate on models of the different stages by which clients enter homes, which gave prominence to formalizing and institutionalizing occasions for resolving conflict between field and residential staff. The project groups came to recognize that no amount of task specificity was felt likely to make a substantial difference to the quality of interaction between field and residential staff. Instead it was thought important to specify the occasions when staff should meet, the tasks upon which agreement was needed and the responsibilities of each party. It was this which was incorporated into the following model processes for admitting clients.

A general model for clients coming into residential care
Each project group designed policy statements for their home which took account of the establishment's particular requirements. Each one sought to lay emphasis upon the organizational components of interaction, to incorporate the collateral model for work between field and residential staff, to give expression to the concept of the prime care agent and to specify the tasks which needed to be agreed upon at critical moments in the client's movement into the home. This is set out diagrammatically in Figure 6.1. The model involves five stages.

Stage 1: initial assessment
This is the first time the client is seen by the agency and the first time the field staff (or residential staff if the client is already in another establishment) recognizes the client as being in need of residential care. At this stage some form of case assessment is being carried out; it was thought desirable that this should be done by a case-account-able member of staff, a trained and experienced person competent to make a full assessment of the client's needs and able to take account of all the alternative modes of care which could be used. The field social worker decides what form of residential care the client needs. Residential staff are not involved at this stage so that there can only be a preliminary decision that the client is in need of residential care.

Stage 2: provisional placement meeting
This stage is different for each of the homes in the project. Again, it does not involve the residential staff. It is a meeting or discussion between the field social worker known to the client and the person who is in control of the placements in residential establishments, who it is hoped understands the pressures on the home. Ideally, and this is crucial for achieving the underlying principles that were being aimed at, the decision here can only be in the form of 'in our opinion this client *could* be cared for in establishment A and can be submitted there for assessment by the Admissions Conference (Stage 3)'. Although the Provisional Placement Meeting is identifiable for each client group, it exists more formally with children.

All children entering the family group home involved in the project were first received into a nursery or observation and assessment centre where all possible placements were considered. One of the complaints of the head of the family group home was that decisions at the assess-

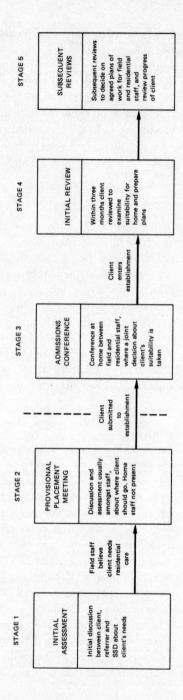

Figure 6.1   Model for clients coming into care

meṅt centre tended to be perceived as binding upon the matron of the home. She could seek to alter the decision once she had seen the child, but this was difficult and was not recognized as one of her understood rights. So this represented a deviation from the collateral model of interaction.

At the time this work was done admissions to the home for the elderly were controlled by a senior field social worker who had liaison responsibilities towards the home. For this home, Stage 2 involved a meeting between the social worker responsible for the case and the liaison social worker. At this time the latter was taking effective decisions as to which clients should enter the home. Instead, in keeping with the principles established, it was decided that it was only appropriate for field staff to rank clients' priority of need, which would then be presented at the Admissions Conference (Stage 3).

To facilitate the next stage when field and residential staff meet, it was decided that each home should prepare a statement of aims and objectives which could be available to field staff seeking to place clients in the home. This is a similar idea to that proposed in the PSSC report, *Living and Working in Residential Homes.*[16]

Statements about each home listed the conditions which needed to obtain before the client could be submitted to the establishment. They covered such matters as the kind of clients the home was prepared to accept, the information that was needed before proper assessments could take place, the manner in which the information should be submitted (some homes produced admission forms), whether visits should take place before the Stage 3 meetings occurred and what information the client should have about the home to assist him in deciding whether he wanted to submit himself to the home. Once these conditions had been fulfilled it was possible to move on to the third stage of the admissions process.

Stage 3: admissions conference
This stage is a meeting between the field and residential staff, chaired by the home's adviser or manager, though there is no reason why the meeting should not be chaired by someone else with the necessary seniority and experience. The project groups decided that an Admissions Conference be held before the client made any visits to the home. Unless this occurred decisions of the conference could be prejudged. Although contact about the client would probably have occurred already, this is the first formal occasion when field and residential staff meet face to face to discuss the client. The prime task

[16] See Personal Social Services Council (1975), op. cit., particularly para. 99.

of the Admissions Conference is for field and residential staff to decide whether a client should be admitted. Such a meeting is needed to implement the collateral model of interaction, which involves residential staff deciding if the home is suitable for the client presented by the field staff. Clearly there will be occasions when the need of the client as perceived by the field social worker, and the absence of alternative placement, may mean they have to appeal over the head of the residential staff for a decision. This was recognized as always being a possibility, but if it occurs frequently the home's manager would have to consider why the home consistently refuses applicants or, on the other hand, why only inappropriate clients are being submitted.

Beyond this, the tasks of the Admissions Conference are to discuss fully the background and needs of the applicant; to enable residential staff to seek additional information on the social history; and (more controversially) examine the client's file if they wish. Residential staff have to decide whether the client will fit in with the particular group of people already in residence. A decision has to be taken here as to who should act as the prime care agent. Usually this would now pass from the field to the residential social worker but this is a decision which needs to be taken explicitly.

Once a decision to admit has been taken there is the further task of agreeing a preliminary action plan which at this stage will probably extend only to deciding how and when initial visits by the client should take place and the purpose of the placement. In all this, considerable emphasis is placed upon preparing and recording specific action plans including the decisions taken at the Admissions Conference. These records are then held by both staff.

Emergency admissions were a possibility for all homes, particularly the adolescent girls' hostel, and, to a lesser extent, the home for the elderly. When these took place without Stage 3 occurring before the client was admitted, the conditions of admission laid down that a meeting equivalent to an Admissions Conference must be held within three days of the client's admission; any actions taken up to this point were conditional upon the subsequent agreement of both parties.

Stage 4: initial review
After the client has been in a home for a short time – three months seemed to be the period most favoured by the staff – there is an initial review. The same staff should be present, the field and residential staff concerned and the home's manager as chairman. The objective of the initial review is to examine the decision and plans

of the Admissions Conference and to see whether they still hold in the light of experience. If the initial decisions seem correct to both parties, fresh plans in as detailed and specific a form as possible are again worked out between the staff. The matters upon which decisions would need to be taken were set out. If a decision has been taken that the client should be present at reviews it would be natural for him to begin attending them at this stage of the process. For both adult homes this is the time to decide whether the field social worker should remain in contact with the client, and this would be a decision taken jointly between field and residential staff. Similarly, decisions are taken here about who should be the prime care agent; by this time it is most likely to be a member of the residential staff.

Stage 5: subsequent reviews

In keeping with the underlying principles, it was agreed that in all homes, both adult and children's, regular reviews should take place on all clients. Detailed objectives of these reviews were set out in each of the documents for the homes. They have three general aims: first, to review whether the client was correctly placed; secondly, to work out detailed, mutually agreed and recorded action plans for both field and residential staff which specify the tasks each agreed to undertake; thirdly, to review plans previously made. Many adult clients do not have social workers. In those cases it was decided that reviews should take place between the head of the home and the home's adviser; the review would have the same objectives. Decisions about clients leaving the home would be taken in review meetings where the views of both staff would be reflected in the final decisions. Here decisions would include agreement about who should remain working with the clients and who should be the clients' prime care agent after they left the home.

Conclusion

Each project group produced a policy statement which systematically set out the tasks of the different meetings and the matters upon which decisions have to be taken as the client enters the home. The form the policy statements took has been described in the last section and these were based upon the principles governing interaction which had already been agreed. Implementation of the new procedures coincided with the assumption by the new divisions of responsibility for running the home and this, together with staff changes amongst field and residential workers, meant progress towards their implementation proceeded at a different rate from home to home.

Beyond the production of agreed ways of admitting clients, changes which occurred included a decision to hold Admissions Conferences on clients in the home for the elderly and the home for the mentally handicapped, where reviews would also take place. In the family group home and hostel for adolescent girls Admissions Conferences and initial reviews were started and there was a clearer understanding about the task of the assessment conference. Files began to be kept on clients by residential staff and these were seen as necessary for the review process. The chairman of the Admissions and Review Conferences came to be seen as someone with prime responsibility for encouraging the process of reaching agreement, though heads of homes could be overruled where the home's manager was the chairman of the Review or Assessment Conferences. There is no easy way of assessing the impact of such arrangements upon clients but among the staff, heads of homes felt they had much to gain from improved clarity about the principles guiding interaction; principles which recognized the shared responsibilities of both groups of staff whilst reflecting a particular responsibility because of a client's relationship with one or other worker.

The discussion has been confined to the four residential homes in the project but the ideas were thought by the department to have application to other residential homes and day care establishments. It was recognized that the implementation of the model would be time consuming and involve more meetings for staff. It involves important changes in work practice. In particular it provides opportunities for heads of homes to decide who should be admitted to the home for which they have responsibility (albeit with a recognition that their decision can be overruled). It was further recognized that there would be occasions when the model would be departed from due to lack of time, personality differences or a shortage of suitable vacancies. Nevertheless, the existence of an agreed set of principles and models to guide interaction provides a framework and a goal to aim at which over a period of time will influence the quality of interaction. Considering the magnitude of the decisions being taken, additional time spent in discussion was thought to be in the interest of the clients and likely to benefit them.

Managers and Community Homes: A Fresh Look at Their Role[1]

by Geoffrey Bromley

Introduction

Before the implementation of the 1969 Children's and Young Persons' Act,[2] the old approved schools were directly responsible to management committees, most of them voluntary. There was a close relationship between management committees and the Home Office who exercised some control through regular visits from the Inspectorate and circulars. One of the major purposes of the 1969 Act was to achieve an improved standard of social care in the former approved schools. It sought to create a stronger link between the new community homes and children's departments or voluntary organizations by making their professional resources more available to the homes. Children's departments ceased to exist at the end of 1970, simultaneously with the introduction of the 1969 Act, and the new SSDs became the bodies whose resources were intended to be made more easily available to the homes.

The Act created a complex triangle of accountability between the responsible authority[3] (the SSD of the local authority), the managers and the home. The present powers and duties are legislated for in the 1969 Act and further defined in Home Office circular 196/70, the Community Homes Regulations 1972 and the individual In-

---

[1] Reprinted (with minor alterations) from *Social Work Service*, (1976), No. 10.

[2] See particularly paras. 39-42.

[3] Controlled status homes, as defined in Section 39 of the 1969 Act, have two-thirds of the managers appointed by the local authority, as responsible authority, and one-third by the voluntary organization. Assisted status homes have one-third appointed by the local authority and two-thirds by the responsible organization, the voluntary organization responsible for the home.

struments of Management.[4] No one, however, could argue that any of these makes the position of managers very clear.

Little has been written about managers and their role and what has predated the 1969 Act. Carlebach[5] provides useful material about managers' perception of their activities and offers an analysis which suggests a shift over time of authority to the Home Office and away from managers. Simultaneously he sees a situation where managers possess responsibility without the accompanying necessary authority. Rose[6] offers a more critical appraisal of managers through an analysis which suggests that, although a perusal of their powers could give an impression of omnipotence, the reverse is the case. The work of Baron and Howell[7] is also relevant to this analysis.

The analysis offered here is based on project work done for a local authority with responsibility for controlled status homes.[8] It strongly suggests that the present unclear division in responsibility between managers, SSDs and homes is preventing the group most responsible for the development of the home from exercising its proper duties.

The project

Faced with the situation of responsibility for two controlled status homes, the SSD invited the author to examine the position of managers *vis à vis* the local authority in the light of the changed status of the homes. Although the work was done with two controlled status homes there are strong reasons for believing the analysis has application to assisted status homes as well.

The SSD began from the point that management committees existed and must be enabled to operate satisfactorily. From this emerged a number of unresolved issues. What does section 41 of the 1969 Act really mean, in practice, by saying that 'the responsible

[4] A statement, unique to each home, of the legal framework within which the managers operate.

[5] Carlebach, J., *Caring for Children in Trouble*, (1970).

[6] Rose, G., *Schools for Young Offenders*, (1967).

[7] Baron, G. and Howell, D. A., *The Government and Management of Schools*, (1974). This authoritative study of the function of school governing and managing bodies is relevant in helping to appreciate the differences of responsibility of community homes management committees. Although the authors highlight unclarity in school governing body functions, there is some greater degree of clarity about what their role should be, compared with management committees.

[8] The work was done with Northamptonshire County Council. It involved work with headmasters, managers, and staff of the SSD connected with two controlled status homes.

body shall exercise their functions in relation to a controlled community home through the body of Managers?

Do the department's responsibilities extend beyond appointing staff and providing finance for the homes to operate? If so, how can they satisfactorily exercise their additional responsibilities? What role is there for managers in this process? In short, what is the role of managers in contrast to the department in enabling homes to oper-ate satisfactorily? As a result of discussion with a selection of man-agers, the headmasters and staff of the SSD, a picture began to emerge of two contrasting ways of viewing the management arrange-ments for the homes.

Managers' changed role

However, before setting these out we need to examine some of the factors which have led managers, and particularly those who have experience, both before and after the changed status of the homes, to see a change in their role. Six main factors emerged as contri-buting to the change in their perception of their role.

First, and perhaps most important in the long run, the local authority had reserved to itself in the Instruments of Management the prime responsibility for the appointment of staff. This important change from the previous arrangement where managers were primarily responsible was modified by the involvement of managers by the local authority in the process of making appointments.[9] Nevertheless, the effect of this important change was to make the headmaster look to the Director of Social Services for his nearest equivalent to an immediate superior. And here words need to be carefully chosen because in no sense does the headmaster have a boss in the way this is normally understood in industry or the largely hierarchical management arrangements experienced in SSDs. What this did create was a strong link between the SSD and the home which affected the headmaster and significantly altered the role of managers.

A second important change relates to finance. Whilst managers must agree to estimates which were then submitted to the local authority for approval, in practice these were worked out between the headmaster and the officers of the local authority, submitted to managers for approval and then to the local authority. Again, this

---

[9] This is, of course, an important difference between the functions of management committees and school governing bodies; see Baron, G., and Howell, D. A., (1974), op. cit.

created a strong link between the SSD and the homes.

Thirdly, the presence of a professional adviser appointed by the SSD had also strengthened the link between the home and the department. As an adviser, it was at the discretion of the headmaster as to how he was used. His contribution extended beyond advising on problems of individual children, to helping the homes examine their ways of treating children by, for instance, examining staffing ratios and responsibilities. Whilst it was recognized that the agreement of managers and of course the headmaster would be needed for any major changes in methods of care or treatment objectives, the regular contact between the adviser and the home necessarily increased the influence of the local authority.

Fourthly, managers were no longer involved in decisions to return children to the community. It was now the SSD, not managers, who were *in loco parentis* on behalf of the children. This duty was relinquished before the SSD assumed responsibility for the homes, but it is a further diminution in their duties and some managers felt it distanced them further from the home.

Fifthly, there had been changes in the frequency of management meetings. From meetings once every month, meetings now occurred quarterly. A significant number of managers came regularly to the home, knew many of the staff and some of the boys. Managers with particular skills were used by the headmaster for a variety of different tasks. However, the reduction in frequency of visits meant managers inevitably knew less about the detailed running of the home and the problems which were being faced.

Sixth, and related to this, was the changed composition of the management committee brought about by the different status of the homes and, more recently, a decision by the local authority to appoint managers who reflected the political composition of the council. In addition the local authority had appointed a small number of non-councillors, a headmaster and educational psychologist. However, one effect of this changed composition may have been to place more discretion with the headmaster and to increase the potential influence of the SSD.

Managers' perception of their activities

If these are some of the background factors against which managers saw their changed role, how did they tend to describe their activities? In discussion emphasis was given to the following activities.

First, managers emphasized the support they gave the headmaster according to their particular knowledge and expertise. Such matters included help with educational provision, comments on architectural designs and assistance with individual boys' schooling.

Secondly, they emphasized agreement or not to policy proposals or recommendations made by the SSD on any aspects relating to how the homes should be run. Managers saw themselves as having authority to agree to all aspects of policy, including those concerned with the detailed ways in which boys are cared for. It meant that, like the officers of the SSD, managers saw themselves as determining within what policy parameters the homes should work.

Thirdly, managers spoke of their responsibility to agree to estimates and be consulted about some staff appointments. The Instruments of Management reserved the authority to appoint staff, other than the headmaster, to the SSD. In practice it seems it was left either to the officers, or headmasters, to involve managers in the process of staff appointments where they acted in an advisory capacity.

Fourthly, headmasters and managers laid particular emphasis upon the value of managers acting as a bridge between the home and the local community to foster good local relationships. Headmasters spoke of this as being something the managers could do better than the officers of the SSD.

Fifthly, managers saw themselves, particularly in informal and the formal monthly visits, as monitoring how well the home kept within the bounds of what society at large might regard as 'reasonable care'.

Sixth, foundation managers particularly, but local authority appointed managers as well, saw an important function in safeguarding the home and seeing that its overall character was maintained. When the Instruments of Management were being negotiated this was clearly an occasion where this was being done, but managers saw this as activity which should be ongoing.

Seventh, many managers were influential members of the community, members of the local authority and senior employees of the County Council. As such they were members of networks which extend beyond their role as managers. Clearly this means they could bring influence to bear in a number of ways beyond their formal role as managers. This may significantly increase the power of managers beyond what they appear on paper.

This list of managers' activities was not exhaustive. The important point which came from an examination of managers' perception of their role was that they, as a whole, did not see themselves as the manager of the home or headmaster, nor even the agent through whom the local authority was exercising its overall management activities. Analysis of their perceptions revealed an accent upon the supportive, social monitoring, advice giving, helping and expressive aspects of management on an *ad hoc* basis. There was little emphasis on the control, accountability and encouragement of developing functions of management. In so far as these were provided, there was an expectation and assumption from managers that they should come from the SSD.

This perception was broadly shared by headmasters who suggested that, so far as control, accountability and encouragement of development needed to be provided, it could and was likely to come most appropriately direct from the officers of the SSD, albeit including managers in certain instances. If this perception is correct, then it has certain major implications for the role of managers, the kind of service the SSD makes available to the homes and the expectations headmasters should have of both managers and the SSD. Using the material obtained from the project situations these issues are now analysed by examining two possible managers' roles.

Models of management

A meaning of management

As soon as one analyses the role of a group called managers the question inevitably arises of what degree of management does a community home need beyond itself? In this project it was found useful to suggest that management in the most general sense embraces four main elements, and any system of government for an institution needs to locate where these lie.

First, there is a quality and standard monitoring function which involves monitoring not just to make sure gross defects in performance are avoided but also to see that certain minimum standards are achieved. Secondly, there is an enabling function of management which involves ensuring the institution or body has the necessary resources of all kinds to carry out its job. Thirdly, there is a developmental function of management which extends to helping the institution or body not just to keep abreast of events but to develop into providing a better and more appropriate service in whatever field it is operating. Fourthly, there is a governmental function which involves the business of appointing key staff and consequently being in some sense responsible for what occurs in the institution. This latter function is something which can be exercised by a committee or corporate body and is similar to the kind of responsibility held by a local authority committee towards its chief officer.

In trying to make some sense of the changed position of managers and the new responsibilities of the SSD, two contrasting models began to emerge. For each, the location of the four management functions presented a very different picture. The two models are the home primarily managed by managers, and the home primarily managed by the SSD.

Home primarily managed by managers
This is the situation which largely prevailed before the changed status of the homes. In present circumstances it would involve the managers operating as a sub-committee of the local authority which delegates its responsibility for that particular institution to the body of managers. It would mean the headmaster looking to managers as the group to whom he is most accountable for the totality of what occurs within the home. It would mean managers were most directly responsible for carrying out the quality and standard monitoring, development and governmental functions of management.

In discharging their functions they would naturally draw on the SSD, who would be exercising an enabling function towards the home. As such the SSD would be operating on what could be regarded as a service-giving basis. The department would clearly be the body the home would draw upon for all material provision, monies, major purchases and the basic wherewithal to enable the home to operate satisfactorily. It might be approached, at the discretion of managers or the headmaster, for help on professional developmental matters relating to the way children are cared for. Equally the home might turn elsewhere for the provision of these items. The SSD under this model would be operating in an essentially passive or *laissez-faire* manner towards the home. It leaves the major functions of management, with the exception of the enabling function, to managers. The SSD provides its services as it is called upon to do so at the managers' and the home's discretion.

Diagrammatically this arrangement could be represented as something like Figure 7.1 Such a representation may appear to be a somewhat stark and extreme model but it is one that is by no means impossible to envisage. Although probably not intended by the spirit of the 1969 Act for controlled status homes, the vestiges of such

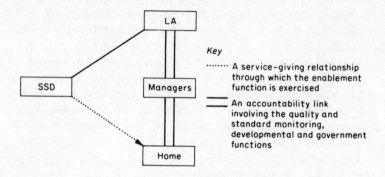

Figure 7.1   Diagram of a home primarily managed by managers

arrangements will exist to some extent. In so far as the SSD has many calls upon its resources and may lack the expertise to offer any service other than a material one to the homes, this situation can be encouraged to exist. Doubtless many headmasters would in fact welcome such an arrangement, which leaves the main line of accountability to managers largely unchanged and allows them to carry on with their job without too much outside interference.

However, there are aspects of this model which strongly suggest there are limitations to its effectiveness.

First, whilst recognizing the relative autonomy of headmasters, the increasing professionalization of residential social work makes senior staff look naturally to full-time professional staff for support, advice and development: the quality and standard monitoring and enabling functions of management. The sheer complexity of residential social work makes it difficult to conceive of managers being able naturally to carry out all four, particularly the developmental function of management.

Secondly, voluntary managers are subject to heavy time pressures from other, usually full-time jobs, which prevent them from undertaking the day-to-day activities inherently involved in management. Of the four functions probably the governmental function is the only one which could be exercised on anything but a full-time basis.

Thirdly, work elsewhere[10] has suggested that, at least for smaller residential establishments, there are severe disadvantages in splitting the activities of management among more than one source. Not only

---

[10] See Chapter 5, and *Social Services Departments*.

does it fail to locate responsibility for management clearly, it means that homes can play one group off against another particularly in times of crisis.

Fourthly, there is the extremely important reality that the 1969 Act has empowered the local authority, as the responsible body, to reserve to itself the power to appoint staff. Responsibility for the appointment of staff necessarily creates a strong link between the SSD and the home which runs counter to the situation of the home being primarily accountable to managers.

Fifthly, the spirit of the 1969 Act and the logic behind the Instruments of Management seem to push in the direction of a stronger link between the home and the responsible body than between the home and managers. In short, managers by their very nature cannot provide the full range of management support needed by a home.

Home primarily managed by the SSD
Turning to the second model, the role of the SSD towards the home is very different from the service-giving and enabling function described in the first model. Instead the dominant link is between the home and the SSD and not with managers whose role is necessarily different from that described above. This model implies that it is the prime responsibility of the department to provide the quality and standard monitoring, enabling, developmental and governmental functions of management. However, there are still some functions and activities which emerge as being realistically valid for managers. These are examined after looking first at the duties of the SSD as the responsible body in this second model.

First, under the 1969 Act the officers of the SSD are primarily responsible through the headmaster for the appointment of staff. The Instruments of Management reserve this power to them. In consequence this seems to create a strong link between the home and the officers. The SSD will appropriately involve managers and headmasters in the process of appointing staff. Nevertheless, the SSD retains this power to itself and, as it also has responsibility for the development of the home, it is able to appoint staff according to the headmaster's and its own conception of what this should be.

Secondly, this model implies the SSD being primarily responsible for budget and expenditure within the homes and accepting the associated developmental opportunities.

Thirdly, the department rather than managers would be responsible for ensuring that the home operates within existing policies relating, for example, to the care and treatment of individual children or to admission and return home procedures.

Fourthly, officers of the SSD, alongside the headmaster, should be primarily responsible for initiating changes as necessary within the homes, particularly those relating to the care, treatment and education of children, taking on board for themselves the developmental function towards the home. In other words, in this model prime responsibility for all four management functions would rest firmly with the SSD and not with managers.

In outlining the role of the SSD it is recognized that very often the department will not be involved in detailed day-to-day matters of the home. These will normally be dealt with by the headmaster, who is likely very often to be the pacemaker in proposing changes and initiating development within the home. In addition, close monitoring of the home by the SSD is often inappropriate and unnecessary or, if it is, it suggests something fundamentally wrong about the appointment of headmaster and staff. The point in spelling out the duties of the SSD in this model is to indicate where accountability and responsibility lie for the management of the home at the margin, and this for some homes can be an extremely crucial margin to identify.

Managers would not be excluded from involvement in these activities. They would be included, not in the day-to-day matters of management, but by being involved in commenting on staff appointments, approving budgets and agreeing to major policy changes affecting the homes. However, and this is crucial, in this model with its strong link between the home and the SSD the managers' role begins to emerge more clearly and realistically, particularly when set against the responsibilities, outlined above, of the officers of the SSD.

In undertaking their duties managers would be responsible for giving advice and help to the headmaster according to their particular speciality and skill. The headmaster is free to accept or reject this advice. In so doing managers would be providing an attitional form of support to the headmaster.

They have responsibility to monitor, particularly in statutory visits, the overall care and education provided to see that it conforms with what society at large regards as adequate. Deliberately it is not suggested that managers monitor adherence to any particular local authority policy, if it exists. This seems more appropriately to be the task of officers of the SSD. They would be involved at the discretion of the headmaster or the SSD in the appointment of staff.

Managers would have a duty to approve expenditure estimates submitted by the SSD, providing supportive links with the community and fostering good local relationships. Foundation managers would additionally have the task of ensuring that the terms of foundation articles were being adhered to.

Finally, there is the extremely important task for managers of approving or not policy proposals relating to all aspects of care in the home, professional and administrative. Clearly, there may be occasions when managers may make policy recommendations but these would need the support of the SSD and headmaster. Such a role for managers means the home must work within a policy framework agreed to by managers. In some respects this responsibility is probably the most important for managers, though the realities of power mean that, for controlled status homes, the local authority can ultimately force the issue on matters of policy.

In laying emphasis upon the policy examination functions of the Committee, it may immediately be objected that it is not at all clear what is meant by policy matters. Part of the problem turns on a difficulty often encountered in residential homes and elsewhere that staff have simply failed to be explicit about the policy within which the home is operating: in consequence it is very difficult to give proper debate to it. Policy issues, beyond such matters as building and equipment, concern such matters as staff ratios, the regime that is being made available to children, home leave policy, arrangements for rewards and punishments, the position of education within the home, and links and relationships with SSDs. It concerns all matters which do not touch on what is being done for a particular child but how children as a whole are being cared for and treated within the home. It is these matters involving not what is being done today with one child but what it is proposed to do with children within the home, tomorrow and thereafter, that are the nub of matters which could be debated within management committees, if within this model they are to be given a proper role.

An objection to this conception may very well be that the kind of policy matters mentioned are really professional matters which should finally be determined by the officers of the local authority. But in this model, management committees would not have any ultimate veto over what policies should exist within the home. This would, in any case, be incompatible with the conception of the home being ultimately accountable to the officers of the SSD. What is suggested is that a logical concomitant function of the management committee is for them to critically examine and scrutinize the policy framework within which the home operates; not so that they should have a final veto on such matters, but in order to expose the proposed mode of work of the home to a wider field of critical scrutiny.

Diagrammatically this second model, the home primarily managed by the SSD, can be represented as in Figure. 7.2.

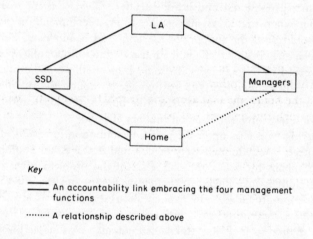

Key

━━━ An accountability link embracing the four management functions

········· A relationship described above

Figure 7.2 Diagram of a home primarily managed by the SSD

Whilst the list of appropriate activities for managers is neither exhaustive nor novel, it does imply a very different role from that outlined for the first model and from the situation which prevailed before the change in status of the homes. It involves managers necessarily acting within the constraints set by the local authority, the responsible authority. It need not reduce managers merely to 'Friends of the Home' – a local sounding board for the SSD, or the home to call upon and use as they think fit. Managers in this model have the power to challenge and resist changes or demand alterations in the policies the SSD may be seeking to impose on the home. And in any case the direct link between the managers and the local authority, frequently with members of the social services committee as managers, means there is a constant check upon the SSD imposing inappropriate constraints and demands upon the home. It is simply not possible for the SSD to deal with the home in the same way as it does with other residential establishments which do not have managers.

The analysis of the possible functions of management committees in controlled status homes is different in emphasis from one offered by the DHSS's Development Group.[11] That Report recommends for controlled status homes that the functions and duties of managers and sub-committees can best be undertaken by the Social Services Committee and the officers of the local authority. Far from suggesting there is a role for committees to scrutinize the policy framework within which the home works, it argues that there is no place for the Committee at all. In contrast however, the same report argues that policy issues for assisted status homes should be brought to the attention of management committees so as to allow them to bring their influence to bear in its development. This is rather nearer the opinion presented in this second model of management.

Clearly, there are other ways of portraying the inter-relationship between the home, the managers and the SSD. Essentially, the project on which this analysis was based suggested that vestiges of the first model, with the home primarily managed by managers, still existed in the minds both of managers and to some extent the responsible body. This in turn was inhibiting the responsible body from exercising its full responsibilities towards the home. Instead the second model, where the home is primarily managed by the SSD, is suggested as an alternative and more appropriate interpretation of the 1969 Act; one that takes far better account of the management needs of homes and the abilities and predispositions of managers. It means in effect that the reality of managers acting as the 'agent' of the responsible authority[12] in management matters has to be critically re-examined. It also strongly suggests that the term 'manager' is probably a misnomer, implying a far greater degree of power and authority than is realistically associated with the post. There are, however, issues which were raised by this analysis in the project authority which are examined in the next section.

Some implications of the analysis

Are managers necessary?
Underlying the discussion so far must be the question of whether

[11] See DHSS Development Group (1977), *Management of Community Homes with Education on the Premises.*
[12] See Section 41(2) of the Children's and Young Persons' Act 1969.

there is still a proper role for managers to play. Why not simply have a direct link between the responsible authority and the home of the kind outlined in the second model, with the responsible authority undertaking managers' remaining activities? This chapter leaves that an open question but does offer an analysis from which a number of conclusions could be drawn – it is not arguing for or against the retention of managers, because the work upon which it is based did not embrace the question.

It is, however, pertinent to record that four possible underlying functions were suggested in the project, both by managers and headmasters, which explained the need for managers. Alternatively they may simply have been advanced as a justification of the *status quo*.

First, the presence of managers was related to the situation of homes dealing with some children who have infringed society's values, where the home was naturally open to the criticism of treating their charges in either too harsh or too lenient a manner. Managers may act as a group helping to determine a right balance between these extremes.

Secondly, as a conventional boss/subordinate relationship does not or cannot exist between a headmaster and the responsible authority, a manager may be the means, additional to the responsible authority, of ensuring that the home is operating within acceptable limits.

Thirdly, managers may be a response to the fact that homes are providing education as well as social care. In so far as the responsible body lacks the expertise to provide the four management functions to the home's school, managers may be a means of making up this deficit.

Fourthly, homes of this size and complexity may simply demand avenues of support additional to those available from the responsible authority. Managers may be a response to this need.

Whether these are justified rationales for the continuation of managers is an open question, outside the scope of this book. However, if the analysis offered of the home primarily managed by the SSD is followed through, there is some reason to doubt the viability of the role in the long term. Indeed, its continuation may be preventing the responsible authority from assuming its full management responsibility.

This line of thinking is paralleled by Baron and Howell[13] who note these underlying explanations for the existence of school governing bodies. 'Their existence is part of a body of assumptions constitut-

---

[13] Baron, G., and Howell, D. A., (1974), op. cit.

ing an administrative mystique concerning the individuality of the school, the leadership role of the headmaster and the freedom of the teacher. Such assumptions, universally expressed in official publications, are essential too for officials working in a situation in which central direction is considered intolerable.' They continue, 'it is part of the carefully worked out set of safeguards, developed over the years for ensuring that the schools can be defended against over-hasty education committees and their officers'. These arguments arise for schools and not community homes. They suggest of course a clearer underlying set of assumptions about the social positioning of schools compared with community homes where, as we have seen, the existence of management committees at all, at least for controlled status homes, is being challenged.[14] Indeed the intervention of the 1969 Act was one of reducing the degree of autonomy of heads of homes. Perhaps the continuation of management committees represents some loss of nerve at the logic of the Act's intentions.

Developmental implications for the responsible authority
The question of how the responsible authority is to interact and effect positive changes in the homes is a complex issue, made more difficult by the fact that these are new institutions for departments to manage. Responsible authorities may simply lack staff with sufficient skill and expertise to contribute towards the development of the homes. In such a situation, the responsible authority may confine its attentions to administrative, financial and building matters and feel that it can make little contribution to fostering the professional development and caring side of the homes.

Doubtless there are some homes where there is no need for changes and these can in any case be left to the headmaster to instigate and sell to the department and managers. However, there was evidence from the project and elsewhere that the very presence of managers, with their ill-defined authority, can make it more difficult for the responsible authority to effect development and change. Managers may in practice be a force for conservation to whom the home may appeal against changes being thrust upon them by the responsible authority. Where the first model, in which the home is primarily managed by managers, is the one under which the different parties are operating, then change can be inhibited. The logic of the analysis is to suggest that the second model is in fact intended by the 1969 Act. Clarity about the implications should enable the

[14] See DHSS Development Group, (1977), op. cit.

responsible authority to assume its full management responsibilities including the developmental function.

Some of the difficulties associated with the full absorption of community homes into SSDs, with the accompanying uncertainty about accountability of heads, may relate to the work strata framework.[15] In so far as community homes have an expected work output at Stratum 3 (and beyond) this would argue for managerial relationships with staff such as assistant and divisional directors. Some departments have taken such decisions even though this creates considerable additional burdens upon those senior members of staff. Professional advisory staff are one way of relieving this burden. The continued existence of management committees may represent hesitation as to how far this logic can be continued.

Educational issues
There is additionally the problem of the SSD having to support an institution with a strong educational element. The presence of managers doubtless partly reflects the situation in the educational field where schools have governors and school management commitees which prevent any strong executive links between the school and Education Department. As things now stand, a strong case can be argued that, despite the 1969 Act emphasizing the social care side of the homes, the education side is still strong and important, and it is difficult for a SSD to provide the management activities towards a part of the homes over which it has no particular expertise. The presence of management committees in part reflects this. One possible solution to this problem could be to split the education side of the home and link it direct to the Education Department of the authority. Responsibility beyond the headmaster for the recruitment and development of the education side would then rest with the Education Department and not with the SSD. The school would then be a resource attached to the home.

This is a radical solution and one which may create as many problems as it solves, particularly over whether it is possible to regard the education and social sides of the home as separate from each other, and responsible to different bodies.

The effectiveness of managers
Finally, there is a problem of how managers can be enabled to do their job effectively. Managers, particularly those who are not councillors, can feel themselves to be the pawn of the SSD or even the

[15] See Chapter 1.

headmaster, asked merely to rubber stamp proposals made else-where. Doubtless, managers of real calibre will not allow this to happen, but certain conditions need to exist to prevent it from occurring. Managers are going to feel impotent and ineffective if they are deprived of real information about the situation under discussion or background information about the proposals made by the authority. As a result apathy may set in. If the functions of managers are broadly correct and their role in the second model is right, then managers need to be given considerable information about the home and alternative strategies for dealing with change. Managers are likely to feel more valuable if they are involved as members of working parties alongside professional staff in formulat-ing new policy proposals. Also continuity of appointment seems vital. This emerged strongly from project discussions where changes in managers brought about by political alterations in the council's com-position led to a decline in the impact the management group as a whole could make. Additionally, though a strong link between the home and the SSD has been argued for, with managers not carry-ing executive responsibility, there does seem a need to have man-agers who are informed about the particular field. Where councillors and others have knowledge of the particular speciality, this is a case for their appointment as managers.

Conclusion

Two alternative roles for managers have been outlined. It has been argued that the logic of the present situation under the 1969 Act points to a strong link between the home and the responsible body, the home primarily managed by the SSD. In attempting to define the relative responsibilities of each of the parties, it has been sug-gested that only by clarification of the relative responsibilities of managers and the responsible authority can each properly assume the duties which seem to be implied by the 1969 Act.

In the second model, besides the expressive, supportive tasks that management committees can undertake, emphasis has been placed on a core function of management committees to scrutinize the policy framework within which the home should work. Whether the need for such a wider examination of the home's policy frame-work is a reflection of real need for homes of this kind, or the very existence of management committees is a superfluous temporary ex-pedient against the day of the ultimate demise, is left as an open question.

The project was not concerned with assisted status homes. Nevertheless, it is suggested that the model has application to this situation as well, where a strong link seems to be demanded between the home and the full-time professional headquarters staff of the Society, the responsible organization. Here again managers would be operating in broadly the role outlined in the second model.

PART IV

Development Work

Introduction

by David Billis

The issues dealt with in this Part are thoroughbred Seebohm. They are distinctive products of the post-integration era. It is not only that, as in the case of Intermediate Treatment, they result from specific central government policy, but also, if our analysis of work is valid, that the problems related in these chapters stem primarily from the impact of the new work expected from SSDs. The officers in charge of intermediate treatment, training, research or development, together with their other colleague consultants and advisers mainly occupy uncharted organizational territory. It is true, of course, that the topics discussed in previous chapters also look very different from the way in which they appeared in the former children's, welfare, or mental health departments. Workers in field, day, domiciliary and residential settings have all, to a greater or lesser degree, been influenced by reorganization. Nevertheless, it can still be claimed – and it is a point which has not insignificant organizational and policy implications – that the new 'developmental' work has led to distinctive problems for the men and women who are often 'in the middle'.

The problems are most comprehensively described in Chapter 8, which is based on project work in nine local authorities reinforced by nine days of workshops. Here are to be found characteristic problems of the Seebohm 'middlemen'. There is a summary of the numerous difficulties confronting those attempting to work in the large, increasing number of posts. Often they are neither working clearly at grass roots level, nor are they part of the departmental headquarters senior management team; sometimes it is unclear whether or not they are expected to engage in operational work, and more often than not their authority *vis à vis* other members of staff is equally vague. A weighty catalogue of problems has been brought forward for collaborative analysis. Chapter 8 examines the problems and the possible reasons for the establishment of such a wide variety of roles. We see that there are a number of models which departments may choose to implement. The model building in this chapter is a detailed and careful attempt to demonstrate the possible pros and cons of seeking to resolve current dilemmas. Four models are outlined: specialist development officers, project officers, staff officers, and consultant practitioners. Only by model building of this sort can we expect to move beyond organizations which are overdependent on goodwill and chance.

Chapter 9 follows the same theme but both narrows and widens the perspective. The text is based on two years' project work reinforced by three two-day workshops with intermediate treatment workers from social services and education departments. In that it is concerned only with intermediate treatment it is obviously narrower in its terms of reference than the preceding chapter. Although the chapter is brief, and the details of the case study no more than telegraphic, it does illustrate the point that explicit models can – and have – formed the basis for executive decision-making. The wider perspective lies in the link which is made between organizational structure and social policy. Too often the interconnections between visionary statements of social policy and the construction of social institutions that have to implement these policies, are either denied or ignored. This chapter is not intended to provide a comprehensive statement about intermediate treatment. It should rather be seen as a modest effort in organizational and policy analysis which is a response to problems raised by a defined group of middle-level staff.

Chapter 10 on 'development' originates from the same broad area of middle-level organizational anxiety. The confusion arising from the indiscriminate use of the word 'development' provides a natural opportunity to explore several major issues confronting those concerned with the personal social services. Thus, the analysis of 'development' indicates that it can be used as a panacea. Underlying its usage may be found extensive disquiet regarding standards of care, co-ordination of services, and the ability of departments to actually deliver the new 'higher-level goods' envisaged by the Seebohm Report.

Although this chapter is directed towards current preoccupations of SSDs, its overall message is one which might have relevance for other social welfare agencies. In discussing the role of research in 'social care', Donnison distinguishes information and technological studies from what he calls 'policy orientated' research.[1] The latter is defined as 'studies in which the researcher is entitled to question

[1] Donnison, D. V. (1978), 'The Economic and Political Context' in Barnes, J. and Connelly, N. (eds.), op. cit., p. 65.

the definition of the problems posed for him by his customers, and to explore the different solutions and their implications'. Policy-orientated research not only helps 'practical men grappling with these problems, it should also help to develop a deeper understanding among other people ... who may have to tackle similar problems in other fields later'. For example, Chapter 9 illustrates how, providing that we are dealing with pressing problems, explorations into what might at first be seen as 'narrow organizational' issues, can lead into a discussion of topics which may have been equally narrowly defined as 'social policy'. In other words, there is a strong case for the development of theories which begin to link the traditional concerns of social administration as Titmuss defined the field in his inaugural lecture:

> On the one hand, then, we are interested in the machinery of administration, which organizes and dispenses various forms of social assistance; on the other, in the lives, the needs, and the mutual relations of those members of the community for whom the services are provided ...[2]

It is time the 'two hands' were brought together! The theory of stratification of work may be seen as an attempt to show the way in which social institutions (the machinery of administration) may be constructed in response to the problems and needs of the community. The middle, Stratum 3, occupants of the new departments are in a unique – if often uncomfortable – position, where 'needs' become translated into what we have described as 'systematic service provision'. It is at this point in the organization that there is an expectation to construct something that might be called 'machinery' to respond to a flow of problems. The Seebohm middlemen have an unenviable task. Their work lacks the obvious rewards of working with individual cases of distress. It lacks too the status and glamour of dealing with long-term strategic issues. At this juncture in the history of the departments they (the workers at this level) are often searching to make sense of job descriptions that do not necessarily provide incumbents with sufficiently clear guidelines for effective action. Analysis of the unease in the middle ground can lead to questioning and reformulation both of the machinery of organization and the definition of the needs that are being met. In this final Part of the book the reader will find three explorations into an area of organizational activity which can be dangerously undervalued by practitioners and by students of social policy and administration.

[2] Titmuss, Richard M. (1958), *Essays on 'The Welfare State'*, pp. 14–15.

8 Advisers, Development Officers and Consultants in Social Services Departments[1]

by Ralph Rowbottom
and Geoffrey Bromley

One of the features of the growth associated with the establishment of large-scale comprehensive SSDs in 1971, and the extension of many of them again in the local government reorganization of 1974, has been the creation of a sizeable band of staff at middle levels in the hierarchy, variously described as 'advisers', 'consultants', 'development officers', principal assistants', and the like. Not on the one hand clear-cut managers of operational services, nor on the other working directly with individual clients, their situation has turned out to be far from problem-free. (We will use the description 'adviser' as a loose cover-all.)

Exploration has revealed a number of characteristic difficulties:[2]

(a) Advisers, or the like, often complain of 'working in a vacuum', of 'losing touch'; that grass-roots workers rarely approach them for help; that they are kept in the dark about many top-level moves and plans;

(b) they complain about frequent lack of interest in such new initiatives and schemes as they do develop, and about their lack of any clear authority to implement changes on their own;

(c) they often report uncertainty or unhappiness about where they

---

[1] An earlier version of this appeared in October 1977 as a Working Paper.

[2] The material of this chapter draws on action-research of the general kind described in the Preface, more particularly on project work in five London Boroughs and four non-metropolitan Counties during the period 1973–7 stemming from specific invitations to help with problems of the kinds of staff just described; on a total of nine days of workshops at Brunel for senior staff of the service spread over the same period, looking at the same issues; and on a wider range of field projects and conferences since the start of the Unit's existence which have had more or less direct relevance as well.

fit in the organizational structure; about who they are really account-able to, and about who is really accountable for their work;

(*d*) certain so-called advisers (many 'domiciliary service advisers' and 'advisers for the handicapped' for example) complain that they are in practice held responsible for the running of operational ser-vices over which in theory they have no management control;

(*e*) on the other hand many operational staff are uneasy about the power that so-called advisers do exercise; for example in deciding placements in care; or in vetting expenditure of various kinds, or in guiding and directing specialist staff;

(*f*) there is frequent unease too on the part of operational staff about vague 'monitoring' duties which may be assigned to advisers, and complaints that advisers intrude in practice into matters which they are not in a position to understand fully and on which they have very little to offer.

Many advisers in SSDs, particularly the more specialized ones, have found themselves in effect thrust into what can best be de-scribed as an 'evangelist' role. Little or nothing is done to define the adviser's exact tasks, or authority, or accountability. Each, being provided with a salary and the minimum of physical facilities, is left as it were to convert others to new points of view on their own initiative, using whatever personal resources of zeal, skill and en-thusiasm that they can muster.

Now, of course, the personal capability of any adviser is a matter of prime importance (as in any job, indeed). If he or she does not have an acceptable personality, appropriate skills and knowledge, and a general ability to tackle work of the level required, then the job will certainly not get well done. However, given this starting point, the organizational arrangements which are then established must, one way or the other, have a profound effect on how well the adviser is able to utilize his own personal resources. Bad organiza-tional arrangements may all but negate the efforts of the individual. Good arrangements, in other words well-devised procedures for link-ing the work of advisers to other established activities, clearly defined roles and authority, and appropriate placing within the organiza-tion, will all considerably enhance them. It is not necessary to assume that superhuman qualities of enthusiasm or diplomacy will be de-manded for this work, more than for any other kind.

When attention is turned to the organizational framework within which advisers are to work, our exploration has shown in fact that there is not just one model for their role but a *range* of possible models amongst which choices have to be made. Moreover, these different models incorporate not one but several different kinds of authority from 'advisory' at one extreme to full 'managerial' at the other.[3] Different models stem from different expectations of what so-called advisers are really there to do.

A variety of reasons are offered for the creation of advisory posts. Frequent reference is made to the need to have staff who can concentrate on 'raising standards'. Particularly in the early days such posts were often seen as a way of filling some of the gaps in the comprehensive ranges of skills necessary for those in the front line of the new general-purpose departments. Other more specific reasons were offered then, as they are still offered now: the need to have staff to 'spearhead' new approaches (for example in community work, or in intermediate treatment, or voluntary work); or to cope with new legislation and its implications; or to monitor standards of actual practice and ensure its consistency across the department; or to maintain specialist excellence; or to co-ordinate and strengthen work in under-developed fields (for example work with the handicapped, under-five-year-old children, the mentally ill); or to strengthen liaison with particular agencies or groups of agencies (for example health authorities or voluntary associations); or to provide specific briefs and information for senior executive staff as and when required; or to investigate continuing problem areas; and so on.

How valid are these justifications? One should start perhaps by reaffirming an obvious point. Staff in the main lines of the managerial structure are themselves responsible for raising standards, co-ordinating, providing information, and so on. Moreover, employing the ideas of Work Strata[4] we should suppose all higher-level operational managers, certainly those expected to work in Stratum 3 or above, to have a strong developmental content to their work and not just to be concerned with staff supervision, or dealing with immediate problems and emergencies.

This still leaves several possible reasons for appointing advisers or the like. They may be required simply to help managers in carrying out detailed explorations and working out detailed schemes. Or they may be appointed in order to provide certain specialist expertise or knowledge which busy generalist managers cannot hope to develop. Again, they may be required to provide an additional dimension of review or co-ordination which 'cuts across' the par-

---

[3] For a discussion of the possible range of authority relationships in organization, see *Social Services Departments,* or *A General Theory of Bureaucracy.*

[4] See Chapter 1.

ticular divisions of responsibility in the existing managerial struc-ture.[5] (For example, it may be felt to be necessary to establish a specialist role to help co-ordinate or review, say, all work with the mentally ill, in a department whose basic structure is divided into field work, residential work, and day care.) In the end, each agency must decide for itself just where such additional posts are necessary at any time, given its own local needs, shortcomings and priorities.

Where any additional post *is* felt to be required, as has become clear from our work, there are four main types or models from which choices must be made according to exactly what kind of need is to be met: (1) a *specialist development officer* model; (2) a *project officer* model; (3) a *staff officer* model; and (4) a *consultant practitioner* model.

We now examine each of the four in detail and the specific needs which each is designed to serve. Finally, we consider certain other activities, not obviously 'advisory' in character, which (it would appear from our research) are nevertheless often undertaken by so-called advisers – the undertaking of monitoring duties, executive decision-making, liaison with other agencies, liaison with geographi-cal sub-units, and the support of more junior specialist staff in the same field. We shall consider how appropriate each may be in its own right, and how it fits or does not fit with any of the four main models.

1. Specialist development officers

The variety of senior specialists already employed in SSDs is legion: specialists in domiciliary care, residential care, fostering and adop-tion, intermediate treatment, casework, group work, community work, the elderly, the mentally ill, the handicapped, the under-five-year olds, etc. Some of these staff carry direct operational responsi-bility, some do not; in other cases again it is unclear. In the course of project work in various authorities and also in conference dis-cussion one possible model for the role of such specialist staff, a model which does not carry any direct operational responsibility, has been identified and defined. It implies not only the possession of appro-priate specialist knowledge and expertise, but also the general ability to work at Stratum 3 level. The main elements of this particular role within the specialist field concerned are as follows:

(*a*) undertaking, as authorized, specific projects: making systematic

---

[5] Thus giving rise to what is often described as 'matrix' organization. See Preface; *Social Services Departments*, Chapter 2; and also Hey, A., (1977), op. cit.

reviews of the level and quality of existing services; producing detailed proposals for improvements in general systems and procedures; and helping to implement agreed proposals;

(*b*) providing on request a continuous source of advice to operational staff who are working on specific cases, and in such specific instances checking for adherence to existing rules or policies (or proposing new ones);

(*c*) keeping abreast generally of new developments and thinking;

(*d*) contributing as required to the development of comprehensive long-term plans, through the provision of advice, ideas and specific information;

(*e*) contributing as required to training and staff-development activities;

(*f*) helping to recruit and select any other more junior staff whose activities or expertise are significantly linked to the field in question, and thus to their special expertise.

Some degree of *co-ordinative* authority will be required both in carrying out investigations and in helping to implement agreed proposals. The provision of advice in particular cases will invariably involve, as we suggest, checking for adherence to rules and policies in the particular case concerned. In some situations (as we discuss later) it may be that the specialist is expected to play an even stronger role in *monitoring* standards in relation to the whole field of activity in question. In none of these instances, however, will it be appropriate for the specialist to carry crucial elements of *managerial* authority in relation to the operational staff at the same level (Stratum 3) or lower level, with whom they deal. It will be inappropriate, for example, for them to intrude into any assessment or appraisal of individual ability or performance; nor will they be expected to arrange for individual training programmes for such staff, reshape their work-roles, or set new policies or limits for them.[6] The only instance in which this last point may not be true may be in relation to lower-level operational staff of the exactly corresponding field of expertise. Here, (as we shall again discuss later) it may be natural for the activity in (f) above to expand into a full 'co-managerial' relationship.

Though the particular kind of model or role which we are dis-

---

[6] For a detailed discussion of the precisely defined concepts of *managerial, co-ordinative*, and *monitoring* relationships, and the differences between them, see *Social Services Departments*, Appendix A. For a brief description see Chapter 2.

cussing here (with or without these additional features) stands distinct from the other three which we shall explore, it is not easy to find a wholly suitable name for it. The identification as a *specialist* is clearly crucial. For the moment we offer 'specialist development officer' (SDO), though this underplays perhaps any monitoring, co-ordinative, or even co-managerial duties that may be built into the role. The title 'specialist adviser' has the same shortcomings. 'Specialist co-ordinator', or 'specialist organizer', both stand as possible alternatives.

2. Project officers

In clear contrast is a second type of role which we have found in a number of departments. Here exploration has revealed the need for members of staff with a high degree of general analytic ability and with certain complementary social skills, but not necessarily with expert knowledge of any particular field, who can devote all their time to undertaking specific investigations on a wide variety of topics as needs and priorities continually shift. Such posts are often referred to simply as 'development officers'. To mark the contrast with SDOs, they may be described alternatively as 'project officers'.

In broad terms, the work expectation of the *project officer* role can be seen as simply to carry out specific projects, as assigned. More fully, it again involves making systematic reviews, producing detailed proposals and helping to implement changes. But, in contrast to the SDO role, the projects may concern any aspect of operational activity, and indeed of supporting service. (The similarity may be noted in passing, between the work of such internal project officers and that of 'organization and methods', 'management services', and 'management consultant', staff who may come into SSDs in order to undertake specific assignments.) Examples of actual projects undertaken by staff of this kind encountered in research include such things as: setting up a new recording system in an area office; reviewing the work of a reception assessment centre; developing a new kind of home help service; exploring the possible use of a new building which had become available by chance.

In certain phases of the work, project officers, like SDOs, will need co-ordinative authority. However, they will not, unlike SDOs, be involved in checking standards in individual cases, or (as for some SDOs) in co-management of more junior operational staff. Senior project officers, or project team leaders, will no doubt be expected to cope with a Stratum 3 level of work. However, in contrast to SDO roles there may be room as well for project officers who, although they may be expected to reach Stratum 3 fairly soon in their careers, are as yet only capable of carrying actual Stratum 2 responsibilities.

Positioning of SDOs and project officers in the departmental structure.
As far as position in the departmental organization is concerned, if the potential work in either an SDO or a project officer post embraces several existing operational divisions, it would seem most logical to place it within some central or support division. If however, the brief only concerns one existing operational division (as say for a specialist in adoption and fostering work in relation to an existing Fieldwork Division) there is an obvious argument for placing it in the division concerned.

In either case, and assuming that the posts in question are pitched somewhere within Stratum 3 (usually corresponding to the lower 'principal officer' grades in present local authority grading structures), their occupants will need the support and guidance of a manager who is firmly in Stratum 4, that is somebody of assistant director or deputy director status or the equivalent. What will probably not serve is a direct line of accountability to a 'senior' adviser who is in fact in terms of grade and capacity only at the top of the third Stratum, and who, for example, is not a regular member of the 'management team' constituted by the director and his immediate subordinates at Stratum 4. In this latter situation our project experience suggests that there are often likely to be complaints from SDOs or project officers of inadequate support and guidance.

Initiating new projects
This last point leads naturally to the question of how work on new projects by either SDOs or project officers is best initiated. Attention has already been drawn to what might be called the 'evangelist' approach. In sharp contrast is what may be described as the 'sanctioned project' approach. In this second approach it is recognized that suggestions for new development projects may come from any source: from middle or senior management, from staff at the service-delivery level, or indeed, from the SDO or project officer him- or herself. However, it is understood that no work can usefully be started on any project of significant size unless the ground has been thoroughly tested, and the existence of adequate sanction established.

Here moreover, 'sanction' must mean a great deal more than the existence of general agreement that the project looks interesting or worthwhile, or that the subject of it justifies attention. At minimum, it must mean that all those who are likely to be affected agree that they are themselves willing to become personally involved in the work to whatever extent is appropriate; and that this particular piece of development work justifies the time and energy that might otherwise be devoted to other competing projects or to dealing with the continual pressure of incoming cases and problems. In order to test sanction, many proposed projects will justify preliminary discussion at full management team meetings of the Director and all his immediate subordinates. Clearly, the sanction of the Head in whose division investigation and change is to take place will be crucial. The agreement of staff at other levels will be important as well.

All this supposes of course that effective procedures exist at various successive strata in the basic management structure itself, for discussing priorities, for sanctioning new investigations, and indeed for discussing recommendations which then flow from them. Our research explorations leave doubt that this is always the case. Indeed, it might be said that the biggest problems in getting systematic development through the use of advisers and the like in SSDs does not lie either with the personality of the individual adviser, or with the precise definition of his role and organizational position, but with the adequacy of functioning of the general departmental management structure, and of the specific machinery for sanctioning and promoting change.

3. *Consultant practitioners*

We come now to a third type of 'adviser' role. In specialist adviser posts, of the type just discussed, the main emphasis is on undertaking specific projects in order to develop procedures and systems applicable to the department as a whole. Detailed intervention in individual cases is minimal or secondary. In the course of project work and conference discussion however, we have become aware of other posts, sometimes still designated as 'advisory', in which the strain is rather the other way; that is, in which the emphasis is on bringing high-level or expert skills to bear in individual cases with the development of general systems or procedures as the secondary function. At the extreme is a conception of a high-level *practitioner*, a practitioner who may also become involved in some limited degree in general departmental co-ordination and development.

Now, there is already a clear move in present-day SSDs towards the creation of more 'senior practitioner', 'career-grade', or 'specialist-practitioner' posts which offer progression for those social workers who do not wish to move to posts with major managerial functions as their careers develop. Our explorations suggest that the majority of such posts are pitched at present within Stratum 2, in the middle or upper zone. Nevertheless, there is scope, in principle at least, for the creation of practitioner posts at Stratum 3 as well.[7] These would almost certainly involve a significant degree of specialization. (Indeed, some specialization of practice is probably implicit in the top Stratum 2 posts as well.) The title 'consultant practitioner' might be an appropriate one. In view of their required level of work, and required specialist knowledge, staff who were considered professionally developed enough to fill them, in addition to direct work with individuals, families, or community groups, might reasonably be expected:

(a) to provide, on request, advice to other practitioners on the handling of specific cases in their specialist field;
(b) to undertake specific development projects in their own field, centred on their own practice;
(c) to contribute to comprehensive long-term planning;
(d) to contribute to training relevant to their own specialism;
(e) to help in staff selection relevant to their own specialism.

Given however, that such staff were primarily practitioners, and that the quality of any other activity undertaken by them was intimately linked to their continuing experience in practice, it follows that any consultant practitioner posts which were established would need to be firmly located in particular operational divisions. If their occupants were to have an influence on thinking and practice through the whole department, it would be likely therefore to be through gradual diffusion of ideas and through training, rather than through their active involvement in general department-wide policy-forming or implementation activities.

Examples of clear Stratum 3 consultant practitioners are few in our own experience, though social workers in hospital or child guidance settings who appear to work at this level often continue to act as direct practitioners in addition to whatever managerial or administrative duties they may perform.[8] It may be that many existing specialist posts in so-called methods such as 'casework', 'group work', or 'community work', are better conceived as consultant practitioner posts, rather than as SDO posts, as just described. How

[7] See Chapter 3, and also Bromley, G. L. (1978), 'Grades and Specialization in Social Work Practice.
[8] See Chapter 3.

large is the potential scope for other full Stratum 3 'consultant' posts, we must however leave as an open question.

The important thing is to mark the distinction between consultant or specialist practitioners on the one hand, and SDOs on the other. Admittedly, there can be consultant practitioners who are frequently involved, say, in department-wide working parties on new practices and procedures; or, on the other hand, SDOs who spend much of their time in giving advice and decisions in individual cases. Particularly where the specialism centres on a type of *service* (for example 'intermediate treatment', or fostering and adoption work) as opposed to a *client group* (for example the mentally ill, or children under-five) it may be felt that the two role-types represent ends of a spectrum rather than distinct categories. But even here it may be useful to consider whether it is primarily the development of a particular point or centre of practice 'excellence' that is required, with spin-offs to other parts of the department as a secondary feature; or whether it is primarily the development of the general approach throughout the whole department that is required, with the establishment of pilot projects as necessary to achieve this object. Even in this case then, the typology may help to identify an important choice.

4. *Staff officers*

Our various contacts with SSDs have revealed another kind of staff, sometimes designated 'advisers' but sometimes given a more general title such as 'principal assistants', who are obviously operating (or intended to operate) at Stratum 3, and whose main job is to help a senior manager in the general task of running a major operational division. Their essential work seems on exploration to be quite a different type again from any of the three main model-types so far described, the specialist development officer, the project officer, or the consultant practitioner. What seems to be present in essence is what may be described as a *staff officer* role. It is a conception for which the general label 'adviser' is in fact particularly ill suited, and at least in order to distinguish it sharply from other models which do lie within the broad umbrella of 'advisory', it demands some attention.

The establishment of a staff officer role may be thought of as a response to a specific need to help those in managerial positions to co-ordinate and control the work of their immediate subordinates, without usurping essential managerial functions or breaking the direct line of accountability. From our work in SSDs, as well as from related work in other fields, it appears that the essential functions of the staff officer are as follows:

(*a*) helping the manager concerned to formulate policies or schemes in the area for which he is responsible, taking into account the experience and views of the manager's other subordinates;

(*b*) seeing that agreed policies or schemes are implemented by the manager's other subordinates: issuing detailed procedures and programmes; ensuring adherence to these programmes; and interpreting agreed policy;

(*c*) dealing with the daily flow of communications and problems coming to the manager: sorting, filtering, exploring and initiating and co-ordinating appropriate responses wherever possible.

Staff officers are expected to be concerned with the internal mechanics: with who does what (staffing and organization) and with what programmes and procedures are necessary to co-ordinate everybody's work in order to reach agreed objectives. They must be available at the manager's right hand, hour by hour, to respond to the constant flow of problems and queries. It is their function to filter these: dealing with some themselves; passing some with or without accompanying comment to the manager; passing some directly to other colleagues for their action. For those matters dealt with personally this means undertaking detailed exploration of the problems posed (usually involving discussion with other staff); issuing instructions to resolve the matter, or raising issues for managerial decision. In this latter case, quite extensive examination of alternative courses of action and their respective pros and cons may be necessary.

It is appropriate for a staff officer to give co-ordinating instructions (though the recipient always has the ultimate right to insist that matters in dispute are referred to the common manager). However, the staff officer should have no authority to set general and continuing limits or policies, or to effect permanent alterations in the role or duties of other colleagues, or to make or contribute to appraisals of personal performance or capacity. Staff officers in fact, regardless of their precise grade, must be seen as working within the same general work stratum as those whose activities they co-ordinate. (On the other hand, the manager concerned is assumed to be working at the next higher Work Stratum.)

Drawing on studies of staff officer posts in various other organizations, it appears that it is often possible to split staff work into a number of distinct parts.[9] So far, however, our work in SSDs has not revealed any natural division of staff work, other than some broad split between 'administrative' topics (finance, logistics, secretarial services and, perhaps, personnel work), and the complementary field of 'operational' issues (treatment of specific cases, introduction of new or revised procedures, etc.). Topics of the first kind are often in fact handled by designated administrative officers or personnel officers.

The essential distinctions between a staff officer role and an SDO role may now be summarized as follows.[10]

Table 8.1   *Distinctions between a staff officer role and an SDO role*

Staff officer	*Specialist development officer*
Always concerned with co-ordination of activities 'across the board'.	May be concerned with services of one particular kind or in one particular sector only.
Works primarily with his or her manager's immediate subordinates only.	Works freely with staff at all levels as needed, as well as with many people from other agencies.
Must work physically close to his or her manager.	Does not need to work physically close to his or her manager.
Issues co-ordinative instructions in continuous flow.	Only issues co-ordinative instructions in implementation phases.

[9] For example in manufacturing it can often be split into three complementary parts: (a) personnel and organizational problems, (b) production planning and scheduling, and (c) production techniques. In the armed forces it is conventionally split into 'A' work (personnel and disciplinary matters), 'Q' work (programming of supplies and services), and 'G' work (operational and training procedures and programmes). Nevertheless, in each case the staff officer still spans the complete range of the manager's (or commander's) responsibility, even if in respect of only one aspect or dimension of work. For further discussion see Brown, W. (1971), *Organization*, Chapter 12, (noting however that he, unlike ourselves, tends to use the expressions 'specialist' and 'staff officer' interchangeably), and Dale and Urwick (1960), *Staff in Organization*, Chapter 5.

[10] In *Social Services Departments* (pp. 73–4) we identified a general kind of activity, namely 'operational co-ordination', which we saw as distinct from a number of other support activities (research, strategic planning, staffing and training, logistics, secretarial and financial work, or public relations), and as justifying the establishment of special support posts in order to carry it out. In effect, we are now able to break such work into two more definite parts, corresponding to the work of 'staff officers' on the one hand, and 'specialist development officers' (or perhaps, 'specialist co-ordinators') on the other.

Other types of work assigned to advisers
Here then are four types or models of roles, none with straightforward operational responsibilities, all carrying an expectation of a Stratum 3 level of work, but otherwise different in most essentials.

It now remains to comment briefly on various other activities which we have found 'advisers', 'development officers', or 'principal assistants' to be carrying out in various departments, and on how fitting each appears to be in its own right, and to all or any of these four main role-types.

Monitoring and inspectorial work
As was noted earlier, the need to have staff who can concentrate on monitoring the standards of operational work actually being achieved in SSDs is one that is frequently mentioned by those who are considering the creation of advisory posts. In practice however, it appears to be very difficult to get such activity effectively established. A closer scrutiny of the very notion of 'monitoring' gives some clues as to why some of the difficulties which occur might be predicted.

In one sense, any exploratory project or review of existing services gives rise automatically to monitoring of standards, at least over the period of time of the investigation concerned and within the limits of its defined scope. In this sense, the problems of monitoring will be integral with the problems of getting *any* development project satisfactorily undertaken (questions of getting adequate sanction for the work, and so on). These problems we have already explored. 'Monitoring' in this sense will be an integral part of any SDO, project officer, or staff officer role, as defined.

We come then to the second, and perhaps stronger, sense in which the word 'monitoring' may be used. Here, some given field or aspect of continuing activity is specified and a duty is established of monitoring it for an indefinite period. The person on whom the duty is laid will be expected to make continuous checks at his discretion, and will need pre-sanctioned right of access at any time, built into the role itself. The carrying out of such work is not unknown in SSDs. There is, for example, a well-established and perfectly viable role for administrative staff in continuously monitoring adherence to budgets and the proper handling of cash.[11]

Could such limited and specific monitoring duties in respect of other aspects of work be assigned to advisers of various kinds without undue conflict? Our project experience for the moment provides no material

[11] See *Social Services Departments,* Chapter 7.

for a very definite answer. Perhaps they might be built into SDO roles at least, without too much difficulty. Indeed, we have already pointed to checking activity intrinsic to the basic SDO role which naturally arises where advice is sought on a particular case. Perhaps such checks at the instigation of those approaching the SDO might be extended also to checks at the instigation or initiative of the SDO himself or herself.

However, the real problems seem to arise when a more general monitoring role is envisaged for any adviser, with a brief to inspect and comment upon a wide range of connected issues in any operational setting. For, the more general and monitoring role the greater the potential conflict with the managerial role. It is after all an integral part of the role of any operational manager to ensure by zooming,[12] personal reviews, visits, and so on, that he has sufficient direct knowledge of the actual services being produced to be able to fulfil his accountability. It must therefore be questioned how far any general inspectorial roles have a place within clear-cut managerial hierarchies, without undermining the position of the managers concerned.[13] In particular, it is questionable, given the basic managerial structure of present-day SSDs, whether such general and continuous monitoring duties are compatible with any of the four role-types which we have considered.

Executive decision-making

We have come across many instances where so-called advisers appear to carry actual executive powers (or something close to them) in relation to specific cases; for example in allocating residential places, or places with foster parents, in making applications to court for rehousing of clients, or in vetting applications for expenditure of various kinds. Clearly, something much more than the offering of take-it-or-leave-it advice is taking place. At the least, advisers doing such work might be conceived as carrying out a monitoring process in order to ensure that established rules and standards are not in danger of being breached, or in helping to develop specifications for new rules and standards. More likely, they might be thought in addition to be making authoritative decisions: to be applying their own best

[12] See Chapter 1.

[13] It is perhaps significant that general inspectorial roles frequently occur precisely where straightforward managerial hierarchy does *not* exist; where, for example, the State wishes to control the basic standards in agencies which it does not directly manage through such things as the Schools Inspectorate, the Factory Inspectorate, or the former Children's Inspectorate.

judgements as to the appropriate action to take in the particular case, thus ensuring perhaps that a consistent response is being achieved by the department as a whole, across all its sections or divisions. Is this appropriate?

The answer depends no doubt on exactly what sort of 'adviser' one has in mind. For example, the making of specific executive decisions which are binding on others, within the framework of given policies, is not in general inconsistent with a staff officer role, as we have already stressed. On the other hand, it would seem obviously inconsistent with a project officer, or a consultant practitioner role. As far as SDOs are concerned, it may be very natural to look to them not only to monitor adherence to policy in certain types of case, but (more positively) to use their specialized skill and experience in judging what is actually the best thing to do in the case concerned. However, if they do so they must necessarily then share some of the accountability for that case and its outcome. The resulting split or diffusion of accountability may or may not be acceptable. If the SDO concerned is sited in the same division as the social workers or others primarily involved in the case, then at least the divisional head concerned will constitute a 'cross-over' point. He, as the common manager of all the staff concerned, will carry ultimate accountability for action in the case concerned, and he will be able to provide a ruling in the event of disagreements. If, however, the SDO is sited within a central, non-operational division (as many will appropriately be), then the departmental director himself will constitute the first common manager, and hence the only firm point of decision in case of disagreement.

Liaison with other agencies

It is far from unusual to find that many 'advisers' have designated liaison duties with other agencies as part of their work, or conversely that those in certain specifically-designated liaison posts are expected to undertake also what are described as 'advisory' functions. Most SSDs currently have, for example, a specifically-designated senior officer with responsibilities for liaison with health services who would also be expected in a general way to 'advise' on health issues. Many SSDs have specialist advisers in designated fields of need – the elderly, children, the handicapped – who carry specific liaison roles with the major voluntary agencies working in these specific fields.

In fact the combination of liaison work with an SDO role seems a very natural one. Liaison work, if carried out at a Stratum 3 level, will involve just the kind of things that SDOs are in any case expected to do, but in respect of two or more agencies at once: developing better systems and procedures, providing advice and help in difficult cases, keeping up-to-date with new developments, contributing to comprehensive planning, and so on. Indeed, even where the *title* of a post happens to be defined solely in terms of liaison with other agencies, the post is nevertheless readily conceivable as an SDO post; one in which the specialist field happens to be defined in terms of a particular external agency and its work, rather than, say, a particular client group or method. It seems unnecessary and confusing to suggest that liaison roles (at Stratum 3) with other agencies, constitute a distinct role type of their own.

Liaison with geographical sub-units
Quite distinct from liaison roles with outside agencies (which should, as we have just suggested, fit easily and naturally with advisory roles of the SDO type) are liaison roles of another type which we have found to exist in several SSDs in which we have worked. Here, head-office staff, often described as 'principal assistants', as well as carrying SDO duties in specialist fields, have assigned to them additional 'liaison' responsibilities in relation to given groups of geographically remote area offices. In practice, this particular combination of duties seems to give rise to problems.

What is really required of advisers in such a situation? Presumably it is something more than that of acting as a two-way message carrier. The danger is that the adviser might be expected to carry something approaching a fully-fledged managerial role. However, this is typically a situation where there is in fact no room for such a role (assuming area officers who work at Stratum 3 and a divisional head who works at Stratum 4).[14] In such situations it is perhaps the case that the need for help in management on the part of the divisional head can better be met by the creation of one or more clear-cut staff officer roles, as we have defined them, each (if more than one) with a particular brief which spans all units of the division concerned.

Supporting more junior staff in the same specialist field
Finally, we come to the complex question of the relationship of specialist 'advisers' to any more junior operational staff who may be working in the same specialist field. Now, the very title 'adviser' might suggest that no responsibility is held for the work of any such staff. In reality it always is the case that close and authoritative links develop

[14] See Chapter 1, for elaboration of the idea of the optimum of one full managerial role per Work Stratum.

between the two, for example between centrally-based 'advisers in domiciliary care' and area-based home help organizers; or between 'advisers for the handicapped' and area-based occupational therapists; or between 'community work advisers' and area-based community workers. Can such special links be justified? If so, what sort of 'advisory' roles result?

Since we are dealing by definition with specialist activity, the most obvious starting point, perhaps, is to test the advisory roles concerned against the SDO pattern. According to the description developed above, any SDO might be expected at least to make a significant contribution to the selection, training, and professional development of more junior staff in their own field of specialism; to co-ordinate them in the introduction of new schemes; and perhaps also to monitor specific aspects of their work on particular cases.

Beyond this, it may well be that some even stronger control or influence of the more junior staff in question is called for. At the extreme, it may be that what is really required in fact, is for the so-called adviser to take full managerial responsibility for the staff concerned and all their work (whether or not the staff are *physically* outposted to work in conjunction with other members of an area team). In this case, of course, the 'advisory' title becomes inappropriate. What results is a straightforward operational manager role.

Often however, it may be some 'co-management' situation that is the most fitting, an arrangement in which the so-called adviser and the local area officer share in a defined way the managerial functions. Here, the local manager would carry operational control, and the specialist manager control over such things as technical methods and career development; both joining in the selection of new staff and in the appraisal of their individual performance in practice.[15]

In any event, what will almost certainly not work is to pretend either that no 'dual influence' situation exists (in the face of all evidence that it does), or that it is unnecessary to try to define the authority and accountability in the two lines of influence concerned.[16]

Conclusion

'Advisers', 'development officers', 'principal assistants' and the like, in posts without clear-cut responsibility for either managing opera-

[15] In this case, generic descriptions such as 'specialist co-ordinator' or 'specialist organizer' might be felt to be more fitting than 'specialist development officer'.

[16] For a further discussion of 'co-management' and the other forms of 'dual influence' organization, see *Social Services Departments*, Chapters 5, 7 and Appendix A.

tional services or for providing services directly to clients, exist in significant numbers in modern large-scale SSDs, and they are probably going to remain. Exactly how many are needed, and with what specific concerns, is another matter, which will depend on where the main managerial structure is seen as in most need of supplementation in any particular department.

However, it appears from our work that reliance on the term 'adviser' as the sole description of such posts is likely only to generate confusion, conflict and frustration. Some further specification is needed, and our finding for the present is that it is probably useful to distinguish at least four main types or models of roles: *specialist development officers* (or some similar title), *project officers*, *staff officers*, and *consultant practitioners*. Each of the four has significantly different implications for behaviour, authority, and often too, for organizational positioning and actual spatial location. General inspectorial roles would constitute a different type again, but their validity in present-day SSDs is doubtful.

9 Intermediate Treatment: In Search of a Policy[1]

by David Billis

Some models and concepts

Flexibility or confusion

The border between flexibility and confusion, if not chaos, can be fragile. We may enter the land of chaos unaware that the boundary has been crossed. Is it too harsh a judgement to suggest that intermediate treatment is slowly sinking in some uncharted marsh? Some observers may feel that this is no bad thing, or that it was always sunk, or that the whole exercise is anyway a metaphysical bluff. The main purpose of this chapter, if we may extend the analogy to the point of exhaustion, is to attempt the business of map construction. The focus will be problems facing SSDs.

From published statements, field projects and conference work it would seem that flexibility does not describe the present situation. At a Brunel conference one intermediate treatment officer saw himself as 'Her Majesty's Loyal Opposition'. Another felt that 'I could talk my head off and nothing happens'. Little progress would appear to have been made since the 1974 Birmingham conference, the report of which clearly indicated widespread discord.[2]

It will be argued that a major cause of confusion is the absence of policy relevant to those entrusted with implementation. Instead we find ambiguous statements of dubious practicability. The ministerial *Guide* seems to abandon the task of policy formulation. In its examination of intermediate treatment the *Guide* states that: 'Given this wide range of possibilities, it is difficult to offer guidance in general terms.'[3]

In the light of the continuing unclarity the Report of the Social Services and Employment Sub-Committee of the House of Commons makes apprehensive reading. It notes: 'with approval that the DHSS

[1] Reprinted (with minor alterations) from *Social Work Service*, no. 11, (1976).
[2] DHSS Development Group (1974), *Intermediate Treatment, Report of a Residential Conference*.
[3] DHSS (1972), *Intermediate Treatment*, para. 17.

is taking a more flexible approach. . . .'⁴ Yet more flexibility – is this the remedy?

We shall refrain from providing any formal description of intermediate treatment or its historical evolution. These can be found in the various references. One lengthy but abbreviated quotation from *Intermediate Treatment Project* may suffice to give the flavour of the minefield laid almost by accident in the 1969 Children and Young Persons Act.⁵ It is pointed out that intermediate treatment is not a term used in the Act but has been adopted since the White Paper 'Children in Trouble' to describe:

> . . . new forms of treatment for children and young persons found to be in need of care or control by a juvenile court. It . . . can only be provided by a requirement . . . added to a supervision order. It is 'intermediate' . . . between (placement) in the care of the local authority, or . . . the care of his parents. It . . . may be exercised at the discretion of the supervisor (who) will have a range of facilities at his disposal, both residential and non-residential, set out under a scheme prepared by the Children's Regional Planning Committee. . . . facilities . . . in the main already being used by (others) not subject to supervision orders. It is intended to enable a child to develop new and beneficial attitudes and activities. . . .⁶

What emerges from this and other documents is the unclarity about:

(*1*) who is the object of attention (the client group);
(*2*) what the clients are going to receive (the work and its objectives);
(*3*) where the work is to take place (the setting);
(*4*) how the work is to be performed (method).

It is hardly surprising that the phrase 'intermediate treatment' has been stretched to the point of an all embracing 'continuum of care'.⁷ Organizational life abhors a vacuum. Lack of explicit frameworks for implementation (e.g. policies) can consequently lead to phenomena such as 'ad hocery', charismatic leadership, personal networks and other informal manifestations replacing rather than complementing agreed objectives. In the absence of policy each of the above variables (*1*) to (*4*) can be seized upon as the panacea for social maladies. Thus we may be excused for occasionally assuming that intermediate treatment is the sole property of some imaginary 'Union for the Propagation

⁴ HMSO (1975), 'Eleventh Report from the Expenditure Committee, Session 1974–1975, vol. 1, para. 117.
⁵ DHSS Development Group (1973), *Intermediate Treatment Project*.
⁶ ibid.
⁷ Paley, J. and Thorpe, D. (1974), *Children: Handle with Care*.

of Group Work', or an 'Anti-Residential League', or even some 'Wholesome Outdoor Activities Society'. We shall suggest that protagonists in the debate are in fact proposing, with varying degrees of precision, alternative models or theories of intermediate treatment. These models do two things: they emphasize different answers to the questions (Who? What? Where? How?), and they imply different levels of provision.

A major task of this chapter will be to construct a limited number of models which appear to be relevant for problem solving inside SSDs. It might then be possible to engage in critical examination of what is really being proposed, the degree of its desirability and feasibility.

The unanswered questions

Theses in plenty await students attempting to answer these questions but limited space compels generalization. If intermediate treatment, whatever model is advocated, is considered as a responsibility of a social services department, either to implement directly or to initiate with other agencies, we might be hard pressed to discover something new. We may find that most of the models could be, and in some cases have been, implemented without the 1969 legislation. Further, that the real novelty and organizational indigestibility of the concept lies in attempts to superimpose packages of 'treatment' for a defined client group upon a qualified 'generic' structure. This point will be returned to later.

(*1*) *Who?* At this stage we wish to stress that, whatever else is in dispute, it is children who are the focal point of intermediate treatment. But which children? Project and some conference work indicates that there exists differentiation, even perhaps an unavoidable gradation, of priorities within this client group. Departments have obligations to children:

(*a*) under court orders which are different and may take precedence over
(*b*) children at risk and which are different still from
(*c*) children in at risk neighbourhoods.

Finally there are 'normal' children in non-risk neighbourhoods, a group which does not fall within the remit of SSDs.

(*2*). *What?* The second question to be answered is: what work is being performed? It is perhaps worth stressing that work is 'purposeful' and that statements about what is being done can easily be transformed into why statements (e.g. objectives). The three broad categories of intermediate treatment work that appear to vie for consideration are those concerned with:

(*a*) improving social functioning
(*b*) improving educational attainment
(*c*) the provision of social, cultural and recreational activities.

(*3*) *Where?* Where is the work taking place? It can be carried out in a variety of settings:

(*a*) in the client's home
(*b*) at a centre or site
(*c*) in a residential establishment.

Like the other subdivisions of the main variables, boundaries need clarification, in particular those between centre and residential establishment. Following but amending the work of Goffman, it is suggested that only when sleep, play and school are the responsibility of the authority, should there be talk of residential care.[8] Weekend and holiday activities would not be residential care, as defined, since school time is not affected. The discussion is not pedantic since confusion over the term's usage is widespread in the documentation. Centre, or perhaps better, site based activities would then be all those which are provided at some distinct site, whether it be a club, a Welsh field, or the corner café.

(*4*) *How?* How is the work being performed? Each individual brings to his or her work a specific style and approach. Whilst styles can be described, we do not intend to attempt the task, which may be neither possible nor desirable, of defining styles to the point where they could be regarded as variables in their own right.

We are content to note three major work methods, remembering that these and the other main variables could be further and more finely divided. The methods are work with:

(*a*) individuals
(*b*) groups
(*c*) communities.

These four major areas of unclarity have been identified in the discussion of intermediate treatment. In turn each such area of confusion can be filled by a number of different and sometimes competing approaches. To take just one area, the clientele, emphasis might be placed primarily on schemes for children and young persons under

[8] Goffman, E. (1961), *Asylums*.

court orders, for children considered at risk, or for those in at risk neighbourhoods. Of course this still does not portray the full complexity since schemes may cover some combination of the different categories of children. But before moving on to further elaborations a table of the variables we have outlined is presented in Table 9.1.

Table 9.1   Key variables in intermediate treatment

(1) Who? Clientele	(2) What? Work	(3) Where? Setting	(4) How? Method
(a) Court orders	(a) Social functioning	(a) Home	(a) With individuals
(b) At risk	(b) Educational	(b) Site	(b) With groups
(c) In at risk neighbourhoods	(c) Social, cultural, recreational	(c) Residential	(c) With communities

Tentative models of intermediate treatment
The variables listed in Table 9.1 might be regarded as discrete parts of a Meccano. With their aid we are enabled to build some tentative models. Indeed our construction is subject to not dissimilar laws, the most pertinent being the thought that there might be natural combinations or clusters of variables.

Before continuing this theme it is necessary to draw attention to one additional cause of confusion. This is the difference between intermediate treatment considered as isolated projects and something wider, as at least the systematic provision of a range of facilities. This distinction will be returned to later. At this juncture it may be noted that these two different notions are rarely disentangled and for the remainder of this chapter, unless specifically qualified, intermediate treatment will refer to both projects and ranges.

To return to model construction. The starting point is the client group, the core element in the controversy. Let us assume that the department wishes to concentrate its efforts on children under court orders. It may be that this decision attracts specific variables. For example it may be necessary to emphasize work in the field of social functioning and education in a residential centre primarily utilizing a one to one method. This model is intended to illustrate the way in which a common and agreed language for comparative discussion can be established. It is not an ideal type or prescriptive suggestion. It is set out in Table 9.2 and for ease of analysis has been called the 'court' model. Likewise four other examples of model building are provided.

We must now consider levels of provision, a crucial refinement to our models if we are to analyse whether and how they can co-exist with SSDs and regional planning committees.

Table 9.2   Examples of intermediate treatment models

Prime client group	Other variables emphasized (from Table 9.1)	Possible title for model
Court orders	$2(a) + 2(b)$; $3(c)$; $4(a)$	Court
At risk	$2(a)$; $3(a) + 3(b)$; $4(a) + 4(b)$	Referral
In at risk areas	$2(c)$; $3(b)$; $4(b) + 4(c)$	Neighbourhood
Court + at risk	Various permutations	Distress
Court, at risk, in at risk areas	Various permutations	Preventive

Different levels of provision – some concepts[9]
Unfortunately we have not exhausted the problems. So far we have indicated the way in which certain variables can be used to build models. One important dimension is still lacking – the level of provision. Some possibilities are outlined below. They will shortly be used to analyse a few of the current problems.

One possibility noted already is that intermediate treatment will be provided as one or more isolated projects (each project could be different). For example a department may have three projects. One project accepts children under court orders (court model); two others are aimed primarily at children thought to be at risk (referral model). Overall the department can be said to be providing intermediate treatment for (some) children under orders and at risk (distress model). Some children in the authority get intermediate treatment, others do not. This limited level of provision will be called situational response (Stratum 2) provision.

Distinct from this is a broader and qualitatively different response. Here projects are regarded as part of a developing and distinct intermediate treatment provision. Projects are seen as inter-related and as part of an intermediate treatment provision which has to be shaped to the needs of a continuing sequence of situations. This will be called Stratum 3 provision.

Yet another distinct jump is made when it is decided that even systematic provision is not enough. What is now required is comprehensive (Stratum 4) provision. The entire territory is to be provided

[9] See Chapter 1.

with a particular model. Some person or group is charged with this comprehensive coverage and must:

(a) have the supporting resources to seek out need;
(b) plan responses;
(c) reallocate existing resources;
(d) recommend capital investments.

We contend, and shall endeavour to illustrate, that confusion concerning the level of provision compounds that already existing from the absence of agreed models.

Models and concepts in action

The intermediate treatment officer
The difference between situational response and systematic service provision can be illustrated by an example from the experience of a London borough. The borough set up and utilized a number of different intermediate treatment projects and facilities with various client groups (from Table 9.1) participating. Although there was an intermediate treatment officer, it was unclear whether his prime concern was to supervise existing activities, develop policy for a range of projects or a mixture of both. The boundaries to the variables outlined in this paper had not been clarified. The officer was caught between organizing group work, outdoor and site activities, and the expectation to be involved in departmental and inter-departmental policy development. He had no agreed authority of any kind over many of the other staff involved in the overall intermediate treatment endeavour. Finally, his place in the hierarchy was too low to provide the right kind of interaction.

After clarification with an external researcher-analyst a policy statement emerges. The preventive model is adopted, but limited to the age group 10 to 18. Emphasis is to be placed primarily, but not exclusively, on group work in a non-residential setting using many of the work variables, including education, with the co-operation of the education department.

The role of the intermediate treatment officer begins to be redefined. Clearer lines of accountability are drawn and his position is seen as roughly equivalent to that of the area officer, assumed to be working at Stratum 3. The move from situational response to systematic service provision begins. Now the officer becomes more of a co-ordinator, in addition to managing other intermediate treatment staff accountable for specific projects. The focal point of the officer must be the initiation of policies for the development of intermediate treatment as defined by the borough. This example shows that an explicit policy embracing both the variables and the level of provision is required, if intermediate treatment officers are to be fitted into existing social services departmental structures.

In the post Seebohm structures it is primarily work in the residential and day care settings which has retained client group as the main defining factor. The community based area office, a key Seebohm concept, provides a flow of services which is not in the main geared to a specific group of clients. Notions of intermediate treatment, however, often imply that resources will also be provided, in the community, for special units, projects and schemes of service delivery for children.

If a situational response model of intermediate treatment is implemented in a functionally organized department, it may well merge, with no more than the occasional hiccup, into one of the mainstreams (fieldwork, residential or day care). Like the community work projects in some authorities, intermediate treatment in this model would have no distinct organizational existence on the systematic service level but would be under the control of the area officer, residential or day care manager. The merger may be particularly bloodless if the (Stratum 2) model of intermediate treatment also emphasizes residential or day care variables, and consequently has a lower propensity to overlap with area field organizations. In other departmental structures, such as those based on geography, intermediate treatment officers might also find themselves subject to the control of development officers or other specialist staff. This narrow interpretation raises question marks over the usage of intermediate treatment as a meaningful term. Is it, cynics might wonder, a case of much ado about very little? The only novelty, noted already, would be the half-hearted attempt to impose a package of treatment for a defined legal category of client. (Paragraph 188 of the Seebohm Report makes salutory reading: '... assistance to children on the basis of legal categories inhibits the use of the most appropriate services ...').

If, as may be likely, SSDs attempt to implement broader models (distress and preventive) as a systematic service provision, major difficulties can be encountered. If in addition these broader models encompass all the possible variables, the continuum of care approach, a new children's department would appear to have been grafted on to the existing structures. Paley and Thorpe are well aware of this, although they hedge their bets by declaring that: 'an analogous structure (to the old children's departments) within the generic social services would not necessarily negate the intentions of the Seebohm Report.'[10] The 'not necessarily' is not elaborated.

The regional planning committee – a comment
What level of intermediate treatment work are the regional planning committees expected to perform? According to Sir Keith Joseph they are meant to 'co-ordinate' the work of voluntary and statutory agencies through 'comprehensive schemes of "intermediate treatment"'.[11] Later the same document strikes a more energetic tone. Their task should be 'the development of a suitable range of facilities ... throughout the country'. Is the work of the committees Stratum 3 where the major limitation is the existence of substantive organizational resources for a particular kind of service? Or are they meant to be in the Stratum 4 business, with the pre-requisites noted earlier?

In the absence of research findings we must be content to raise logical questions that appear to stem from our analysis. At a guess it would seem that it is hoped that committees will provide a 'comprehensive intermediate treatment' (Stratum 4) response without being provided with the necessary resources or authority.

Conclusion
What we appear to have is a statutory expectation to establish a network of ill-defined social work provisions for children in trouble. We have discussed the way in which various theories of intermediate treatment vie for primacy and have touched upon some of the organizational problems. In the short term the slogan of flexibility can permit confusion to be tucked under departmental carpets. It is questionable how long this state of indecision can be maintained. Project officers are looking for guidance. Too often they can be the rejected foreign matter in a statutory heart transplant. Their natural linkages with area officers and other operational sections will continue to be uneasy unless higher level policy is enunciated.

In formulating policies departments have to decide what model to adopt and whether it is to be a peripheral situational response or a major systematic service provision. Expectations may prove to be unrealistic. Failure to provide guidelines could lead to a rapid turnover of intermediate treatment staff. There are already precedents in the short lives of the new departments.

[10] Paley and Thorpe (1974), op. cit., p. 97.
[11] DHSS (1972), op. cit., p. 5.

This paper is both brief and preliminary. We have concentrated on SSDs since it is difficult to see that intermediate treatment could be analysed in a realistic manner until departments clarify their own positions. In so doing less than justice has been done to other involved statutory and voluntary agencies. It is believed, however, that the concepts and models will be valid even when these additional bodies are included.

10 'Development' in Social Services Departments: the Birth of Administrative Obscurity[1]

by David Billis

In defence of hair-splitting

It is not often that we have the opportunity to explore in some detail the introduction of a new administrative concept. Sometimes the exploration is not a luxury but a necessity. An organization, or set of organizations, may embark on an anticipated mild flirtation with the newcomer. The affair becomes more serious. The term spreads, takes root, and over the years its origins become shrouded in mystery. There may even be a correlation between ambiguity and administrative longevity. Portmanteau terms implying much and saying little may suit a particular strategy.[2] Enquiry into the meanings behind organizational vocabulary may appear to be fruitless, or counterproductive. Why bother? Undertaking the daunting task of analysing the word 'administration', Dunsire finds it necessary to pose a similar question. 'Does it matter?' After all: 'To a practising administrator, of all men, cerebration about "administration" in the abstract goes decidedly against the grain ...'[3] Dunsire's defence of 'hair-splitting' suits well our own purposes. 'Distinctions are hair-splitting (he argues), only so long as we do not need them for purposes of our own; if we do come to need them, yet do not quite realize it, we may go on using one term in several senses, and fail to communicate.'[4] W. Brown writes in similar vein. He points out that concepts depend on

[1] Reprinted (with minor alterations) from *Public Administration*, no. 54, Summer 1977.
[2] Donnison, D. V. *et al.* (1970), *Social Policy and Administration*, pp. 118–19.
[3] Dunsire, A. (1973), *Administration: The Word and the Science*, p. viii.
[4] ibid., p. ix.

'shared perceptions', that mental models depend on concepts and that without such models we cannot understand social institutions.[5] Hair-splitting may therefore be seen as an essential component of concept and model building. And on this more general issue of model building we close the defence with a comment of the late Richard Titmuss: 'The purpose of model building is not to admire the architecture of the building, but to help us to see some order in all the disorder and confusion of facts, systems and choices concerning certain areas of our economic and social life.'[6] Analysis has its dangers. Bell and Newby discussing theories of 'community' refer to the 'thriving sociological industry' in which the *pièce de résistance* was Hillery's analysis of no fewer than ninety-four definitions.[7] Our discussion of development is not intended to join that particular industrial scene. We are concerned with disentanglement, with hair-splitting as a prelude to model-building and organizational problem solving.

Development as a phenomenon of social services departments

Of course the introduction of a particular term in one context may be greeted elsewhere with yawns of *déjà vu*. The analysis that follows may have, at least in part, wider significance. The main purpose however, is the attempt to capture a phase in the history of a set of organizations (SSDs) in order to illustrate the way in which new terminology is introduced in response to changed objectives and the ease with which problems become buried and obscured by the new language.

We start by noting that the term we shall be exploring is essentially a 'post Seebohm' phenomenon.[8] It can hardly be accidental that the creation of SSDs after 1970 brought in its wake a trail of new distinctive phrases. Development, research, planning, training (amongst others) have blossomed in the wake of the mainstream activities. The Seebohm Committee was anxious lest its proposals be seen merely as a reshuffle of existing functions: '... we have stressed that we see our proposals ... as embodying a wider conception of social service, directed to the well-being of the whole of the community and not

[5] Brown, W. (1971), op. cit., pp. 19–20.
[6] Titmuss, R. M. (1974), *Social Policy*, p. 30.
[7] Bell, C. and Newby, H. (1971), *Community Studies*, p. 27.
[8] HMSO, the Home Office *et al.* (1968), *Report of the Committee on Local Authority and Allied Personal Social Services* (the Seebohm Report), Cmnd 3703.

only of social casualties ...'[9] Whether the brave new role allocated to the departments has in fact materialized is a moot point. These are early days to be passing judgements. The relevant point for our discussion is, however, precisely the organizational consequence of the changed objectives. The Committee itself was quite aware that the leap to 'community tasks' would necessitate a 'community focus' and talked somewhat vaguely about '... developing and utilizing research and intelligence services ...'[10] Indeed, one member of the Committee, writing just before the implementation of the Report, saw the proposed intelligence and research units not only as providing data on 'real needs', but also as a political lever at local and national level. That is to say that local authorities would have an eye on what level of provision their neighbours were providing and central government might also '... encourage the less ambitious authorities to raise their standards' where such authorities were below the average.[11] Other authors used development as an activity in its own right.[12] We are suggesting therefore, that development is one of those terms that stems from the creation of departments which are not merely *amalgamations* but 'creative innovations'.[13]

We shall see that the term has now become an organizational potpourri, the ingredients of which are no longer readily identifiable. One of our central themes will be that by establishing duties, posts and sections with a development tag, SSDs might be responding to a number of different phenomena and that the absence of 'shared perceptions' can leave the real problems to fester. The following exploration highlights a number of major situations where development has been utilized as a convenient organizational response, i.e. as a response to: (1) criticism of existing standards; (2) problems of organizational structure; (3) absence of new activities. Finally, we shall consider the notion of development as social experimentation.

Development as a criticism of existing standards

A familiar complaint is that standards of service in SSDs have

[9] ibid., para. 474.

[10] ibid., para. 502.

[11] Parker, R. A. (1970), 'The Future of the Personal Social Services', p. 113.

[12] Kogan, M. and Terry, J., (1971); *The Organization of a Social Services Department: A Blueprint*, Rowbottom, R. W. and Hey, A. M., (1970). 'Towards an Organization of Social Services Departments'.

[13] Shumpeter, J. A., 'The Creative Response in Industry', *Journal of Economic History*, vol. 7, pp. 149–59, November 1947.

deteriorated. The accuracy, or otherwise, of this criticism is not a direct preoccupation of this paper (although it is difficult to imagine that standards could be raised without solving some of the acute problems illustrated). Here the important factor is that some departments judge that standards have fallen. Consequently, in an effort to make good the shortfall, new posts may be established. Has a genuine diagnosis been made? Will the new post provide a remedy? In many cases, we suggest, criticisms made about the quality of service delivery are in fact judgements of the work of specific individuals and groups and their inability to achieve expected levels of performance, an inability which might be attributed to a failure in personal capacity or other reasons, such as inadequate resources.[14] These two possibilities are illustrated in Figures 10.1 and 10.2.

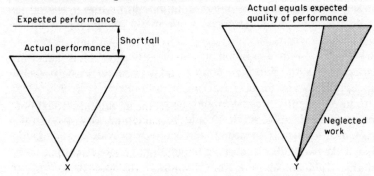

Figure 10.1 (*left*)   *The shortfall between expected and actual performance*
Figure 10.2 (*right*)   *Amount of work neglected when the actual quality of performance equals that expected*

In both examples staff x and y are expected to attain a more or less specific level of performance. As Jaques has shown, all work contains both prescribed and discretionary elements, although: 'At times it may seem that so much of the content of responsibility may be prescribed that little or no discretion appears to be left in a job.'[15] If we reduce the discretionary content of a job to near zero we 'dehumanize it. It can be better done by a machine'.[16] Building on the work of Jaques, the author and colleagues have been engaged in developing a theory of the stratification of work in organizations. From this emerging

[14] For a comprehensive statement of the nature of 'capacity', see *A General Theory of Bureaucracy*. Also Billis, D. (1977), 'Differential Administrative Capacity and Organizational Development', pp. 109–27.

[15] Jaques, E. (1967), op. cit., p. 79.

[16] ibid., p. 81.

theory we put forward the thesis that there is a hierarchy of discrete work strata in which the range of the ends or objectives to be achieved, and the range of environmental circumstances to be taken into account, both broadens and changes in quality at each successive step.[17] The relevance for our present discussion is that it is only in the lowest stratum of work (Stratum 1) that output can be completely specified (as far as is significant) beforehand; i.e. that *output* (not discretion) can be prescribed. At Stratum 2 and above, the output can only be partially specified beforehand – appraisal and assessment of the situation are required. In social work the critical boundary would be between those staff who are judged to be capable of being accountable for a case (Stratum 2), and those who are not (Stratum 1). This is a distinction of considerable significance for departments and society. More detailed examination of this theme would take us far afield; its application for social work in the residential setting is analysed elsewhere.[18]

We are now in a position to see that the level of performance expected of x and y in Figures 10.1 and 10.2 might be more or less susceptible to any form of external measurement. It is only where outputs are tightly prescribed and discretion minimal that measurement of 'standards of service' could be attempted. And even in this case measurement is hazardous and can only provide a crude guideline. Take two authorities whose populations cannot be distinguished in any significant way one from the other in terms of their needs for meals on wheels. Both authorities provide exactly the same number of meals per thousand of the population. Can we deduce that 'standards of service' are identical in both departments? Closer investigation would be required before any conclusion was reached. How, for example, are the meals being delivered? What is the nature of the interaction between the deliverer of the meal and the recipient? Are the meals being provided with courtesy and sensitivity – or deposited on the doorstep as a chore to be completed as rapidly as possible? When we attempt the more difficult task of measuring in quantitative terms outputs which can be partially prescribed – not meals but social work intervention – the link with reality becomes tenuous to the point of illusion.

Diagrammatic representation, as in Figures 10.1 and 10.2, should not be misconstrued. Performance, both actual and expected, assumes the presence of human evaluation – an elementary observation, but one which sometimes gets lost in the rush for the comforting concrete-

[17] See Chapter 1.
[18] See Chapter 5.

ness of mathematical data. The figures depict a situation where an 'area' of work, represented by the clear triangles, needs to be covered by x and y. But the two examples represent different situations.

In Figure 10.1 the judgement is that x really cannot 'deliver the goods'. Perhaps x has been over-promoted. Narrowing the spectrum of work is not seen to be a solution. The prognosis is that this would lead to less work being performed without any significant improvement in quality. Yet departments sometimes create new posts, possibly graded more highly than x, in the hope that the missing quality will be injected into the scene. In addition to x, who in all probability is retaining his original post and title, a new 'super x' is brought in to cover the same area of work. The missing quality (development) may, depending on local custom, appear as part of the new title. Alternatively, or in addition, it may loom large in the more detailed job description. Burns and Stalker refer to the familiar managerial strategy of 'bringing somebody in': 'A new job, or possibly a whole new department, may then be created, which depends for its survival on the perpetuation of the difficulty.'[19]

Organizational man, like the battery-hen, requires a minimum of space to survive. It is a puzzling thought that SSDs with their particular approach and core of staff trained in interpersonal skills appear to be, as yet, as prone to the same bureau-pathologies as other organizations.

Figure 10.2 is different. Here y is judged to be suitable, but not to have been provided with adequate resources – he is overloaded. Consequently, an area of work (shaded in the Figure) is neglected. Some of the choices available to the department would appear to be:

(*a*) to do nothing:
(*b*) to reallocate y's workload, some (not necessarily the shaded) functions being neglected;
(*c*) to reduce y's workload;
(*d*) to increase resources;
(*e*) to provide 'specialist' manpower.

This last strategy is of particular interest since it can lead to a second possible use of the word 'development'. Not, as in Figure 10.1, an injection of required quality. And not, as in choice (*d*) above, the provision of additional 'conventional' workers; but the introduction of some 'specialist' worker. Specialist is relative. It depends for its existence and meaning on that which is regarded as generalist. If there is no *qualitative* change in the work performed – a move to another work

[19] Burns, T. and Stalker, G. M. (1968), op. cit., p. x.

stratum – it merely means, in the words of Simon, 'that different persons are doing different things'.[20]

So we have identified two distinct and conflicting usages of the term 'development'. In Figure 10.1 an infusion of additional quality, a striving to attain an appropriate level of performance. But who is not in this form of the development business? Certainly, if top and middle management are not engaged in development of this sort something may be thought to have gone seriously astray. If, on the other hand, development is equated with a move into specialist work, why use the term at all? Used in this fashion, the word can be misleading, implying that other staff are not engaged in 'development'.

Job titles attract expectations. Advisers will expect to advise, consultants to be consulted, training officers to train. The title may not reflect that which is really expected from the role holder. Advice and consultancy may not be sought, training officers may be bewildered to discover that there is little direct training for them to do. As yet we have by no means exhausted the situations to which the title 'development' is a response.

Development as a response to problems of organizational structure

SSDs are not only much larger than the sum of their predecessors, they are vastly more complex. One director, presumably with some feeling, has referred to them as 'growing monsters'.[21] They are faced with a wide range of structural problems which are manifested in difficulties of the co-ordination of services, systems, 'awkward' and small scale activities. A tempting response has been to label everything that is not easily integrated – development. In other words: 'getting it together' (co-ordination) = development.

Essentially, problems of co-ordination flow from a well-known conundrum. How do we cut the organizational cake and still retain its wholeness – and wholesomeness? The more complex and ambitious the work of the organization, the greater the problems of co-ordinating the various parts.[22] When we are discussing departments which are not just growing in numbers of staff employed but are also passing through a stage of creative innovation, we discover problems of co-ordinating existing activities – and the 'non-existent'. First we shall examine in this section that which exists.

[20] Simon, H. A. (1967), *Administrative Behaviour*, p. 22.

[21] Westland, P., reviewing a book in *British Journal of Social Work*, vol. 4, no. 4, Winter 1974.

[22] Greenwood, R. *et al.* (1975), 'Contingency Theory and the Organization of Local Authorities: Part I, Differentiation and Integration'.

In general, SSDs have moved towards either a functional or geographical model of organization. That is to say, that the second tier of operational management is either assistant directors, fieldwork, residential and day care (or some similar titles), or divisional directors of 'mini-departments'. We will not discuss here the minutae of departmental structures; it is sufficient to note that both models have advantages and disadvantages, and that local circumstances play a large part in shaping the preferred structure. In both instances co-ordination can be considered at least at two distinct levels. At the grass roots, the delivery of Stratum 2 services to clients; and at the level of systems (Stratum 3) the provision of frameworks within which those services can be provided in an integrated and acceptable fashion. Whilst the different overall structures will lead to variations in the precise nature of service and systems co-ordination, it is contended that the same approach can be adopted. Experience indicates that the term 'development' is primarily used in the context of systems co-ordination. However, in view of the weaknesses in the area of service co-ordination identified in a number of reports of individual tragedies which have aroused much public concern, a brief digression would appear to be warranted.

Clients receive services from the department in a number of different settings and from a number of different specialist workers and occupational groups. It may well prove necessary to create some mechanism for co-ordinating *cases*, where a case is defined as: '. . . an instance of the situation presented by any person or family registered by the department as in need of help or action by the department.'[23] The mechanism suggested in *Social Services Departments* is that of case co-ordination.[24] This is illustrated in Figure 10.3, where x_2, y_2 and z_2 represent workers providing services to the client. We turn next to

[23] See *Social Services Departments*, p. 251.

[24] The definition of case co-ordination provided in *Social Services Departments*, p. 252, is as follows:

(a) proposing necessary tasks in relation to the total needs, short- and long-term, of the case; (and then, assuming agreement):
(b) negotiating co-ordinated work programmes and procedures;
(c) arranging the allocation of existing resources to colleagues or arranging the provision of additional resources where necessary;
(d) keeping informed of action and progress in the case;
(e) helping to overcome problems encountered by other colleagues;
(f) providing relevant information to other colleagues, including information on progress;
(g) reporting on progress to superior.

systems co-ordination, a more fertile and complex field for the introduction of development.

If we return to the problem of the division of activities and the
analogy of the organizational cake, we can identify two Stratum 3
(systems) activities – within and across the 'slices'.

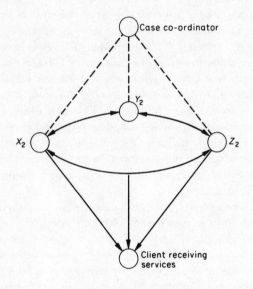

Figure 10.3   Case co-ordination

The production of 'within the slice' systems should be straightforward or simple, resulting from the existence of one clear-cut
accountable manager (see Figure 10.4). It is the increasing number
of 'cross-slice' or complex interactions which present more intractable
problems. The differentiation associated with the division of labour
calls forth a wide variety of integrative devices – the ubiquitous
working party being an outstanding example. Another possibility,
where integration is required on an ongoing basis, is to create a
separate role with general cross-slice duties, possibly a common reason
for the establishment of 'development officer' posts (see Figure 10.5).
This kind of role which stems from integrative reasons can be distinguished from the sort of specialist illustrated in Figure 10.2.

The examples in Figures 10.3, 10.4 and 10.5 attempt to illustrate
the propositions made so far. For diagrammatic simplicity the organi-

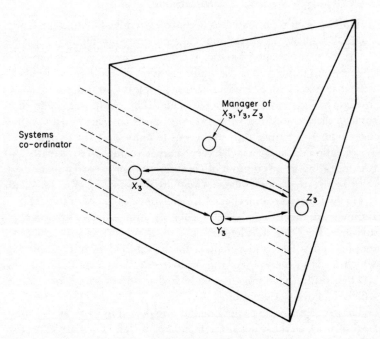

Figure 10.4   Simple systems co-ordination

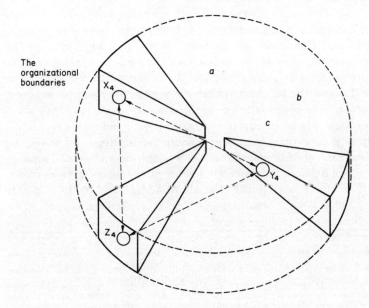

Figure 10.5   Complex systems co-ordination

zation has been represented as a closed system.[25] The diagrams, the single slice of the organizational cake illustrated in Figure 10.4, and the more complex position represented in Figure 10.5, ignore the open-system implications. In reality, systems co-ordinators are likely to be in contact with a large number of people inside and, particularly in Figure 10.5, outside the department. The point was made that some of these co-ordinative (Stratum 3) posts have attracted the title 'development'. Figure 10.5 enables us to appreciate the dynamics of organizational change which have led to such titling. We reiterate that it is mistitling as a symptom of confusion which we are pursuing.

In Figure 10.5 six members of staff are depicted: x_4, y_4, z_4, a, b and c. The first three are entrenched in an explicit segment of the organization – in the case of SSDs probably functional or geographic divisions. Each has an identifiable boss, a network of colleagues for support and advice, and a chain of command (whatever its problems) which leads to the apex of the department. Now consider a, b and c. Their duties have not been indicated in the diagram for reasons which demand examination.

They (a, b and c) are appointed and expected to work at the same level of work as the other three members of staff. They are expected to provide frameworks within which cohesive service-delivery can take place, although they may also, in varying degrees, become involved in the direct provision of services. But, in this example, they have no firm organizational base since the focus of their work does not fit precisely into one of the existing segments, nor is there any real common denominator spanning these 'isolates'. They may be working on their own, or with a few subordinate staff. Their line of accountability might be dubious, the post itself is likely to be new, the result perhaps of a sudden piece of legislation or of the creative innovation. They share only one common feature – organizational indigestibility. They straddle the existing bases of organization. Sometimes, at one and the same time, they represent the exciting and the awkward. Training, community work, intermediate treatment, voluntary service officers, liaison officers with health – all are candidates for the development tag. In like fashion, organizational bases that have been abandoned, or never implemented, re-emerge in the guise of specialist or 'development' posts (for example, those based on client group or social work method). These too have now an 'across the slice' focus. Co-ordination, integration, policy making (as we have defined it) – this is what all these posts are really about. Why not use a title that provides a less confusing sense of the main thrust of the work?

Further difficulties can arise when *a*, *b* and *c* are integrated into one development division with terms of reference which do not stand up to scrutiny. It is highly debatable whether the small SSD development divisions (usually combined with some additional title) can sustain substantial inner tensions. It might be more logical to link *a*, *b* and *c* into the segment with the closest mutual interest. That, of course, on the assumption that having removed any obscurity buried by mistitling, the need for the posts still exists! Combining a number of roles such as those we are now describing into one 'convenient' group causes (in the experience of this researcher) tensions at two levels. Staff at the same level strongly miss the existence of a collegiate or sentient group – it is difficult, if not impossible, to create any 'team spirit', any sense of common purpose. Above this their manager is placed in an invidious position. Where is he or she leading this disparate group? What widespread range of talent is necessary to guide and support these middle level policy makers (*a*, *b* and *c*)? There *is* an attempt at rationalization. All are concerned with the development of systems and 'resources'. Some of the individual components of development divisions make strange bedfellows: covering them with a seemingly attractive bedcover may not be a long-term alternative to the provision of a good home. At this juncture the notion of any shared perception about the meaning of development collapses. This would appear to be an extension of the argument used when discussing Figures 10.1 and 10.2. The same answer can be given. Which higher-level staff are not in the development business?

Development as a response to the absence of new higher-level activities

Functions or activities can be absent in two senses:

(*1*) We may *state* that they are present; but this manifest statement may not match reality.
(*2*) They really can be absent in explicit form from organizational life.

(*1*) *The manifest-reality mismatch*

We have already mentioned cases where recognized work was not being performed. We are concerned in this section with a very different situation. What is absent is a qualitatively higher level (or stratum) of work. Indeed, a large part of the difficulty lies in the absence of a comparative organizational language which would facilitate a constructive dialogue. Sadly, many existing job descriptions raise a hollow laugh from their incumbents. They (job descriptions) would appear to be most effective at the most tangible level – what we would call Stratum 1 work, where the output is prescribed. Not the least of our research problems is the continuing pursuit, where the need is felt, for a more precise and acceptable language. But more of this later. We are suggesting that some new, expected, qualitatively 'higher' (above Stratum 2) activities might in fact exist only at lower levels, and that part of the trouble flows from the fact that there is no common agreement about the nature of the work. Some examples may aid in the elaboration of this theme.

A cursory glance at the formal headquarters hierarchy of SSDs is adequate to impress us with the bewildering number of permutations of planning, research, training and development.[26] Indeed, each of these is often preceded by some qualifying term, e.g. forward planning, capital development, social environmental development.... What do these titles really mean? What is a 'research officer'?[27] Are departments hiring staff who are expected: to collect some prescribed data (Stratum 1); to respond to some research situation themselves and perhaps instruct others what data will be needed for a specific project (Stratum 2); to provide a systematic research service, dealing with a continuous flow of departmental research needs and helping to formulate a policy to meet those needs (Stratum 3); to provide a comprehensive departmental research service encompassing not only the current flow of research needs, but also dealing with emerging or as yet unmanifested research requirements (Stratum 4)?

It is critical to be aware of the real and expected level at which an activity is to be pursued. We have illustrated above very briefly the essence of what might be Stratum 1, 2, 3 and 4 research roles. It would appear that some departments have placed Stratum 3 or even 4 expectations on staff who, by virtue of their experience, could realistically be expected to produce Stratum 2 research work. A gap, reflecting the mismatch, is created with widespread consequences. The particular consequence that concerns us is the departmental response that 'fills' this gap by undefined development.

A similar exercise could be repeated in respect of other activities. The newer activities are thus prone to attack on two fronts. Since they are new, their boundries are unclear. And secondly, when sufficient boundary clarification is achieved, the whole complex question of level of work remains to be analysed. It is all too easy to regard 'develop-

---

[26] See (1975/6) *Social Services Yearbook*, (1969), Councils and Education Press.

[27] For a discussion of research, see *Social Services Departments*, p. 45.

ment' as the repository of social work aspirations for the future, a future where 'real' needs will be 'researched', agency policy will be 'planned' and staff will be 'trained' – laudable objectives – providing these slogans do not hinder the critical examination of what work is actually being performed.[28]

(2) *The absence of relevant high-level activities*
A more subtle variant of the absence of higher-level functions seems almost metaphysical. We might, in fact, be inclined to ignore this phenomenon were it not for its obvious importance for administrative problem solving and organizational design. What we are describing is a situation where there is as yet no institutional articulation of 'below-the-surface' unease. Here and there individuals sense that something is awry, that something important is not being done, but no authoritative forum is able to conceptualize the problem and propose a remedy. This is the fertile ground where the invited outsider can work in a collaborative manner analysing together with organizational members their problems.[29] It is by the utilization of this methodology that the researcher-analyst is enabled to get into the skin of the organization to obtain shared perceptions. In the absence of internal or collaborative analyses 'development' can eventually be found in a variety of titles which do not necessarily tackle the real need but are rather a stumbling response to the general sense of unease.

Development as social experimentation
Is there a case for the utilization of development as a term in its own right? To answer this question we draw a distinction between development as a *state* or act, and development as the *process* by which that

[28] A Working Party set up by the British Association of Social Workers echoes the same theme: 'One of the problems has undoubtedly been a lack of clear definition about the various tasks (and personnel required to perform them) which needs to be undertaken by social services departments'. *BASW News*, 24 July 1975.
[29] The social science methodology that is being described is known as 'social analysis'. A definitive account of the method is to be found in Jaques, E. (1965), 'Social Analysis and the Glacier Project', op. cit. An elaboration of the application of the method in the hospital setting is included in Rowbottom, R. W., *et al.*, (1973), op. cit. An account of social analysis utilized in the Social Services Department of Brent is related in Billis, D., (1973), op. cit. There is a wide body of literature concerned with what is often called 'action research', within which social analysis might be considered to be subsumed. A useful overview of this research field is in Clark, Peter A. (1972), *Action Research and Organizational Change*.

state is reached.[30] Much of this chapter so far can therefore be regarded as an examination of the organizational responses intended to achieve a state of 'normality' or 'improvement'. (We have seen that in most cases other and more suitable titles could be advantageously employed.) The responses take the form of processes, activities or strategies. Improvement is regarded as a rather vague new state which is accompanied by specialization, co-ordination or planning as necessary prerequisites.

There is a more specific usage. This occurs when development is primarily associated with a defined new state or act, i.e. with a project or experiment. To be involved in development is now to be engaged in the production of a new product – to be 'experimenting'. So there are some SSDs where posts have been established with project development duties. Called development officers, their role would appear to be modelled on the manufacturing mode of organization.

According to the manufacturing model, experiments can be isolated, controlled and guarded. There is an end product which may, or may not, be launched onto the market. Research is the process which, it is hoped, will result in an act of creation, or an idea. Once this is achieved development is the process of conversion of: '. . . converting an idea . . . into an article which a factory . . . can make in sufficient quantities and sufficiently cheaply to make the whole venture profitable.'[31]

This is a simplistic summary of research and development in the industrial setting; there are many problems widely reported in the literature.[32] Nevertheless, the outline is sufficient for our purposes. What we wish to question is the validity of the approach for SSDs or for many service organizations. Do departments really launch experimental projects? It is suggested that they are actually involved in the very different act of social exploration.[33]

Clients, the department's raw material, cannot be controlled in laboratory conditions, even in 'regulatory total institutions'.[34] Marris and Rein, in their comprehensive and powerful critique of the American Community Action projects, pinpoint the dilemma: 'In practice, then, the projects could not realize their claim to be experi-

[30] See Nieuwenhuijze, C. A. O. van, 'Public Administration, Comparative Administration, Development Administration: Concepts and Theory in their Struggle for Relevance'.
[31] Burns and Stalker (1968), op. cit., p. 158.
[32] For example, Brown, W. (1971), op. cit., Chapter 23.
[33] Marris, P. and Rein, M. (1974), *Dilemmas of Social Reform*, pp. 242–61.
[34] Webb, A. (1971). 'Social Service Administration: A Typology for Research'.

ments without abandoning their determination to benefit the communities in which they worked. They were not demonstrations but explorations of the possibilities of reform.'[35] Explorations, the authors point out, are an integral part of the field of operation, they are pragmatic and flexible and consequently need to be retrospectively interpreted in a different manner from an experiment: 'The whole process – the false starts, frustrations, adaptations, the successive recasting of intentions, the detours and conflicts – need to be comprehended.'[36] Self's strictures about cost-benefit techniques in examining policy issues may be seen as part of the same broad approach. He points to the predicament of the economist who 'can guard the purity of his research by eschewing all contact with policy making', but if so '... the practical utility of their work also dwindles ...'[37]

It would seem that labelling social explorations 'experiments' often springs from political motives. In a study of detention centres Hilary Land concludes that:

> The controversial detention centre policy gained acceptance by being labelled 'experimental', because it is very difficult to oppose an experiment. Such a tactic allowed its proponents to remain vague about the actual methods to be employed in implementing the policy on the grounds that it would restrict the experiment too much.[38]

In passing we might note that the exploration-experimentation conjuring trick is a problem for academic commentators, as well as agencies and practitioners. This is neatly illustrated by Land's interesting study which although, as we have seen, fully appreciates the political character of the detention centre exercise, still does not question the ground rules. There is the usual emphasis on statistical data, in this instance since reconviction rates remained high, the experiment, Land states, '... could not, in 1961, be judged a great success'. The unsurprising conclusion is reached that the rapid expansion of detention centre provision in the early 1960s was not 'soundly based on the *successful* outcome of an experiment'.[39] Since it is patently clear from her own analysis that the centres were never experiments (but explorations) we appear to have an example of kicking down an already open door.

[35] Marris and Rein (1974), op. cit., p. 260.
[36] ibid., p. 260.
[37] Self, P. (1974), *Administrative Theories and Politics*, p. 214.
[38] Land, H., in Hall, P., Land, H., Parker, R. and Webb, A. (1975). *Change, Choice and Conflict in Social Policy*, p. 369.
[39] ibid., p. 367.

If, as we are arguing, SSDs are concerned with explorations, not experiments, the case for project officer posts, distinct from operational staff, is questionable. Explorations, once embarked upon, become an integral part of the social territory. New explorations, whilst they may have a lengthy planning phase, rapidly become enmeshed in false starts, frustrations, adaptations and associated phenomena. It might be difficult to discern precisely when the exploration moves into a full operational state. Why not involve those who will eventually be accountable for the project, as soon as possible? Overcoming the problems encountered by new explorations might be considered invaluable experience, not to be isolated into discrete project roles. Still, we have here an issue with many more pros and cons than those mentioned. Those who decide have to live with the consequence of their decisions; which leads us back to our main purpose.

Summary – what's in a name?

The word 'development' poses problems for SSDs (and not just them).[40] Words, titles, can have unintended and unwanted consequences. Unrealistic expectations lead to difficulties. Take, for example, the title 'senior social worker' – a post held at some time by thousands of staff. In a small case-study undertaken soon after the Seebohm reorganization the author writes: 'No job descriptions had been written and no discussions about their role in the newly-formed department had taken place, leaving seniors unsure of what was expected of them. Such ambiguity and conflict of role expectation encouraged a dissipation of energy and resulted in a lower standard of work.'[41]

So it is with development. Dissection of the term causes us to reflect, perhaps to reconsider. A number of possibilities have been uncovered:

(*1*) Development considered as a response to the failure to achieve some desired 'standard'. Assuming that no new qualitatively different level of work is demanded, two types of 'development people' were identified:

(*a*) those brought in to boost up personal inadequacies (Figure 10.1);
(*b*) those who become 'specialists', who concentrate on a narrower

[40] In this connection, see Milne, R. S. (1973), 'Bureaucracy and Development Administration', pp. 411–25. Whilst he is dealing with a much greater spectrum, some of the similarities are interesting, in particular the different usages of the term 'development administration' (pp. 411–12).

[41] Glasgow, S. (1972), 'Senior Social Workers after Seebohm', p. 8.

range of activities of the same degree of complexity as the 'general-ists' (Figure 10.2).

(2) Development can be regarded as co-ordination – responding at different levels to the difficulties encountered in integrating activities of growing and complex organizations. Co-ordination was considered at two distinct points:

(a) at the grass roots, putting together the delivery of direct services to clients (Figure 10.3);

(b) systems co-ordination, providing frameworks within which the grass roots work can be implemented (Figures 10.4 and 10.5).

(3) Development reflecting the absence of higher level work:

(a) as a response to the mismatch between stated, expected perform-ance and reality;

(b) as a response to a general sense of unease.

(4) Development as social experimentation. An implicit manufactur-ing approach is adopted and project officers launch the new pseudo-experiments.

What then is in a name? Sometimes very little. Certainly not always sufficient to justify the effort of serious investigation. If, on the other hand, there is widespread evidence of distress and unease felt concerning the usage of a particular term, this surely is a storm signal to be taken seriously by researchers in the field of administration.

Our initial starting point has been the weighty problems faced by staff in SSDs. The question might be raised whether this approach *merely* justifies the status quo and makes life easier for departmental staff. Such an assumption would be gross misrepresentation and under-evaluation of the nature of the relationship between 'outsider' (researcher–analyst) and 'insider'. That is a task beyond the bound-aries of the present study and has been dealt with elsewhere.[42]. We must be content to emphasize that a genuine collaborative relationship is not entered into lightly. There need be few limits to the search for shared perceptions and alternative models. The case-study, already mentioned, traces the often painful twists and turns which a joint search can invoke; at least one participant was quite explicit that he might be 'talking myself out of a job.[43] Uncovering the meanings of the term 'development' may be no less painful. As we have tried to illustrate, departmental aims and objectives might be seen in a different light. In this discussion we have attempted to indicate some

[42] See *Social Analysis*, op. cit.
[43] Billis, D. (1973), op. cit., p. 459.

of the misconceptions which are already enmeshed in the new SSDs.

We are thus, it is hoped, providing potential tools for administrative problem solving in a set of public service agencies whose impact is already felt by vast numbers of citizens in critical areas of their social lives.

References

Baron, G. and Howell, D. A. (1974), *The Government and Management of Schools*, London: Athlone Press, University of London.

Bartlett, Harriet, M. (1970), *The Common Base of Social Work Practice*, New York: NASW.

Beedell, C. (1970), *Residential Life with Children*, London: Routledge & Kegan Paul.

Bell, C. and Newby, H. (1971), *Community Studies*, London: Allen & Unwin.

Bendix, R. and Lipset, S. M. (eds.) (1953), *Class, Status and Power*, London: Routledge & Kegan Paul.

Billis, D. (1973), 'Entry into Residential Care', *The British Journal of Social Work*, vol. 3, no. 4.

Billis, D. (1975), 'Managing to Care', *Social Work Today*, vol. 6, no. 2.

Billis, D. (1976), 'Intermediate Treatment: In Search of a Policy', *Social Work Service*, no. 11, DHSS.

Billis, D. (1977a), 'Organizational Responses to Social Problems'. Unpublished Paper presented to the United National Social Welfare Workshop, Baden. Brunel University.

Billis, D. (1977b), ' "Development" in Social Services Departments: The Birth of Administrative Obscurity', *Public Administration*, no. 54, Summer.

Billis, D. (1977c), 'Differential Administrative Capacity and Organizational Development', *Human Relations*, vol. 30, no. 2.

Blau, P. and Scott, W. (1963), *Formal Organizations*, London: Routledge & Kegan Paul.

British Association of Social Workers (1975), *A Code of Ethics*, Birmingham: BASW Publication.

British Association of Social Workers (1976), 'Accredited in Social Work', A Report of the Professional Development and Practice Committee, *Social Work Today*, vol. 7, no. 7.

British Association of Social Workers (1978), *Residential Care, Staffing and Training*, A Report by the Social Services Liaison Group.

Bromley, G. (1976), 'Managers and Community Homes: A Fresh Look at Their Role', *Social Work Service*, no. 10, DHSS.

Bromley, G. (1977), 'Interaction Between Field and Residential Social Workers', *British Journal of Social Work*, vol. 7, no. 3.

Bromley, G. (1978), 'Grades and Specialization in Social Work Practice', *Social Work Today*, 31 October.

Brown, W. (1960), *Exploration in Management*, London: Heinemann.

Brown, W. and Jaques, E. (1965), *Glacier Project Papers*, London: Heinemann.

Brown, W. (1971), *Organization*, London: Heinemann.

Brunel Institute of Organization and Social Studies, Social Services Organization Research Unit (1974), *Social Services Departments: Developing Patterns of Work and Organization*, London: Heinemann.

Burns, T. and Stalker, G. M. (1961), *The Management of Innovation*, London: Tavistock.

Cambridge Social Services Training Workshop (1976), 'The Role of the Social Work Assistant', *Social Work Today*, vol. 7, no. 9.

Carlebach, J. (1970), *Caring for Children in Trouble*, London: Routledge & Kegan Paul.

Central Council for Education and Training of Social Workers (1973), 'Training for Residential Work' (Discussion Document).

Central Council for Education and Training of Social Workers (1976/77/78), *Consultation Papers 1, 2 and 3 on CQSW Training*.

Chandler, A. D. (1963), *Strategy and Structure*, Cambridge, Mass.: M.I.T. Press.

Child, J. (1972), 'Organizational Structure, Environment and Performance: The Role of Strategic Choice', *Sociology*, vol. 6, no. 1.

City of Wakefield Metropolitan District Social Services Department (1976), *Neighbourhood Work*, Wakefield.

Clark, Peter, A. (1972), *Action Research and Organizational Change*, London: Harper & Row.

Cooper, J. (1978), 'The Collective and the Personal – A Decade of Tension', *Community Care*, no. 243.

Cypher, J. (1977), *Personal Social Services, Manpower and Training*, Birmingham: Social Workers Educational Trust.

Dahrendorf, R. (1968), 'On the Origin of Inequality Among Men' *Essays in The Theory of Society*, London: Routledge & Kegan Paul.

Dale, E. and Urwick, Lyndall, F. (1960), *Staff in Organization*, New York: McGraw-Hill.

Department of Health and Social Security (1967 and 1972), 'Organization of Medical Work in Hospitals' (Cogwheel) (First and Second Reports of the Joint Working Party), London: HMSO.

Department of Health and Social Security (1972), *Intermediate Treatment*, London: HMSO.

Department of Health and Social Security Development Group (1973) *Intermediate Treatment Project*, London: HMSO.

Department of Health and Social Security (1974), *Intermediate Treatment, A Report of a Residential Conference*, London: HMSO.

Department of Health and Social Security (1976), *Manpower and Training for the Social Services* (The Birch Report), Report of the Working Party, London: HMSO.

Department of Health and Social Security (1977a), *Health and Personal Social Service Statistics for England 1977*, London: HMSO.

Department of Health and Social Security Development Group (1977b) *Management of Community Homes with Education on the Premises*, London: DHSS.

Department of Health and Social Security (1978), 'The DHSS Perspective' in Barnes, J. and Connelly, N. (eds.) (1978), *Social Care Research*, London: Bedford Square Press.

Devon County Council (1975), *Career Grade – A National Study*, Exeter.

Donnison, D. V. *et al.* (1970), *Social Policy and Administration*, London: Allen & Unwin.

Donnison, D. V. (1978), 'The Economic and Political Context' in Barnes and Connelly (eds.) (1978), *op. cit.*

Dunsire, A. (1973), *Administration: The Word and the Science*, London: Martin Robertson.

Emery, F. E. and Trist, E. L. (1965), 'The Causal Texture of Organizational Environments', *Human Relations*, vol. 18.

Emery, F. E. (ed.) (1969), *Systems Thinking*, Harmondsworth: Penguin.

Etzioni, A. (1964), *Modern Organizations*, Englewood Cliffs, N. J., Prentice-Hall.

Evans, J. S. (1970), 'Managerial Accountability – Chief Officers, Consultants and Boards'. Unpublished Paper, Brunel University.

Forder, A. (ed.) (1963), *Penelope Hall's Social Services of England and Wales*, London: Routledge & Kegan Paul.

Forder, A. (1974), *Concepts in Social Administration*, London: Routledge & Kegan Paul.

Glasgow, S. (1972), 'Senior Social Social Workers after Seebohm', *British Hospital Journal and Social Service Review*, January.

Goffman, E. (1961), *Asylums*, Harmondsworth: Penguin.

Goldberg, E. M. *et al.* (1977), 'Towards Accountability in Social Work: One Year's Intake to an Area Office', *British Journal of Social Work*, vol. 7, no. 3.

Goldberg, E. M. *et al.* (1978a), 'Towards Accountability in Social Work: Long Term Social Work in an Area Office' *British Journal of Social Work*, vol. 8, no. 3.

Goldberg, E. M. and Connelly, N. (1978b), 'Reviewing Services for the Old', *Community Care*, December.

Goldstein, H. (1973), *Social Work Practice*, Columbia, S. Carolina: University of Carolina Press.

Goode, W. J. (1969), 'The Theoretical Limits of Professionalisation' in Etzioni (ed.) (1969), *The Semi-Professions and their Organization*, New York: The Free Press.

Greenwood, R. *et al.* (1975), 'Contingency Theory and the Organization of Local Authorities, Part I: Differentiation and Integration', *Public Administration*, vol. 53, Spring.

Greiner, E. L. (1972), 'Evolution and Revolution as Organizations Grow', *Harvard Business Review*, vol. 50, no. 4.

Health Services Organisation Research Unit (1977), *Organization of Physiotherapy and Occupational Therapy in the NHS, A Working Paper*, Brunel Institute of Organization and Social Studies.

Heraud, B. J. (1970), *Sociology and Social Work, Perspectives and Problems*, London: Pergamon.

Hey, A. M. (1973), 'Analysis and Definition of the Function of Caring Establishments', in Ainsworth, F. (ed.) (1973), *Residential Establishments: The Evolving of Caring Systems*, Dundee University.

Hey, A. M. (1977), 'Local Authority Social Services Departments, Examples of Matrix Organization' in Knight, K. (ed.) (1977), *Matrix Management*, London: Gower Press.

Hey, A. M. (1978), *Social Work – Careers, Practice and Organization in Area Teams, A Working Paper*, Social Services Unit, Brunel Institute of Organization and Social Studies.

Hickson, D. J. and Thomas, M. W. (1969), 'Professionalisation in Britain, A Preliminary Measurement', *Sociology*, vol. 3, no. 1.

Hill, M. (1976), *The State, Administration and the Individual*, Glasgow: Collins.

Home Office *et al.* (1968), *Report of the Committee on Local Authority and Allied Personal Social Services (Seebohm)*, Cmnd. 3703, HMSO.

Home Office (1969), *Report of the Care of Young Children*, London: HMSO.

Home Office (1975), 'Eleventh Report from the Expenditure Committee' Session 1974–5, vol. 1, London: HMSO.

Jaques, E. (1965a), 'Social-Analysis and the Glacier Project' in Brown and Jaques (eds.) (1965), op. cit.

Jaques, E. (1965b), 'Preliminary Sketch of a General Structure of Executive Strata' in Brown and Jaques (eds.) (1965), op. cit.

Jaques, E. (1965c), 'Speculations Concerning Level of Capacity' in Brown and Jaques (eds.) (1965), op. cit.

Jaques, E. (1970), (2nd edn.), *Equitable Payment*, Harmondsworth: Penguin.

Jaques, E. (1976), *A General Theory of Bureaucracy*, London: Heinemann.

Jaques, E. (ed.) (1978), *Health Services*, London: Heinemann.

Johnson, T. J. (1972), *Professions and Power*, London: Macmillan.

Joint RCA/BASW Report (1976), 'How can Residential and Field Social Workers Co-operate?', *Social Work Today*, vol. 7, no. 12.

Judge, K. (1978), *Rationing Social Services*, London: Heinemann.

Kassels, M. (1973), 'Guidelines for the Design of Career Systems' in Austin, M. (ed.) (1973), *Human Service Agencies in Statewide Career Planning*, University of Florida.

Kogan, M. and Terry, J. (1971), *The Organization of a Social Services Department, A Blueprint*, London: Bookstall Publications.

Land, H. in Hall, P. *et al.* (1975), *Change, Choice and Conflict in Social Policy*, London: Heinemann.

Marris, P. and Rein, M. (1974), *Dilemmas of Social Reform*, Harmondsworth: Penguin.

McGregor, D. (1960), *The Human Side of Enterprise*, New York: McGraw-Hill.

Miller, E. J. and Rice, A. K. (1967), *Systems of Organization*, London: Tavistock.

Milne, R. S. (1973), 'Bureaucracy and Development Administration', *Public Administration*, Winter.

Muluccio, A. N. and Marlowe, W. D. (1972), 'Residential Treatment of Emotionally Disturbed Children: A Review of the Literature', *The Social Service Review* (June).

National Council of Home Help Services (1978), *Home Help Services in Great Britain*, London: Published by National Council of Home Helps.

Nieuwenhuijze, C. A. O. van, 'Public Administration, Comparative Administration, Development Administration: Concepts and Theory in their Struggle for Relevance'.

Paley, J. and Thorpe, D. (1974), *Children: Handle with Care*, National Youth Bureau.

Parker, R. A. (1970), 'The Future of the Personal Social Services' in Robson, W. A. and Crick, B. (eds.) *The Future of the Social Services*, Harmondsworth: Penguin.

Patterson, T. T. (1972), *Job Evaluation*, vols. 1 and 2, London: Business Books.

Personal Social Services Council (1975), *Living and Working in Residential Homes, Interim Report of a Working Group*, PSSC.

Personal Social Services Council (1975), *Residential Care Reviewed*, PSSC.

Pettes, D. E. (1967), *Supervision in Social Work, A Method of Student Training and Staff Development*, London: Allen & Unwin.

Residential Services Advisory Group (1973), *Staff Support and Development – A First Report*.

Righton, P. (1971), 'The Objectives and Methods of Residential Social Work' in Residential Child Care Association (1971), *Child in Care*.

Rose, G. (1967), *Schools for Young Offenders*, London: Tavistock.

Rowbottom, R. W. and Hey, A. M. (1970), 'Towards and Organization of Social Services Departments', *Local Government Chronicle*, no. 5403.

Rowbottom, R. W. (1973), 'Organizing Social Services, Hierarchy or ...?' *Public Administration*, vol. 51.

Rowbottom, R. W. *et al.* (1973), *Hospital Organization*, London: Heinemann.

Rowbottom, R. W. (1977), *Social Analysis*, London: Heinemann.

Rowbottom, R. W. and Billis, D. (1977), 'The Stratification of Work and Organizational Design' *Human Relations*, vol. 30, no. 1.

Rowbottom, R. W. and Bromley, G. L. (1978), 'The Future of Child Guidance – A Study in Multi-Disciplinary Teamwork' in Jaques, E. (ed.) (1978), op. cit.

Rowbottom, R. W. and Hey, A. M. (1978), 'Collaboration Between Health and Social Services' in Jaques (ed.) (1978), op. cit.

Rowbottom, R. W. and Hey, A. M. (1978), *Organization of Services for the Mentally Ill, A Working Paper*, Published jointly by Health Services Organization Research Unit and Social Services Unit, Brunel Institute of Organization and Social Studies.

Schon, D. A. (1971), *Beyond the Stable State*, London: Temple Smith.

Self, P. (1974), *Administrative Theories and Politics*, London: Allen & Unwin.

Shumpeter, J. A. (1947), 'The Creative Response in Industry', *Journal of Economic History*, vol. 7.

Silverman, D. (1970), *The Theory of Organizations*, London: Heinemann.

Simon, H. A. (1967), *Administrative Behaviour*, New York: The Free Press.

Smith, G. (1970), *Social Work and the Sociology of Organizations*, London: Routledge & Kegan Paul.

Social Services Liaison Group (1978), *Residential Care, Staffing and Training, A Report of a Working Party*, BASW.

Social Services Organization Research Unit (1976), *Professionals in Health and Social Services Organisations, A Working Paper*, Brunel Institute of Organization and Social Studies.

Social Services Organization Research Unit (1977), *Advisors, Development Officers and Consultants in Social Services Departments, A Working Paper*, Brunel Institute of Organization and Social Studies.

Social Services Year Book – 1975/76, London: Councils and Education Press.

Stevenson, O. (1963), 'Reception into Care: Its Meanings for all Concerned', *Case Conference*, vol. 10, no. 4.

Strauss, A. *et al.* (1963), 'The Hospital and Its Negotiated Order' in Friedson, E. (ed.) (1963), *The Hospital in Modern Society*, London: Macmillan.

Tavistock Centre (1978), *Statutory Registration of Psychotherapists, A Report of a Working Party*, London: Tavistock.

Thomas, J. (1978), 'Which Way for Social Work?' *Social Work Service*, no. 18, DHSS.

Titmuss, R. M. (1958), *Essays on 'The Welfare State'*, London: Allen & Unwin.

Titmuss, R. M. (1974), *Social Policy*, London: Allen & Unwin.

Tod, R. J. N. (ed.) (1968), 'Staff Roles and Relationships in Residential Work' in *Papers on Residential Work, Vol.1: Children in Care*, London: Longmans.

Toren, N. (1969), 'Semi-Professionalism and Social Work: A Theoretical Perspective' in Etzioni, A. (ed.) (1969), op. cit.

Wareham, J. (1977), *An Open Case, The Organizational Context of Social Work*, London: Routledge & Kegan Paul.

Webb, A. (1971), 'Social Service Administration: A Typology for Research', *Public Administration*, Autumn.

Westland, P. (1974), Review of a book in *British Journal of Social Work*, vol. 4, no. 4, Winter.

Wilensky, H. L. (1964), 'The Professionalisation of Everyone?', *American Journal of Sociology*, vol. 70, no. 2.

Williams, G. (1967), *Caring for People*, London: Allen & Unwin.

Winnicott, C. (1964), 'Casework and the Residential Treatment of Children', *Child Care and Social Work*, Hitchin: Codicote Press.

Index